JESUS AND GIN

EVANGELICALISM, THE ROARING TWENTIES AND TODAY'S CULTURE WARS

BARRY HANKINS

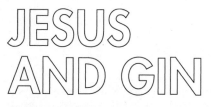

palgrave
macmillan

JESUS AND GIN
Copyright © Barry Hankins, 2010.
All rights reserved.

First published in 2010 by PALGRAVE MACMILLAN® in the US-a division of St. Martin's Press LLC, 175 Fifth Avenue, New York, NY 10010.

Where this book is distributed in the UK, Europe and the rest of the world, this is by Palgrave Macmillan, a division of Macmillan Publishers Limited, registered in England, company number 785998, of Houndmills, Basingstoke, Hampshire RG21 6XS.

Palgrave Macmillan is the global academic imprint of the above companies and has companies and representatives throughout the world.

Palgrave® and Macmillan® are registered trademarks in the United States, the United Kingdom, Europe and other countries.

ISBN: 978-0-230-61419-2

Library of Congress Cataloging-in-Publication Data

Hankins, Barry, 1956–
    Jesus and gin : evangelicalism, the Roaring Twenties and today's culture wars / Barry Hankins.
        p.   cm.
    ISBN 978-0-230-61419-2 (hardback)
    1. Evangelicalism—United States—History—20th century.   2. United States—Church history—20th century.   3. Nineteen twenties.   I. Title.
BR1642.U5H363   2010
270.8'2--dc22

2009051993

A catalogue record of the book is available from the British Library.

Design by Letra Libre

First edition: August 2010

10 9 8 7 6 5 4 3 2 1

Printed in the United States of America.

CONTENTS

ACKNOWLEDGMENTS

Several individuals and institutions aided and encouraged this project. None is responsible for any errors of fact, judgment, or interpretation herein. Giles Anderson of the Anderson Literary Agency helped brainstorm and conceptualize the book and then guided meticulously the formulation of the original proposal. Editor Jake Klisivitch brought the proposal into the Palgrave Macmillan fold and did a great job of editing. The book is sharper and more focused as a result of his skill and hard work and that of production editor Yasmin Mathew. The Earhart Foundation of Ann Arbor, Michigan, provided funds that made it possible for me to take a semester off my teaching duties at Baylor University in order to write the original draft. Baylor's Institute for Studies of Religion and its director, Byron Johnson, have generously provided summer funding for my research over the past several years. As always, Baylor University, particularly history department chair Jeff Hamilton and arts and sciences dean Lee Nordt, supported the project in innumerable ways, not the least of which was working out the logistics of the Earhart Grant and my sabbatical. Graduate assistant Lindsay Cleveland tracked down numerous research items over the course of several months, always with good cheer, and Ben Wetzel aided in proof reading and the development of the index. Wayne Weber of the Billy Graham Center Library/Archives and Maria David of the Charlotte *Observer* library helped locate documents at their respective archives. Historians P. C. Kemeny of Grove City College and Larry Eskridge at the Institute for the Study of American Evangelicals were kind enough to read various chapters and give me helpful comments and criticism.

As always, I wish to express a special thanks to my wife, Becky, who remains my greatest earthly source of encouragement.

PREFACE

During the presidential election of 1980, religion entered the political fray in the guise of Christian Right groups such as the Moral Majority led by the famous fundamentalist preacher Jerry Falwell. Such overtly religious activism seemed brand new, and many journalists and scholars were shocked and outraged at the intrusion. Religion was a *private* matter, pundits believed, and had been since the Scopes trial of 1925. In that case, John Scopes was tried for teaching evolution in violation of Tennessee law. Although technically winning the trial, William Jennings Bryan and the fundamentalists found themselves humiliated by Clarence Darrow and the American Civil Liberties Union, then ostracized in news reports. Fundamentalists seemed to disappear shortly thereafter and stay pretty much out of sight for a half century.

With fundamentalists out of the picture, the period from 1930 to 1980 appears to have been remarkable for its liberal religious harmony that dovetailed nicely with modern cultural and political liberalism. The twin pillars of modern liberalism are freedom, based on the autonomy of the individual, and religion as a private matter. Even amid the secular tumults of the 1960s, public religion in America was broad, amorphous, and devoid of sectarian stridency. When religion did enter public life in a major way in the Civil Rights movement, the emphasis on freedom and equality for all people was something that both secular and religious liberals applauded. Fundamentalists and other evangelical types worked behind the scenes and out of sight in the pre-1980 period, building their own subculture and largely keeping to themselves. Then, in the 1980s and 1990s, it seemed as if religious fundamentalists were suddenly crashing the party, reentering politics in overt ways with dangerously divisive ideas that harkened back to the 1920s. The twin pillars of the Christian Right were that religion was properly public and that freedom might be something other than the idea that autonomous individuals could do whatever they wanted. The appearance of the Christian Right ignited a series of culture wars, the roots of which go back to the 1920s.

It should be said that the absence of conservative religion and culture war in public life from 1930 to 1980 may have been more apparent than real. It is possible that the media just ignored evangelicals and fundamentalists except when they acted in ways that embodied the liberal stereotype that was created at the Scopes trial—or when their name was Billy Graham. Historians will no doubt revise our view that there was less religion in politics before 1980 than after. Whichever the case, this book will argue that with respect to religion and American culture war, the twenties were quite a bit like the era from 1980 to the present.

❧❖❧

If the half century between 1930 and 1980 was a time of little religiously inspired culture war, that era was the outlier, the aberration. What if we took the first and last quarters of the twentieth century as normal bookends that bracketed an unusual half century of religious harmony? This book is about religion during the earlier era. Religion in the 1920s was like religion today—divisive, flamboyant, controversial, and, most of all, a central feature of American culture. While everyone certainly touted freedom, there were fundamentally different ideas about what freedom meant and how far it should go, and people fought about that.

The decade under discussion is usually referred to as the Roaring Twenties and the Jazz Age. Both terms evoke a loud, swinging era filled with jazz halls, flappers, speakeasies, gangsters, and people on the make. Religious folk were full participants in this bombastic spirit, even as they condemned it. Beginning with a media star evangelist whose real name was Billy Sunday, fundamentalists were no less outlandish than the modernizing liberals they set out to defeat. Nor were religious personalities less scandalous than others. Although Sunday stayed clean, another high-profile fundamentalist preacher went to trial for murder, and the nation's best-known Pentecostal had a high-profile adulterous affair that rocked the news media. Both scandals came on the heels of the infamous Scopes trial, and together the three events derailed a fundamentalist movement that had arguably been winning its culture war against liberal Protestantism.

And culture war it was. The 1920s saw a titanic battle between fundamentalists and liberals in the northern Protestant denominations, with both groups convinced that America would be ruined if the other side won. There were smart, articulate, and even wise leaders in both camps, a fact that is often obscured by the apparent demise of the fundamentalist movement after Scopes. Ironically, as fundamentalists and liberals battled for the hearts and minds of Americans, neither could have contemplated that this decade was actually the last gasp for Protestant domination. Losing their hegemony in the face of an influx of Catholics and Jews, fundamentalist and liberal Protestants were forced into an uneasy alliance as they came to grips with their diminished control of the culture. Little wonder that when faced with a Catholic candidate for president in 1928, liberal and fundamentalist Protestants fought on the same side and occasionally together, supporting the Republican Protestant Herbert Hoover against the Democratic nominee Al Smith.

As in the election of 1928, liberal and fundamentalist Protestants were also allies in the obscenity wars focusing on a series of novels that dealt frankly, and some said obscenely, with human sexuality. Secular liberals defended the individual freedom of novelists to express themselves as they saw fit, while Protestant liberals tried to maintain a sense of corporate or communitarian values they believed constituted a good society. This particular battle pitted liberals of one kind against liberals of another, with fundamentalists mostly cheering the censorship campaign from the sidelines. Complicating Roaring Twenties culture wars further, several Catholic leaders and organizations that opposed Protestant liberals in the election of 1928 supported the liberal Protestant crusade against obscenity. There was no simple fundamentalist-liberal dichotomy during the Roaring Twenties.

⋙❈⋘

Following the election of 1928, as the censorship wars raged, the country plunged into the Great Depression. Although Hoover was unsuccessful in stanching the early effects of the economic catastrophe, at least the new president's Protestant supporters could say that he maintained Prohibition. In the face of a Democratic critique that seemed to be fueled by non–Anglo-Saxon immigrants and secularizing leaders who wore their religion pretty loosely, Prohibition survived until the inauguration of Franklin Roosevelt in 1933. Prohibition has been called America's "last Protestant crusade," but the title was given before 1980, when observers thought there would never again be a viable evangelical political movement like that of the twenties. That assumption was wrong, of course. The 1920s had Prohibition; the 1980s, abortion.

Although the nominally Protestant Hoover's reputation suffered for decades as a result of the depression, few Americans remember the first president elected in the 1920s who happened to be a lifelong Baptist. Hoover was an upstanding genius compared to Warren G. Harding, the most morally corrupt and wisdom-deficient man ever to occupy the White House. Richard Nixon rivaled Harding in public corruption, and Bill Clinton in personal immorality, but no president before or since has combined both into one tidy package of misdeeds. It has been said that George Washington could not tell a lie; someone once quipped that Harding "couldn't tell a liar" and thus filled his administration with an Ohio gang that seemed to believe government positions were personal investment opportunities. Moreover, while his cabinet bilked the country, Harding engaged in multiple adulterous affairs.

≈✢≈

The religious story of the 1920s was certainly not all scandal and warfare. Many Americans continued to live as they always had, religiously or otherwise, but this book is about the folks who made the decade roar religiously: Harry Emerson Fosdick, the first theological liberal to become a household name; Aimee Semple McPherson and J. Frank Norris, who made headlines in church and in court; and black mega-church preachers such as Daddy Grace and Father Divine.

Given what has happened in America since 1980, it appears today that the Roaring Twenties was not the last gasp of religious traditionalism in favor of a broader, more liberal and harmonious ethos. Rather, the 1920s were religiously typical while the half century from 1930 to 1980 was the anomaly. In short, the religiously fueled culture wars of the 1920s were a prologue to our own age: a time when religion was culturally central, participating fully in politics, media stardom, social life, and scandal.

CHAPTER 1

WARREN HARDING AND THE MORAL AMBIGUITY OF THE ROARING TWENTIES

S candal was part of what made the 1920s roar, and no one set the tone more than America's first Baptist president, Warren G. Harding (1921–1923). He wore his religion loosely and his morality not at all. Neither made him particularly typical of public figures of the era, but this combination of religious and moral indifference symbolized an anything-goes decade. Although the criminal misdeeds of his cabinet and his own personal immorality came to light only after his death, they symbolized what the religious culture warriors of the Roaring Twenties feared most—a society that was losing its moorings, adrift in a sea of ethical chaos. For the devout, Harding was exactly what one should expect when religion lost its central place in the culture.

ALL THE PRESIDENT'S WOMEN

In 1964 author Francis Russell traveled to Harding's hometown of Marion, Ohio, doing research for a biography.[1] After getting to know the townsfolk, Russell was taken to lunch at the Harding Hotel, where lawyers and businessmen gathered frequently. In the course of conversation, Russell heard that a Marion attorney named Don Williamson possessed a box of Harding letters that he had found while serving as the executor of the estate of Marion resident Carrie Phillips after she died in 1960. Williamson took Russell to his home and let the author read the contents of the secret archive, which turned out to be love letters from Harding to Phillips. Once Russell pieced together the story, it became clear that Harding had had an affair with Carrie for 15 years and that while cheating on his wife with Carrie, Harding had been cheating on both with Nan Britton.

Carrie and her husband, Jim, were the Hardings' friends. Jim owned a dry goods store in Marion and had married Carrie Fulton from the nearby town of Bucyrus in 1896, when he was 30 and she 21. By all accounts Carrie was a beautiful and vivacious young woman. In 1905, when Jim Phillips was ailing, Harding assisted in sending him to the Battle Creek (Michigan) Sanatorium, which was run by the health-conscious Seventh-day Adventist J. H. Kellogg, the inventor of corn flakes. By that time, Harding was Ohio's lieutenant governor, serving office in the state capital of Columbus. While Jim Phillips was in Battle Creek convalescing and Harding's wife was recovering from a kidney operation, Harding dropped in to check on Carrie, who was still grieving the loss of her son, who had died the year before. Harding and Carrie Phillips fell in love.

The affair lasted until 1920, when Harding ran for president. During the election campaign, the Republican Party helped keep the affair secret by sending Jim and Carrie on a cruise to the Far East and paying them $20,000 plus a monthly stipend as long as Harding was in office.

While doing his research, biographer Russell learned that the Harding-Phillips affair was well known among the upper echelons of Marion society. Carrie had continued to live in Marion long after the death of both her husband and Harding. By the late 1950s she was living in squalor created by a mass of dogs she tried to raise for a profit, many of which were not housebroken. Before her death, a local judge appointed attorney Williamson as Phillips's guardian. Williamson had her placed in a home for the elderly then arranged to have the house sold and Phillips's belongings cataloged. That was when he found a locked box in the back of a closet that contained the many letters Harding had sent to Carrie. Some of the letters ran 30 to 40 pages, and many were written on U.S. Senate stationery while Harding was a senator.

Williamson believed that if he turned the letters over to the Harding family, they would be destroyed, so he kept them hidden until Russell came to town. After reading and cataloging the letters, Russell contacted the Ohio Historical

Society, which set in motion a chain of events that lasted for years. The Harding Memorial Association was preparing for the centenary celebration of Harding's birth when trustees got wind of the letters. They persuaded a judge to create a Carrie Phillips estate consisting of the papers. A member of the Memorial Association board was appointed executor of Phillips's estate, which meant that the Ohio Historical Society had to relinquish the papers to the group most likely to destroy them. The agent of the Ohio Historical Society, however, had made a microfilm copy of the letters, which he then sent to *American Heritage* magazine in New York. When word leaked of the contest over the Harding love letters, the story became front-page news across the country. In some areas the coverage of this Republican scandal from the 1920s dwarfed coverage of the 1964 Republican National Convention taking place at the same time the story broke. Russell wanted to go forward with his biography, but the Harding family thwarted his plan to quote from the love letters by persuading a judge to issue a restraining order. After wrangling unsuccessfully for three years, Russell published his nearly 700-page book anyway, leaving blank lines where the direct quotations would have been and paraphrasing the content in his own words. Eventually, the letters ended up in the Manuscript Division of the Library of Congress, where they are sealed until 2014, 50 years after Williamson gave them to Russell.[2]

Emerging from Russell's story is a portrait of Harding as a hapless philanderer, more repulsive than evil. He simply did not seem have the moral fortitude to say no, either to temptation or to other people who prevailed on him. Even Harding's marriage appears to have been not so much a loving choice as an inability to resist the persistent importuning of Florence Kling. In 1880, at the age of 20, Flossie, as she was known, had eloped, pregnant, with her boyfriend, Henry DeWolfe. The marriage lasted four years before she filed for separation and divorce. She sent her son to live with her wealthy parents and took up piano teaching in an attempt to make ends meet. One of her students was Harding's sister, and when Florence met Warren Harding, she began to woo him with the same ardor she had hounded her first husband into marriage.

Harding was at this time the editor of the Marion *Star* newspaper. Flattered by the attention and affection Flossie Kling sent his way, it also could not have been lost on Harding that she was well connected, being from one of the wealthiest families in town. As Russell put it, once Flossie decided to have Harding, "he had no chance," and the same had been true of her first husband.[3]

Flossie was a forceful woman, and eventually Harding took to calling her "the Duchess." He tried to resist her, at least at first. On one occasion Florence met him unexpectedly at the train station when he returned from a business trip. Harding saw her out the window and exited the opposite side of the train, only to hear her yell, "You needn't try to run away, Warren Harding. I see your big feet."[4] Eventually, he gave in and married her in 1891.

After entering politics in the 1880s, Harding moved steadily up the ranks of the Republican Party to lieutenant governor, Republican candidate for governor (he lost in 1910), and U.S. Senator before winning his party's presidential nomination in 1920. That year, following his victory in the election, three reporters were dining at the home of a Marion widow. The woman's eight-year-old daughter took the reporters on a tour of the house, pointing out the president-elect's toothbrush in the upstairs bathroom and reporting "He always stays here when Mrs. Harding goes away."[5]

Today it would be hard to imagine the press not investigating and exposing the affair, especially after Harding became the Republican presidential nominee. If the story of the reporters seeing his toothbrush is true, however, it illustrates a kind of deference to elites that no longer exists. The reporters never followed up on the hot tip from the eight-year-old. Still, Republican Party officials feared the Phillips affair would come to light during the campaign, thus the Far East cruise and payoff to Jim and Carrie.

Harding's affair with Carrie Phillips ended as he campaigned for the Republican nomination in 1920, in part because Carrie suspected he was seeing other women. He was. In fact, he had been carrying on a torrid affair with Nan Britton for at least four years. In 1910, when Harding ran for governor of Ohio, Nan was in ninth grade. Her favorite teacher was Abigail "Daisy" Harding, Warren's sister.[6] Nan became infatuated with Harding and hung his campaign photos on her bedroom wall. She placed one at the foot of her bed so he would be the first thing she saw after waking in the morning. Nan met Harding for the first time while on a Sunday afternoon horse-and-buggy jaunt with her elder sister, Elizabeth. Passing by the Hardings' house, they saw the candidate and the Duchess sitting on their porch and decided to double back to say hello. After idle conversation, mostly between Elizabeth and Mrs. Harding, Elizabeth exclaimed, "You know, Mr. Harding, Nan talks of nothing but you."

Over the next three years of high school, Nan attempted to catch the attention of Marion's most famous resident, even stopping by the Harding home as a 16-year-old in 1914 when Harding won election to the U.S. Senate. In 1917 she moved to New York to attend secretarial school, and that year wrote a letter to Senator Harding. Beginning with the line "I wonder if you will remember me," she inquired if perhaps he might be able to employ her or recommend her for employment. Harding wrote back, "You may be sure that [I remember you], and I remember you most agreeably, too."[7]

Shortly thereafter, Harding traveled to New York, called Nan, and told her to meet him at the Manhattan Hotel. After a morning of conversation in a hotel reception room, Harding invited the 21-year-old to his room, explaining that with vacancies scarce because of a business convention in the city, he had secured the last available accommodation in the hotel—the bridal suite. They were scarcely in the room when they began to kiss passionately, hesitating from time to time to discuss her secretarial skills and job prospects. Harding gave her $30 at the end of their liaison, the first installment on mistress upkeep that would last for the rest of his life.

Harding juggled the two women, along with the Duchess and his senatorial duties, from 1917 until 1920, when the pressure of a wife, two mistresses, and a presidential election campaign proved too much. Actually, the relationship with Carrie had long since run its course. Accusing him of having affairs with other women, she also ridiculed his presidential ambitions as he began angling for the Republican nomination. Carrie knew what the country would learn the hard way—Warren Harding was not presidential timber.[8]

Had party officials known the rest of Harding's story, they would have arranged for two cruises, one for Carrie and her husband and a second for Nan, who was carrying Harding's child—not pregnant, but literally carrying in her arms little Elizabeth Ann, who had been born on October 22, 1919.[9] For nearly two years Harding had been visiting Nan in New York and arranging for her to travel by train to meet with him while he was on a various speaking tours. During one of their New York trysts, a hotel employee tipped off the police that a 50-ish man, probably married, had a young woman alone in one of the rooms. Harding and Nan were still dressing when the officers burst in to arrest them. This was an age when adultery was not yet a private matter and could be grounds for state prosecution. Harding pleaded with the two policemen to let Nan go. "You can tell it to the judge," one of the officers replied. As the policemen proceeded to rouse the couple out of the room, one picked up Harding's hat and saw "W. G. Harding" embossed in gold lettering. Realizing they had invaded the room of a U.S. Senator, the instinctive deference to elites that marked the era kicked in, and the officer began to apologize. Harding and Nan packed up their belongings, and the officers escorted them to a side exit and let them go, but not before Harding tipped them $20. Out of their sight, Harding told Nan, "I thought I wouldn't get out of that under $1000."[10]

As the affair intensified, Harding began arranging for Nan to visit him in Washington. She would take the train, register at a hotel, and slip over to the U.S. Senate building, where the couple would have sex in Harding's office. It was there, Nan would write later, that their daughter was conceived in January 1919. By late February she was sure she was pregnant and wrote Senator Harding with the news. They discussed "handling" the problem, but Nan was determined to have the baby. Harding had never fathered a child with the Duchess, and Nan was convinced Harding wanted this child, his first, as badly as she did. This was a delusion, of course, but Harding never pressed the issue of abortion, leaving the decision to her. She went to Chicago where her sister Elizabeth arranged a meeting with an abortionist. The doctor told Nan that she was quite frail for such an operation and that 13 weeks into a pregnancy made the procedure even riskier. On the advice of a friend, Elizabeth then concocted a potion that was said to induce miscarriage, but Nan decided she could not take it, writing later: "I could not bring myself to destroy the precious treasure within me."[11]

Some months after Elizabeth Ann's arrival, Nan went back to Chicago to convalesce at her sister's apartment. She was living there in the summer of 1920 when the Republican National Convention convened in the same city and nominated Harding for president. In spring and early summer, as he moved steadily toward nomination, Harding warned Nan that it would become increasingly difficult for him to see her. He would be "shadowed" by the press, he said, and he gave her instructions to act naturally and ignore reporters who followed her. Still, he managed to slip away from the convention hall and across town to Elizabeth's apartment to see Nan. Elizabeth, her husband, and the baby would absent themselves so the couple could spend time alone. Nan spent much of her time that summer clipping newspaper articles about Harding while cooing to the infant beside her, "Your daddy's going to be president."[12]

While Harding ran his "front porch" campaign from his home in Marion, Nan secured a job with the Republican National Committee in Chicago, where she joined unsuspecting office mates in stuffing envelopes and mailing posters for the Harding campaign effort. She also resumed contact with her old high school teacher, Harding's sister Daisy, who told Nan in a letter "You must be very happy working for your hero."[13]

Ironically, the Democratic Party's main attempt to throw mud on Harding was the resurrection of the old rumor that he had "negro blood." The newspapers vetted Harding well, even telling the story of Mrs. Harding's first marriage to the miserable alcoholic DeWolfe, but they never learned the big secret of his life, and we can only imagine what might have happened had they found out that he had a "kept" woman and child. After reading several of the stories of Harding's private life, Nan recalled thinking "But they haven't got our story."[14]

Trysts with Nan became ever more difficult after Harding was sworn into office in March 1921. The president decided it would be safer to smuggle Nan in and out of Washington than to rendezvous with her in New York or elsewhere. She made her first White House visit in June after the inauguration. Nan arranged her trip through presidential bodyguard Tim Slade, who picked her up at her hotel and escorted her to the White House. When Harding appeared, he instructed Slade to stay put while he took Nan through an anteroom and into his private office. Afraid armed guards outside the office window might see them, they repaired to a five-by-five closet off the anteroom. Harding then gave Nan a tour of his office, showing her the fireplace where he burned her letters after reading them. The closet trysts remained their custom until Harding's death.

Nan claimed that Harding promised to provide for her financially as long as she and Elizabeth Ann lived, but Harding died slightly more than two years after her first White House visit. In the summer of 1923 Harding embarked on a "Voyage of Understanding" tour of the West Coast. After becoming the first president to visit Alaska, he became ill en route to Seattle, Washington, and died suddenly a few days later in San Francisco. Nan spent the next four years attempting to scrounge up enough money to take her daughter back from her sister Elizabeth and support the child on her own. She briefly married a man who was involved in the shipping industry. When she learned his claims of wealth were exaggerated, she had the marriage annulled.

Nan turned to Daisy, eventually telling the president's sister about the affair and Elizabeth Ann. Concerned that her brother's posthumous reputation not be tarnished by a sex scandal along with the early rumors of official corruption in the Harding administration, Daisy was nevertheless sympathetic and offered Nan small amounts of money. When Daisy was unable to raise the desired sum of $50,000, however, Nan took legal action against the Harding estate. In preparing her case, she wrote an outline of the facts of her affair with the president. The outline grew into an essay and eventually a 400-page book that Nan sought to publish. No publisher would accept her manuscript, however, for fear of libeling a president and incurring the wrath of an American public that still revered its leaders, especially recently deceased ones. Undeterred, Nan secured funding for a private printing. When production began, the head of the New York Society for the Suppression of Vice led six policemen on a raid of the print shop and, under the guise of the state's obscenity laws, seized the printing plates. Nan challenged the police action in court and won. The plates were returned, and the book appeared in print in 1927 bearing the title *The President's Daughter*. After a slow start, sales took off when famed journalist H. L. Mencken gave the book a favorable review. Aiding publicity were a number of condemnations, including one from an Arkansas Democratic senator who denounced the book from the Senate floor, calling it "obscene, filthy, and lewd, . . . a blast from hell."[15] In addition to supporting her daughter, Nan used book royalties to set up a charity for illegitimate children called The Elizabeth Ann League.

Harding's moral lapses illustrate a weak personal constitution and inability to repress his basest appetites, but they also symbolize an age when Victorian mores were publicly challenged. Although he exercised illicit passions privately, the flappers and fops of the speakeasies and juke joints flaunted sexual freedom in public. Neither he nor they were particularly troubled in conscience. In short, like many others in the decade, Harding had lost his moral bearings. Not surprisingly, the circle of friends that became his administration consisted of individuals more audacious than he. His private lack of judgment became their public scandals.

TEAPOT DOME

By the time *The President's Daughter* appeared, two Harding administration officials had committed suicide while under investigation for corruption, two others were involved in legal battles that would eventually send them to prison, and several were well on their way to public disgrace. Much of this resulted from Teapot Dome, one of the most infamous public scandals in American history.

Although the term became a catchall name for a host of scandals that took place in the Harding administration, Teapot Dome itself was an oil field in Wyoming set aside for use by the Navy. There was a similar field in California called Elk Hills. In April 1921, just a month after Harding's inauguration, Secretary of the Interior Albert Fall persuaded Harding to transfer these oil reserves from the secretary of the navy's jurisdiction to his own. Several oil companies desired access to these fields, including Edward Doheny's Pan-American Petroleum and Transport Company. Doheny was Fall's friend and was already leasing some of the Elk Hills fields for drilling. In return for the right to drill on government lands, Doheny paid a percentage of his profits to the U.S. government and also agreed to build fuel storage facilities for the military in Pearl Harbor, Hawaii.

At the same time the oilmen wanted access to the fields, Fall needed money to close an important land deal in his home state of New Mexico. In return for increased access to Elk Hills oil, therefore, Doheny provided Fall with a personal "loan" of $100,000. The money was organized in five bundles of $20,000 each, put in a black bag, and transported to Fall by Doheny's son Edward Jr.[16] A few weeks later Fall met oilman Harry Sinclair. Sinclair wanted to know if Fall would grant him the same access to Teapot Dome that Doheny had secured in Elk Hills. Typically, such a government venture would have been opened for bidding, and several companies would have competed for the rights to the fields. There was no such bidding, and by April 12, 1922, Sinclair's newly formed Mammoth Oil had a 20-year lease on Teapot Dome signed by Fall and the secretary of the navy. On May 8 Sinclair paid Fall roughly $270,000, much of it in Liberty Bonds.

Just two days after Fall signed the Teapot Dome lease over to Sinclair, the *Wall Street Journal* broke a front-page story that quoted unnamed officials of the Department of Interior saying "The arrangement [between the government and Mammoth Oil] marks one of the greatest petroleum undertakings of the age . . . and signalizes a notable departure on the part of the government in seeking partnership with private capital for the working of government-owned natural resources."[17] Newspapers in New Mexico and other parts of the West had already been investigating a possible connection between Fall's growing landholdings and his friendships with oilmen. A few days after the *Wall Street Journal* story, Fall claimed there was nothing unusual about the arrangement with Sinclair.

It is difficult to determine if Harding had anything to do with the Teapot Dome scandal. A report written by Fall, which the president signed, said that Harding had approved the plan for the naval oil reserves.[18] Given Harding's notorious disinterest in details, however, it is unlikely that he ever read the report, especially given that it was 75 pages long and padded with facts, charts, and diagrams intended to obfuscate more than clarify. In October, after Fall had awarded Sinclair another contract giving the oil baron even more rights in Teapot Dome, Harding wrote to Fall, "I have no concern about Wyoming oil matters. I am confident you have adopted the correct policy and will carry it through in a way altogether to be approved."[19] Harding's confidence was misplaced; Fall resigned in January 1923.

Fall was hardly the lone crook in the Harding administration. During the same period that Fall was selling government oil leases, Veterans Affairs (VA) chief Charles R. Forbes took bribes from construction company owners in return for favorable contracts for the building of VA hospitals. Forbes also took kickbacks after arranging for the government to purchase land from real estate friends at inflated prices. On one occasion the government paid $105,000 for property valued at $20,000. Forbes and another official split a kickback of $25,000 while the property owner kept the rest.

In the fall of 1922 Forbes gained authority over government warehouses in Maryland filled with medical supplies left over from World War I. Forbes made a deal with a Boston company to sell off the supplies, ostensibly claiming that the sale would save the government money on storage. Bed sheets the government had purchased for a dollar apiece were sold to the Boston company for 20 cents. Other supplies included drugs, alcohol, towels, gauze, and even pajamas. The Surgeon General and the chairman of the Federal Hospitalization Board complained, so Harding summoned Forbes to the White House for an explanation and ordered him to stop selling the supplies. Forbes continued, then he left the country for Europe and tendered his resignation in February 1923, one month after Fall's resignation. The next month, Forbes's accomplice, the VA general counsel Charles Cramer, committed suicide by shooting himself in the head. The official investigation into Forbes's activities commenced in October, the day before the congressional hearings on Fall began. Following the investigation, Forbes was indicted, tried, and convicted of conspiracy. In 1926 Forbes became the first from the Harding administration to go to prison, where he served two years.[20]

While Forbes and Fall were enriching themselves through kickbacks and oil leases, Attorney General Harry Daugherty took bribes from bootleggers and businessmen under indictment. He also secured pardons and paroles for wealthy white-collar criminals doing time in federal prison. Daugherty's underling Jess Smith did much of the legwork for these operations. By 1923 Smith was telling his girlfriend there were people out to get him. He was probably right. Later investigations revealed that he had been collecting bribes for favors and that some of the favors were never delivered. Criminals who had paid hundreds of thousands of dollars for a pardon or parole were cheated out of their money and were angry with Smith. Moreover, Smith began to suspect that the misdeeds of the Justice Department might be pinned on him. In other words, if the crooks didn't get him, the feds would.

On Memorial Day, Smith set up an appointment with Thomas Walsh (D-Montana), one of the senators looking into Harding administration misdeeds. (Walsh would later head the Senate investigation.) After the appointment, Smith took care of some errands, then returned to the Wardman Park apartment that he shared with Daugherty and retired to his room. Early the next morning, Daugherty was awakened by a loud crash. When he walked into the living room, he found Smith dead of a gunshot wound to the head, his head stuck in a wastebasket. By the time the police arrived, the gun was missing, never to be found. There was no autopsy, and most of the police report disappeared shortly thereafter. What remained of the report said that the bullet had entered the left side of Smith's head and exited his right temple, the opposite direction one would expect in a suicide committed by the right-handed Smith. Moreover, there were no bullet holes in the wastebasket. Still, the death was ruled a suicide.

⁂

Senator Walsh's Committee on Public Lands and Surveys began its investigation into Fall's activities on October 23, 1923, roughly two months after Harding's death. The hearings took the form that would be replicated later in the century during the Watergate scandal of the 1970s and the Iran-Contra scandal of the 1980s. The proceedings started with congressional hearings, then broadened when President Coolidge appointed special prosecutors.

Fall testified most of the first two days of the hearing. He and Walsh sparred over the power of the president to issue direct orders having to do with public lands, specifically the Teapot Dome and Elk Hills leases. Fall held his ground in arguing that the president and his cabinet were within their power to issue contracts as they saw fit to protect the vital interests of the United States. Then the questioning shifted to whether Fall himself had received compensation. Walsh asked Fall pointedly, "Did you get any compensation at all [in these land deals]?" Under oath, Fall nevertheless replied with the first of many lies: "I have never even suggested any compensation and have received none."[21]

Harry Sinclair also appeared before the Senate committee and admitted to nothing. Then, after a one-month recess, Edward Doheny testified, beginning on December 3. Doheny eventually told the committee that he had lent Fall $100,000 and that Fall had tried to keep this a secret for fear that it would be misunderstood as a bribe rather than a loan. Walsh noted for the record the oddity that a business loan that large would be made in cash stuffed into a black bag. Walsh got Doheny to admit that Fall had paid nothing back on the loan—no interest, no payments on principal. Doheny also claimed that Fall had given him a legal IOU for the $100,000 but that the note had been lost.

Doheny's testimony suddenly raised the Teapot Dome scandal to a level of corruption not seen since the Grant administration of the 1870s. In March Secretary of the Navy Denby and Attorney General Daugherty resigned for their roles in transferring the leases to Fall's jurisdiction. Coolidge then appointed two special prosecutors—Atlee Pomerene, a Democrat, and Owen Roberts, a Republican. Coolidge told Roberts, "If you are confirmed, there is one thing you must bear in mind. You will be working for the government of the United States—not for the Republican Party, and not for me."[22] Coolidge's moral clarity stood in stark contrast to Harding's slovenly ethics, both private and public. The charge of the special prosecutors was twofold: secure cancellation of the leases between the government and Sinclair and Doheny's oil companies and bring to justice those who had committed crimes in conjunction with the leases.

Roberts used the same investigative strategy that Bob Woodward and Carl Bernstein would use a half century later in cracking open the Watergate case against Richard Nixon: Follow the money. The investigation was complicated because the bonds Sinclair had given to Fall changed hands so many times. Lead investigator Thomas Foster tracked the bonds through individuals, corporations, dummy corporations, Canadian banks, and finally Sinclair's Mammoth Oil Company. In June 1924 Roberts secured indictments against Fall, Sinclair,

Doheny, and Doheny's son Edward Jr., charging they had conspired to defraud the U.S. government.

Fall and Doheny were found not guilty, while Sinclair was found guilty only of contempt of Congress, essentially for lying to the investigating committee. He was sentenced to three months in jail and a $500 fine. Former Attorney General Daugherty was also tried and found not guilty. All was not lost, however. In addition to the criminal cases against individuals, the government also challenged the legitimacy of the Elk Hills and Teapot Dome contracts. The cases wended their ways to the U.S. Supreme Court, and in October 1927 the contracts were voided because the Court ruled they were the result of fraud and conspiracy. The oil leases were returned to the government, while Doheny and Sinclair had to repay the government nearly $35 million. Essentially, although the government could not persuade juries to convict former U.S. cabinet members, judges found that government officials and the heads of the two oil companies had engaged in fraud and conspiracy and thus the contracts were voided. The Supreme Court decision cited Fall as a "faithless public officer . . . willing to conspire against the public interest."[23]

Following the Supreme Court decision on the lease cases, there was one more criminal trial. Juries had failed to convict Fall and Doheny of conspiring together in the Elk Hills case, but Fall and Sinclair were yet to be tried in the Teapot Dome case.

In April 1928 Sinclair's second trial for conspiracy began. Fall was too ill to be tried at the time, so his case was separated from Sinclair's. Fall's son-in-law, M. T. Everhart, testified that he had taken large amounts of cash and bonds from Sinclair and delivered them to Fall. The only question was whether these were bribes, loans, or a purchase of part interest in Fall's New Mexico ranch. Given that there had never been a loan note or certificate for the sale of land, this seemed an open-and-shut case of bribery. The jury deliberated only a few hours before returning with a verdict: not guilty.

Congress, the press, and the American people were flabbergasted and outraged. Sinclair had essentially been confirmed a conspirator by the U.S. Supreme Court in the oil lease civil cases and by Walsh's Senate committee, yet a Washington, D.C., jury refused to convict him. After his acquittal he was called back before the Walsh committee. He could not plead the Fifth Amendment because he had been found not guilty and therefore could not be tried for bribing Fall. Before Walsh's committee, he admitted that he had given cash and Liberty Bonds to Fall but insisted the money was an investment in Fall's ranch.

Walsh's committee hearings ended on May 2, 1928, immediately after Sinclair's testimony. After four years the committee had shown conclusively that four oilmen had profited illegally and that one of them, Sinclair, had given some of those profits to members of Harding's cabinet and to the Republican Party. Still, no one had gone to prison for these misdeeds. That changed a year later when Sinclair reported to the Washington, D.C. jail and asylum to serve his sentence for contempt of Congress, the result of his two conflicting testimonies before Walsh's committee. Like the oil lease civil cases, Sinclair's appeal had gone all the way to the Supreme Court, where his contempt conviction was upheld. He served seven and a half months during which time he worked in the jail pharmacy rolling pills and assisting the jailhouse doctor. Sinclair had also been convicted of jury tampering, and while he was in jail an appeals court upheld that conviction. His sentences ran concurrently. During his time in jail the board of his company, now called Sinclair Oil, unanimously decided to retain him as chief executive. Likewise, a large bank in Tulsa decided to retain him as vice president and director. When he was released in November, he issued a statement saying he had been railroaded by Democrats (Walsh's committee) and that he had never done anything wrong.

Matters did not turn out so well for Fall. His 700,000-acre New Mexico ranch was seized by the sheriff for back taxes and debt. The day after Sinclair went to jail, the ranch was sold at auction. Doheny bought the property for $168,250, which amounted to 24 cents an acre, and allowed Fall to continue living there.[24] In October 1929 Fall went on trial for bribery. The ailing 67-year-old sat in a large, comfortable chair with cloaks draped over his shoulders throughout the trial. He was ushered in and out of the courtroom in a wheelchair, attended by a doctor and nurse. Jurors were locked up through the three-week ordeal to avoid a repeat of the jury tampering that had taken place in Sinclair's trial. They concluded that the $100,000 Doheny had given Fall back in 1921 was a bribe. The judge sentenced Fall to a year in jail and a fine of $100,000, about a third of the maximum sentence allowable. The following March Doheny went on trial. After 10 days another sequestered Washington jury took but an hour to return from deliberations with a verdict of not guilty.

Fall's supporters appealed to President Herbert Hoover for a pardon. The request was pending when Hoover spoke at the dedication of the Harding Memorial in Marion, Ohio, in June 1931. In his speech the president cited the men around Harding who had betrayed the former president's trust. He no doubt had Fall in mind and was signaling that he was not about to pardon him. When an ambulance delivered Fall to a Santa Fe correctional facility in July 1931, he became the first cabinet officer in the history of the United States to go to prison.

PRODIGAL NATION

Some years after Harding's presidency, nationally renowned Kansas journalist William Allen White compared America during the Harding years to the story of the Prodigal Son in the gospel of Luke. In that story, one son of a wealthy landowner asks for his share of the inheritance then goes to a far country and squanders his fortune on riotous living. Eventually, penniless, hungry, and jealous of the swine he worked among because at least they had enough to eat, the prodigal journeys back to his father. White's gloss was that America during the Harding years had "turned away some of the things of the spirit, got its share of the patrimony ruthlessly, and went out and lived riotously and ended it by feeding among the swine." "God what a story," White declared. "The story of Babylon is a Sunday school story compared to the story of Washington from June 1919 until July 1923. . . . We haven't even yet got back to our Father's house."[25] Author Alice Longworth was even more severe. She wrote, "Harding was not a bad man. He was just a slob."[26]

There is a sense in which Harding's story is the story of America during the Roaring Twenties: unbridled opportunism leading to corruption, scandal on a monumental scale, moral degeneration, and contempt for the rule of law. Harding, like the country itself, was formally religious, a member and trustee of the First Baptist Church of Marion. While religion was an official part of his life, however, it was neither deep nor personal. Church membership was like belonging to a country club. It was a public association somewhat detached from important matters. As his biographer Russell put it, "Religion was for Harding like the Constitution, something to be honored and let alone."[27]

But this is hardly the only story of the era. Religion in the Roaring Twenties could be deep or superficial, genuine or pretentious, personal or a mere formality. But any way we cut it, religion was central to the culture, and its proper role in public life was highly contested. At the same time the Harding mess was unfolding in the White House, America was three years into the great social and moral experiment known as Prohibition.

CHAPTER 2

PROHIBITION AS CULTURE WAR

Less than eight months after the official start of the Prohibition era in 1920, a still was found on the farm of Senator Morris Sheppard (D-Texas), the "Father of National Prohibition." The federal Prohibition officer and local sheriff's deputies had to wait for the contraption, hot from a night of use, to cool before removing it. Nearby stood eight barrels of mash ready to be turned into alcohol. Another Roaring Twenties scandal? Actually, Senator Sheppard had nothing to do with the still. In fact, his family no longer owned the farm on which it was found. Symbolically, however, the proximity of a bootlegging operation to the boyhood home of one of America's leading Prohibitionists symbolized the difficulty federal authorities would have enforcing the Eighteenth Amendment. The same Texas soil that sustained Sheppard in his youth had the capacity to produce over 100 gallons of alcohol per day. Similarly, the same restless Progressive Era reform impulse that made national Prohibition possible also brought about innovations of the kind that made the 1920s roar and resulted in the law's eventual repeal.

In December 1917 the Eighteenth Amendment passed both houses of Congress by the required two-thirds majority. By mid-January 1919 it had been ratified by three-fourths of the states and was set to take effect exactly one year later. The year of limbo meant that when the troops came home from World War I in 1918 and early 1919, they could buy a drink without fear of arrest, unless they lived in the 75 percent of America that was already dry before the amendment took effect. In reality, neither the Eighteenth Amendment nor the

Volstead Act that was passed to enforce it stopped the use of alcoholic beverages everywhere. Rather, in some areas Prohibition merely drove what had been
a legal business underground and seemed to help several crime bosses become
wealthy, most notoriously the millionaire gangster Al Capone. As Capone once
said, "Prohibition is business. All I do is supply a demand." This is not to say
that Prohibition failed entirely. In some areas the law did reduce alcohol consumption. Alcohol use did not decline uniformly across the nation, however.
In many areas, particularly large urban centers, enforcement was nearly impossible. Prohibition advocate William Jennings Bryan acknowledged in 1923
that Prohibition sentiment had not yet captured the cities. In New York City
reporter Stanley Walker estimated in the mid-1920s that there were 9,000 establishments that served alcohol, while a recent historian has put the number
at 30,000. When the mayor of Berlin, Germany, toured New York in 1929 he
saw so many liquor establishments that he became confused and asked his host
when Prohibition was supposed to start.[1]

Someone once called Prohibition "a bad idea whose time had come," but in
some ways it was a good idea whose time had passed. Prohibition is often
viewed as an attempt to bring people's private habits in line with some sort of
Puritan behavioral norm, and even some scholars and pundits have portrayed
it this way. Journalist H. L. Mencken viewed Prohibition the way he viewed
everything supported by fundamentalists: as a backward-looking attempt to
spoil other people's fun. Prominent historian Richard Hofstadter wrote in the
1960s that Prohibition "was carried about America by the rural-evangelical
virus" that had an aversion "to the pleasures and amenities of city life, and to the
well-to-do classes of cultivated men."[2] Such a view has been laid to rest by scholars who interpret Prohibition as part of the Progressive Era (1900–1925), when
reformers tackled a series of abuses that threatened society's bold march into
the future. "If the Progressive movement was nourished on a belief in the moral
law," wrote historian James Timberlake in 1963, "so was Prohibition, which
sought to remove from commerce an article that was believed to despoil man's
reason and undermine the foundation of religion and representative government."[3] Seen this way, Prohibition was a sibling to child labor laws, legal limits
on the working hours of wage earners, and other regulations on industrial working conditions. Prohibition reflected the progressive belief in efficiency that
resulted from scientific progress. Science showed that alcohol diminished the
capacity of human beings to be productive, that it led to crime, poverty, and

disease. Eliminating the liquor trade, reformers hoped, would remove these obstacles to progress. This is not to say that all progressives supported Prohibition. Old-stock, Anglo-Protestant reformers did, while ethnic, urban reformers often did not.

Although part of the progressive spirit, in another sense Prohibition symbolized the last gasp of traditional America that was at war with a new conception of freedom. The older, Victorian ethos of the nineteenth century consisted of an American culture in which the family was the basic unit that promoted the values of self-confidence, character, conscience, hard work, and self-sufficiency. "The purpose of Prohibition was to protect the values sheltered by the American nuclear family," Prohibition historian Norman Clark has written. Prohibition was an expression of anxiety about the industrial world in both Europe and America. In that new world "industrialism, opportunity, and social turmoil (new in Europe as well as in America) was [sic] a moral frontier . . . [that] demanded new patterns of interpersonal relationships." Prohibition reformers understood "that these new relationships were threatened by the unrestricted use of distilled spirits."[4]

Such a communitarian notion that the family was the basic unit of freedom clashed with a newer idea of individual rights. In this view, often known as modern liberalism, a family or any other group was merely a voluntary or biological gathering of free individuals. The existence of Prohibition in a decade such as the 1920s revealed two competing views of America. The older, Anglo-Protestant, Victorian view emphasized the corporate nature of public morality. The newer, liberal view trumpeted personal freedom, individual rights, and privacy to do as one pleased so long as no one else was hurt. Standing often between these two camps, but siding against Prohibition, were America's newer arrivals—principally Roman Catholics, ethnic Lutherans, and Jews—most of whom simply did not accept the moral position of abstinence from alcohol. Moderation was their watchword.

THE BACKGROUND FOR PROHIBITION

Along with antislavery, education reform, and women's rights, temperance grew out of the revivals of the Second Great Awakening. These revivals swept over the young nation between 1800 and 1840. They produced many individual conversions to evangelical Christianity and ensured that revivalist Protestantism would be the dominant religion in America for the rest of the century. The revivals also spurred social reform on the part of those who were converted. Initially, temperance reformers emphasized moral suasion as the means by which Americans would cut alcohol consumption. According to the best statistics available, absolute alcohol consumption in the United States in 1830 was 7.1 gallons per year for those 15 years or older, the highest it has ever been in American history, including in our own time. Drinking was not merely a nighttime activity for those prone to party. Rather, workers imbibed throughout the day, owners of businesses often providing the booze. Of course, alcohol consumption was not uniform across the population. About half of the adult males drank two-thirds of the alcohol that was consumed, and consumption shifted from beer and wine, with relatively low absolute alcohol content, to distilled spirits.

The situation worsened as the American people moved westward across the frontier, but America was hardly the only nation with a drinking problem. As a historian of early American alcoholism puts it, "Americans drank more than the English, Irish, or Prussians, but about the same as the Scots or French, and less than the Swedes." One study in the 1970s showed that only France had a higher per capita intake during the nineteenth century.[5] Heavier-drinking nations, such as Scotland, Sweden, and the United States, tended to have a strong agricultural base that produced cheap and abundant grain, they were rural and lightly populated, and they were Protestant. The hardships of the plains combined with the lack of churches and other civic organizations seemed to facilitate a growing American alcohol problem and the social dysfunction that accompanied it—abuse of women and neglect of children the most obvious effects. One historian has called America in the first half of the nineteenth century *The Alcoholic Republic*.[6]

By 1850 the temperance movement had succeeded in reducing per capita consumption of absolute alcohol for those 15 years or older from 7.1 to 1.8 gallons per year. Living in the era before sophisticated social science data, however, many reformers were unaware how effective their efforts over the previous two decades had been. They wanted to do more, especially those with an ethic of abstinence. Instead of continuing with the program of moral suasion, therefore, temperance reformers became Prohibitionists, shifting their efforts toward outlawing the manufacture and sale of alcoholic beverages. Maine was the first state to pass Prohibition legislation in 1851, and many others followed with their own "Maine laws." Eight of the 13 states where such laws were passed saw the legislation struck down by state supreme courts. The trauma of the Civil War interrupted the progress of the Prohibition movement as slavery increasingly occupied the attention of legislators. The Prohibition movement paused before resuming with renewed vigor after the war.[7]

The National Prohibition Party was founded in 1869 followed by the Woman's Christian Temperance Union (WCTU) in 1874 and the Anti-Saloon League (ASL) in 1893. The ASL became the most important organization in the move toward a dry Constitution. As with the Maine laws of the 1850s, much of the Prohibition work before World War I took place in state legislatures. Progressive reformers promoted initiatives and referenda as democratic mechanisms fostering state and local dry laws. Using these instruments of democracy, several states passed local option laws that permitted cities, towns, or counties to vote on whether they preferred to be dry or wet. By 1917, 26 states were dry, representing more than half of the U.S. population. In 17 of them, legal Prohibition resulted from local option voting on the part of the people, as opposed to acts of the legislatures. Meanwhile, Frances Willard and the WCTU promoted state laws mandating temperance education in public schools. Eventually, all states had such laws.

The efforts in the individual states, however, were problematic. Specifically, there were issues concerning legal shipments of alcohol originating in wet states then moving through areas where alcohol was illegal. The U.S. Constitution reserves to the U.S. Congress the right to regulate interstate commerce, which left dry states helpless to keep alcohol shipments out so long as they originated elsewhere. More generally, from the perspective of Prohibitionists, the very existence of wet states was an affront to dry reformers. For this and other reasons, in 1913 the ASL launched its drive for national Prohibition. By that time ASL legal counsel Wayne Wheeler had mastered the technique of lobbying state legislators for local option laws. Arguably the most important force behind legal Prohibition, Wheeler led the ASL effort to convince the U.S. Congress to pass the Eighteenth Amendment.

As Wheeler and the ASL effectively lobbied representatives and senators, Morris Sheppard of Texas became a leader within Congress. Elected to the U.S. House of Representatives in 1902 and moving into the Senate in 1913, he helped write the Webb-Kenyon Act (1913), which aimed to regulate the interstate shipment of alcoholic beverages, thus alleviating one of the problems faced by dry states. In 1916 he wrote a bill that bore his name to prohibit the sale of alcohol in Washington, D.C., where the U.S. Congress has direct jurisdiction. Following passage of the D.C. law, Sheppard received a death threat. Postmarked Washington, D.C., the letter read in part: "The people of the District are not going to put up with your despotism and I am willing to go to the electric chair for killing a devil like you."[8] Undeterred by the threat, the next year Sheppard introduced the Senate resolution that led to passage of the Eighteenth Amendment, and he also aided the enactment of the Volstead Bill, which took its name from Andrew Volstead, who introduced it in the House of Representatives.

The efforts of the ASL's Wheeler and Senator Sheppard notwithstanding, it is doubtful that the Eighteenth Amendment would have succeeded in the absence of World War I. War often accelerates social reform. As the soldiers trained, reformers emphasized the need for moral fitness. The U.S. government pressured cities to rid themselves of houses of prostitution and saloons near military training facilities. Congress then outlawed the selling of liquor to soldiers and also banned the use of grain and other foodstuffs for the distilling of alcohol. The official slogan was "Shall the many have food or the few have drink?" Moreover, Prohibitionists linked German breweries with the German enemy in the war, turning Prohibition into patriotism. As one propagandist put it, "We have German enemies across the water. We have German enemies in this country too. And the worst of all our German enemies, the most treacherous, the most menacing are Pabst, Schlitz, Blatz, and Miller."[9] The efforts of the ASL from 1913 to 1917 put the nation in the position of having to decide on national Prohibition; the war tipped the scales toward yes.

PROHIBITION AND THE ROARING TWENTIES

The year Prohibition went into effect, Fort Worth, Texas, fundamentalist J. Frank Norris presented his U.S. senator with an engraved silver set bearing the words "Presented to Senator Morris Sheppard by the largest Sunday School in America, The First Baptist Church, Fort Worth, Texas as an appreciation of his successful work in securing constitutional Prohibition." Like Norris, almost all fundamentalists supported Prohibition. William Jennings Bryan campaigned against alcohol long before he took up the mantle of anti-evolution. When he was secretary of state in the Woodrow Wilson administration from 1913 to 1915, he refused to serve alcohol at State Department functions. It was no accident that as soon as the Eighteenth Amendment passed Congress, Bryan took to serious anti-evolution work that would lead eventually to his role in the Scopes trial of 1925. With one social ill disposed of, he turned his energies to the other. Likewise, renowned Pentecostal preacher Aimee Semple McPherson fought the twin evils of alcohol and evolution. In 1924 the WCTU chose her to announce the nomination of Marie Brehn for vice president on the Prohibition Party ticket, and McPherson campaigned for vigorous enforcement of the Eighteenth Amendment via her radio program emanating from her Angelus Temple in Los Angeles.

Neither Norris nor McPherson, however, had the Prohibition cachet of Billy Sunday, the most famous evangelist of the era. Around 1909 he developed a 12,000-word sermon entitled "Booze" and went on to preach it many times as the campaign for Prohibition gained momentum. The sermon was not centered on the need for holy living; Sunday did not expect the unconverted to live holy lives. Those who came down the aisle for conversion at his revivals were instructed to immediately give up alcohol and stop sinning as best they could. But that would not stop the unconverted from continuing to wreak havoc through drink. Prohibition was intended to make the unconverted stop drinking. Sunday, like the progressive reformers, supported legal Prohibition because he believed it would result in a reduction of crime, violence, and a host of other societal ills. He used a dizzying array of statistics to prove the ill effects of alcohol. For example, he claimed that the state of Illinois appropriated $6 million in 1908 to care for the state's insane people. Alcohol, he claimed, produced 75 percent of the insane. (The actual figure from science at that time was closer to 25 percent.) The insane were housed in state-run asylums or jails. He concluded, therefore, that if alcohol were outlawed, the measure would save the taxpayers a great deal of money. "Do away with the saloons and you will close these institutions. The saloons make them necessary." He went on to calculate that the average factory worker made $450 a year, while it took $1,200 per year to support each "whiskey criminal" in a jail or prison somewhere in the nation. Sunday's solution was to outlaw alcohol so the whiskey criminal would reform and start earning his $450 per year instead of costing the state $1,200.

With an argument that might have impressed a careful logician, even if leaving one suspicious of his premises, Sunday declared passionately:

Now listen! Last year the income of the United States government and the cities and towns and counties, from the whisky business was $350,000,000.

That is putting it liberally. You say that is a lot of money. Well, last year the workingmen spent $2,000,000,000 for drink, and it cost $1,200,000,000 to care for the judicial machinery. In other words, the whisky business cost us last year $3,400,000,000. I will subtract from that the dirty $350,000,000 which we got, and it leaves $3,050,000,000 in favor of knocking the whisky business out on purely a money basis.[10]

It is doubtful anyone in his audience could follow the particulars of such an argument, but the point was clear, and Sunday was just getting warmed up. Much more moving were anecdotes about the drunken young man who became enraged when his mother would not give him money for alcohol. He pulled a pistol and intended to force a nearby saloonkeeper to give him a drink. His mother and sister tried to stop him, but he pushed them away. When a neighbor heard the commotion and tried to intervene, the young man shot the neighbor dead. The young man was convicted and sentenced to life in prison. When his mother heard the verdict, she fell in a swoon and died three hours later.[11]

In this anecdote Sunday hit upon two important cultural factors that fueled Prohibition. The first was the nature of drunkenness in America. In Sunday's story, the drinking man is prone to violence. Alcohol lessens inhibitions, making it difficult to control emotions. As philosopher William James once put it, alcohol is "the great exciter of the Yes function in man."[12] Historically, among American males, drunkenness has most often meant yes to sex and violence. Such is not the case in all cultures. In some places, drunken males are overly sentimental, passive, or given to religious transcendence—useless, perhaps, but also harmless.[13] One can conjecture about why drunkenness in America leads to violence and sex, but there is little wonder why these manifestations were considered harmful to the family structure. The male breadwinner of the Victorian family needed to maintain and model industry, thrift, and character, which is difficult when one is chasing women and engaging in barroom brawls.

The boozing, footloose male puts women and children at risk. In Sunday's story two women attempt to rescue the young alcoholic—his mother and sister—but it might just as well have been a wife and daughter, as was the case in the classic temperance novel *Ten Nights in a Barroom, and What I Saw There.* Written in the wake of the Maine law of 1851 and then turned into a stage drama, the story focuses on Joe Morgan, who becomes an alcoholic, mistreats his wife, and abandons his family to poverty. Morgan's daughter Mary comes to the saloon to rescue him, singing "Father, Dear Father, Come Home with Me Now." The scene turns violent when the bartender throws a mug at the worthless Morgan but misses and hits Mary instead, killing her. The play continues with the alcoholic ruin of other males in the village of Cedarville, where Morgan lived. The story climaxes when the bartender is murdered by his own son. The alcohol-induced mayhem eventually leads Morgan to the same conclusion as Sunday 60 years later: "The accursed [liquor] traffic must cease among us," Morgan says. "If you would save the young, the weak, the innocent . . . , let us resolve this night, that from henceforth, the traffic shall cease in Cedarville."[14] Morgan reformed himself, while Sunday's nameless young man could not be saved, and he took down his mother with him when she died of a broken heart following his conviction.

The second cultural component in Sunday's story was the saloon. To Prohibitionists, the saloon symbolized the greatest institutional threat to society. There was a positive side to the local saloon, especially for the ethnic working classes in the cities. Anglo-Protestants, however, saw only the negative. Sunday's young man commits murder outside a saloon. It is no accident that the most influential Prohibition organization was the Anti-Saloon League and not the anti-alcohol league. Saloons were considered anti–middle class — that is, anti-Victorian and anti-family. They cultivated nonvirtues of sex, violence, sloth, and slovenliness. Breweries sponsored saloons with exclusive contracts that encouraged saloonkeepers to push for ever growing consumption. Saloonkeepers in turn provided all sorts of inducements to encourage working males to go straight from the factory to the bar, and the inducements worked. After the decline in alcohol consumption as a result of the Temperance movement from 1830 to 1850, the period from 1850 to 1890 saw a 24-fold increase in total consumption of beer, while the population merely tripled. Moreover, houses of prostitution usually stood near saloons, and the two institutions worked in cooperation with each other, as alcohol excited the Yes function. Many Prohibition reformers made clear that the saloon was the object of their wrath, not the drinking of fermented beverages in the quietness of one's own home. Morris Sheppard said in 1917, "I am not a Prohibitionist in the strict sense of the word. I am fighting the liquor traffic. I am against the saloon. I am not in any sense aiming to prevent the personal use of alcoholic beverages."[15] In keeping with such sentiment, neither the Eighteenth Amendment nor the Volstead Act outlawed possession or private consumption of alcohol, only its production, transportation, and sale. Oddly, this meant that if one had stock-piled enough booze to make it through the Prohibition era and only drank in private, all would be well.

While Sunday, Norris, and McPherson all campaigned tirelessly for Prohibition, Presbyterian J. Gresham Machen stood virtually alone among fundamentalists in his opposition to the law. Machen was the most important fundamentalist intellectual of the 1920s. Politically, he was a small-government libertarian who viewed Prohibition and similar efforts to control behavior as evidence of creeping statism that would eventually curtail personal liberty. He also opposed child labor laws, the creation of the Department of Education, and even prayer and Bible reading in public schools because such measures interfered with the rights of families and churches to make decisions about work, education, and theology. Machen was originally from Baltimore, born of parents from the Old South. He identified with Thomas Jefferson's dictum that the government that governs least, governs best. But he also had theological reasons for opposing Prohibition that complemented his political views. Essentially, he believed that the church was the proper institution to police the morals of its members. The state should protect individual liberty, while churches, families, and voluntary organizations should build character. Moreover, Machen hailed from a wing of Reformed (i.e., Calvinist) Protestantism that stressed moderation in the use of alcohol, not total abstinence.[16] In short, Prohibition interfered with his personal liberty to enjoy a glass of wine in the evening as he studied scripture, wrote theology, or contemplated how best to defeat the theological liberals in the Presbyterian church.

Like many secular journalists of the 1920s, twenty-first-century pundits see Prohibition as a failed fundamentalist crusade to control the private lives of Americans. Ironically, among the religious of the time, Prohibition was hardly a fundamentalist cause. The liberal-leaning Federal Council of Churches (FCC) endorsed the Eighteenth Amendment and espoused "total abstinence for the individual and Prohibition for the state and nation." This, the FCC said, "is the path of wisdom and safety."[17] Liberal Protestant elites were just as often at the forefront of Prohibition as were fundamentalists. In 1926 liberals in the Presbyterian Church U.S.A. used Machen's opposition to Prohibition to deny him a promotion at Princeton. The underlying reasons may have been Machen's fundamentalism and personality conflicts with liberals, but the liberals knew that citing opposition to the Eighteenth Amendment as their reason for barring

Machen from an endowed professor's chair would cash out better among rank-and-file church members. Along with many liberal Protestants, Harry Emerson Fosdick, the leading liberal preacher of the era, campaigned vigorously at the local level to rid Montclair, New Jersey, of saloons while he pastored there from 1904 to 1915. Although he preferred the local option approach over national Prohibition, once the Eighteenth Amendment was in force, he usually favored it over alternatives. In theory he sometimes entertained the general notion that legalizing beer and light wines might be acceptable, but in practice he spoke against almost all specific measures that would have weakened Prohibition. As one reporter noted of Fosdick's view, "He admits the desirability of changing the law as long as the proposition remains general. But let anyone advance a particular change, and he is up in arms."[18]

Liberal Protestants such as Fosdick were imbued with the modern spirit of progress. Like secular progressives, they believed that if they applied the technical expertise of social science to social problems, better and better societies would emerge. In his immensely popular book *Christianity and Progress,* Fosdick contrasted the traditional view of nature as a fixed, unchanging reality with the modern temperament that accepted, welcomed, and promoted change, all for the better. He classed Prohibition as an example of progress that even the most ardent conservative accepted, writing: "[Even] the most conservative of us so hates the colossal abomination of the liquor traffic, that we do not propose to cease our fight until victory has been won."[19]

In the liberal camp Charles Stelzle was the most ardent champion of Prohibition. He served as superintendent of the Presbyterian Church U.S.A.'s Department of Church Labor from 1903 to 1913. He virtually created this agency, the purpose of which was to apply Christianity to social problems in the spirit of the Social Gospel movement. Social Gospel advocates were especially concerned about the plight of working-class people in the cities. When the Department of Church Labor foundered financially, Stelzle resigned and took on social service fieldwork for the Federal Council of Churches and the Red Cross. Like the fundamentalist Billy Sunday, Stelzle was fond of citing statistics, usually drawn from sociological studies. He wrote a book titled *Why Prohibition* and in his 1926 autobiography devoted an entire chapter to the cause. He argued that the movement was not started by people who wanted to force their personal ethic of abstinence on everyone. Rather, he claimed, "Prohibition was brought about because large numbers of the nearly two hundred thousand saloons and places where liquor was sold in this country had become a distinct menace." In other words, Prohibition aimed to protect the public, not police private lives. He pointed out that Prohibition was aimed at those who manufactured alcohol and at the saloons that retailed it to the public. "[I]t was the Anti-Saloon, not the Anti-Liquor League, that was the most active organization in temperance reform," he noted.[20]

Even while Prohibition was the law of the land in the 1920s, Stelzle emphasized that it could not be forced on Americans. In 1925 he spoke to the executive committee of the Federal Council of Churches at its Detroit meeting. "Prohibition will produce its best results," he said, "only when the people of our country accept it sincerely, warm-heartedly, and enthusiastically." Having grown up in the Bowery neighborhood of south Manhattan, Stelzle was one of the few Prohibitionists who understood both the positive and negative sides of the saloon. He pointed out that when Prohibition was enacted, no substitute for the saloon emerged. For many workers, the saloon stood as their chief place of fellowship and recreation. With nothing to take its place, these workers became bitter. He argued that Prohibition needed to be connected to a larger program of Progressive reform aimed at remedying the ills of the city, where urban workers lived. By implication Stelzle targeted his criticism at those who believed that strict enforcement alone could reform society.

On this point he surely had many of his Protestant brothers and sisters in mind, and among them fundamentalists in particular. Of all the supporters of Prohibition, fundamentalists were the most likely to make militant pronouncements concerning the need to abide by Prohibition law. As Stelzle wrote in his autobiography, "It is unfortunate that many Prohibition reformers have assumed an arrogant attitude toward this entire situation. They have insisted with irritating finality that because the Eighteenth Amendment to the Constitution was passed in a perfectly legal way that the question is forever closed." Similarly, he told his Detroit audience, "It is not sufficient merely to insist upon obedience to the law. There should be more of an inclination on the part of the Prohibitionists to rest the claim for observance of the Volstead Act upon its merits as a social measure."[21]

Both Stelzle and Bryan combined the nineteenth-century temperance movement's moral suasion with the legally enforced Prohibition of the 1920s. In other words, even as the manufacture and sale of alcohol remained illegal, they continued to persuade people of the social benefits of Prohibition. As anyone could see in any American city, Prohibition enforcement failed when people lost faith in the cause. In stressing the need for continued moral suasion, Stelzle warned against abusive and bombastic tactics, telling a story of one of his own debates with a prominent New York attorney. Warned ahead of time that his opponent would certainly belittle Stelzle and the Prohibition position, Stelzle decided to disarm the man with reason and peace. Speaking first, Stelzle made no reference to the attorney or the organization he represented but instead lectured on the economic aspects of the liquor problem. According to Stelzle, when the attorney took to the podium, he turned to Stelzle and said, "You are too much the gentleman to be in this business. You have not abused the liquor men nor the saloon-keepers, and this sort of procedure is altogether too uncommon among your friends."[22] The attorney then told the audience a few funny stories and ceded the floor, declining his 10-minute rebuttal later in the debate. Stelzle knew all too well the kind of rhetoric that often came from fundamentalist Prohibitionists, and he and the attorney might well have had J. Frank Norris in mind when they denounced abusive and offensive Prohibition speech.

In 1921 Norris believed that Fort Worth federal judge James C. Wilson was too lenient on bootleggers. In his newspaper, the *Searchlight,* Norris ran a series of vitriolic articles against the judge in which he pitted Wilson on the side of the bootleggers and opposed to the Ku Klux Klan. In addition to being a racist organization, the Klan was also in favor of moral reform, Prohibition in particular. The KKK was also powerful enough in Texas that if Norris could convince the public that Wilson opposed the organization, the charge would hinder the judge's social and legal standing. As the articles and sermons continued weekly, Norris's charges escalated from lax enforcement of Prohibition, to corruption, then to Wilson's alleged public drunkenness (the latter the same charge Prohibitionists would use in 1928 against Democratic presidential candidate Al Smith). When Wilson announced that he was considering contempt of court charges against Norris, Norris told his followers that he could not be held in contempt of court because the court itself had become contemptible. Eventually Norris backed down and stopped his anti-Wilson campaign.[23]

Norris tended to stress vigorous enforcement of the law rather than the kind of persuasion that Stelzle believed necessary. Playing on racial fears, and combining the alcohol question with sex, Norris said on at least one occasion that the bootlegger was just as bad as a "black rapist." The clear implication was that vigilant police power was the answer. "I want to service notice on the whole bootleg gang and all of their officials, you must as well to get ready to fold your tent, for America is going to be as dry as the Sahara."[24] Norris's self-appointed role was to help elect public officials who were staunchly for Prohibition. To that end, the liquor question became the litmus test election issue for Norris and many other fundamentalists, much as abortion is for Christian Right forces today. In 1924, when the wife of impeached Texas governor Jim Ferguson ran for governor herself, Norris assumed the maneuver was a ruse. Norris believed that Jim would continue to run the state over his wife's shoulder, which was especially troubling because Norris believed Jim Ferguson was soft on Prohibition. Norris's newspaper ran headlines such as "Robertson vs. Jim Ferguson: Rum, Romanism, Russianism, the Issue," "Is Liquor Coming Back?" and "Can You Vote with the Bootlegger?" To his chagrin, Ma Ferguson, as she was affectionately known, won the election. Then, to Norris's surprise, she came out for Prohibition.

Presbyterian Mark Matthews represented the West Coast for fundamentalism the way Norris represented the Baptist South. On the issue of enforcement, he once said that law was sovereign and eternal and therefore Prohibition "ought to be enforced if every street in America had to run with blood and every cobble stone had to be made of a human skull."[25] So much for moral suasion. Ironically, in 1929 the irascible Matthews criticized the Anti-Saloon League for its "fanatical stress" of Prohibition law to the exclusion of concern for other crimes, such as murder. Claiming that only about 100 suspects had been prosecuted for the 13,000 murders committed in 1928, he thundered, "What we need in this country is a League that will prevent establishment of leagues for specific purposes and which will bring the American people back to a sense of their responsibility to the government and to law."[26] As one would expect, anti-Prohibition forces used Matthews's statement against the ASL as an example of waning support for the Volstead Act. The ASL was stunned, and other Prohibition forces accused Matthews of hypocrisy, all the more so when the next year he tried to maneuver himself into the position of United States Prohibition Commissioner. In requesting that his U.S. senator nominate him, he wrote, "I would like to give Prohibition a real enforcement test, and if they will let me organize it I can do it."[27] Both Matthews's biographer and one of the leading historians of Prohibition believe that his rant against the Anti-Saloon League was an attempt to split the dry movement so he could lead it himself.[28]

Fundamentalist enforcement rhetoric like that of Norris and Matthews sometimes jeopardized the fragile Prohibition coalition of fundamentalist and liberal Protestants. Many found revolting the growing stridency of fundamentalist anti-liquor rhetoric. As one liberal Prohibitionist was heard to say after feeling alienated at a 1928 Prohibition convention, "I am going home on the 12:30 train because we Congregationalists and Catholics are merely scenery at this convention; it is altogether a Methodist and Baptist movement."[29] Such sentiment worried the editor of the liberal journal *Christian Century.* Specifically, he feared that Prohibition was becoming a sectarian affair, too narrow to attract wide support. "It is . . . important that national Prohibition shall not become the special interest of any group of churches," he editorialized. "This danger does exist. . . . It is a result of the vigor displayed in behalf of Prohibition by certain evangelical denominations."[30]

Like Stelzle, secular journalist and renowned social commentator Walter Lippmann had people like Norris and Matthews in mind when he wrote in 1929 that fundamentalism "has become entangled with all sorts of bizarre and barbarous agitations, with the Ku Klux Klan, with fanatical Prohibition, with 'anti-evolution laws,' and with much persecution and intolerance."[31] Lippmann was careful to point out that such was not the essence of fundamentalism, but he also understood something that fundamentalists such as Norris and Matthews apparently forgot: Prohibition enforcement was very difficult. The reason, Lippmann said, was that "unless the enforcement of the law is taken in hand by the citizenry, the officials as such are quite helpless." An injured party will report a violation of a contract, and almost everyone will report a burglary. By contrast, Lippmann continued, "The reason Prohibition is unenforceable in the great cities is that the citizens will not report the names and addresses of their bootleggers to Prohibition officials."[32] Stelzle, Bryan, and the editors of *Christian Century* understood this and so continued even at the height of the Prohibition era to persuade people to abide by the law. By contrast, Norris went after Judge Wilson for lax enforcement, failing to acknowledge that lax enforcement against bootleggers was what many people wanted.

DECLINE AND REPEAL

One of the myths of Prohibition was that it was a failure. Myths can be true, false, or partly true. They are essentially stories that people use to make sense of themselves and their culture. To say that Prohibition was a failure is to say something that has been believed widely since the 1920s, and it helps Americans make sense of Prohibition's repeal. One can believe that Prohibition was a noble experiment that just could not work, that it was the stupidest reform ever known to man and therefore doomed to failure, that it represented the last gasp of rural and Christian America against urban and secular America, or that it was another indication that religious fundamentalists want to control people's private lives. All those positions have been argued by scholars, pundits, and folks on the street, but whether Prohibition was a failure depends on what one believes it was intended to do.

In February 1925, after nearly five years of Prohibition, the otherwise unknown Stanwood Lee Henderson wrote a letter to the editor of the New York *Times* titled "Failure of the Dry Law." He cataloged some of the typical arguments against Prohibition, most of which were patently false. Referring to the Volstead Act as an exercise in "tyranny," he claimed that Prohibition had been foisted on the nation by "a tiny body of drys [who] forced their will, through 3000 odd legislators, upon 110,000,000 people." He then said that Prohibition led to bootlegged liquor of such poor quality that thousands of drinkers had been poisoned, many fatally. "Following Prohibition thousands of deaths have been recorded from poisonous wines and liquors," Henderson wrote. "Thousands more have died whose deaths were not so recorded." (It is not clear how he became aware of the unreported thousands who had died.) Henderson went on to list "gastric and renal hospital cases" that were caused by "green beverages," home-brewed beers and wines. He said that these afflictions "kill by slow degrees." Moreover, he claimed, "Murder, robbery and poisoned death for the past four years have formed a fearful triad of daily performances in every portion of the United States." He asked how many of the hundreds treated for alcoholism at New York's Bellevue Hospital in the past six months "would have been there at all had it been possible for them to observe true temperance at their homes with light wines and beer, purely made and legally sold"?[33]

Moving to slightly less deadly issues, Henderson argued that Prohibition was responsible for corrupting women and degrading public decorum. He claimed that before Prohibition, it was a social taboo for a woman to sip liquor from her date's hip flask, but not anymore. After nearly five years of the Volstead Act, such occurrences were "viewed by all with tolerance as 'sporting.'"[34]

Henderson said that if the Volstead Act were modified, Americans could return to true temperance—that is, voluntary self-control and drinking within the privacy of their homes. Like many other opponents of Prohibition, he implied that the reason alcohol dominated so many social functions was that it was hip to defy the law, and there is evidence that this was so in some cases and in some places. Henderson was mimicking a book he may have read. In 1921 author Michael Monahan published *Dry America* in which he blamed Prohibition for religious bigotry, crime, drug addiction, and a general decline in "social happiness." He claimed that Prohibition had brought America a "train of miseries and annoyances quite surpassing any with which we were actually threatened during [World War I]."[35]

Henderson's letter was answered four days later by Gifford Gordon, an Australian who had come to North America with his brother, Coningsby Gordon, to study Prohibition in the United States and Canada. Entitled *35,000 Miles of Prohibition,* their book was published in 1923 by the Victorian Anti-Liquor League. In his letter to the editor Gordon admonished Henderson to "[s]tudy this problem before you rush into print with statements which cannot be substantiated by facts." He then cited statistics for alcohol-related deaths in the four years before Prohibition went into effect as compared to the first four years of the Prohibition era. During "the last four wet years," as he called them, there were 2,061 such deaths, compared to only 835 for the first four dry years. Gordon then cited a Dr. Neal from Los Angeles who owned 66 alcohol rehabilitation centers that had treated 123,000 patients in the 12 years before the Eighteenth Amendment. All 66 centers had been put out of business during the first two years of Prohibition. Similarly, claimed Gordon, the largest alcohol treatment facility in the nation, located in Dwight, Illinois, was being leased to the U.S. government and used as a hospital for disabled soldiers because alcohol treatment was no longer needed.

Gordon said that in his study of Prohibition, he had found many individuals who like Henderson generalized from their New York City and New York state experiences. This was faulty reasoning, Gordon argued, not only because "there are some other States and some other cities in this great Republic," but even more so because New York had recently repealed its state Prohibition law, the Mullen-Gage Act. How could a state and city that clearly refused to cooperate in national Prohibition be used to judge whether Prohibition was a success or failure?[36]

Who was right, Henderson or Gordon? Most studies show that alcohol consumption decreased significantly during the Prohibition era. As one historian puts it, "Americans after Prohibition were drinking less than at any time since they had learned the technology of distillation."[37] This was not so much because it was impossible to buy booze. H. L. Mencken noted in his satirical essay "The Noble Experiment" that there were only two isolated incidents during the entire Prohibition era when he had difficulty procuring a drink. In most cities anyone with the cash could find a place to purchase bootlegged liquor. But having the cash was the problem. Bootlegging was a costly and dangerous business that drove up the price of alcohol, putting it out of reach for many working-class people. With fewer able to afford liquor, arrests for public drunkenness dropped significantly, saving cities and towns jail expenses. One study from the 1960s showed that for many years during Prohibition, articles on alcoholism virtually disappeared from the literature of the medical professions, which would be in keeping with Gordon's claim that many alcohol rehabilitation hospitals closed. Some critics during the 1920s and since claimed that Prohibition caused a crime wave—that it virtually created the Al Capones of the world. Criminologists, however, find little evidence for this argument. For crime bosses, bootlegging liquor became part of their enterprises that already trafficked in prostitution, gambling, racketeering, bribery, and so forth. With its high overhead costs, one might even question whether bootlegging was as profitable as other prohibited enterprises. Was it more or less profitable for mobsters to bootleg than to own a legal saloon where they provided illegal gambling and prostitution?[38]

Besides the now widely accepted fact that alcohol consumption fell significantly as a result of Prohibition, some qualifiers seem equally true.

1. Prohibition was much more effective before 1925 than after.
2. It was more effective in states that had dry laws before the Eighteenth Amendment.
3. Whether in previously dry or wet states, Prohibition was more effective in rural areas than in urban ones.
4. In urban areas, the cost of alcohol became prohibitive for the lower classes. In other words, after the saloons closed, very few speakeasies became working-class or poor man's clubs.[39]

PROHIBITION'S ENDURING LEGACY

If the goal of Prohibition was to eliminate drinking in America, then it failed. If the goal was to significantly reduce drinking and reduce the influence of the saloon in American culture, then Prohibition was a success. If Prohibition succeeded, why was it repealed? The key is to go back to the interpretation of Prohibition as a reform movement intended to protect the Victorian family and its values—industry, thrift, and character. Interpreted this way, Prohibition relied on a view of America that held the family as the basic unit of freedom and identity. In the family, an individual learned the duties and obligations of citizenship. For prohibitionists, the saloon was a poor substitute for the family, so reducing the likelihood that individuals would go there protected the family and the individual's ability to function properly in a free society. Only within a family-based culture could an individual learn how to exercise freedom. A threat to family values, therefore, was a threat to the individual.

The 1920s saw a culture war between those who believed that community values preceded individual rights and those who believed that individuals had rights that the community could not violate. Prohibitionists believed they had the right to outlaw the saloon if it threatened the family and any other institution on which a free society had been built. Many on the other side favored a new version of freedom. They believed that individual rights came before the community or even family. The family was merely the unit in which the individual found self-expression. Individuals, therefore, had the right to go to the saloon if they wanted to, so long as their actions did not pick someone's pocket or break someone's leg, to paraphrase Thomas Jefferson, one of the founders from whom one can draw both communitarian and liberal lessons. Not all who opposed Prohibition were liberal in their views of individual rights, of course. In particular, Roman Catholics believed in strong families nurtured by a church that held authority over individuals. Such Catholic views came up for public debate later, in the election of 1928.

The liberal view of individual freedom was certainly a minority position in the 1920s. This liberal view peaked in the 1960s. In that decade historian Samuel Eliot Morison claimed in his immensely popular textbook *Oxford History of the American People* that Prohibition encouraged "the building up of a criminal class that turned to gambling and drugs when Amendment XVIII was repealed." Moreover, Prohibition affected women who were emancipated by the Nineteenth Amendment so they could violate the Eighteenth. "Hip-flask drinking certainly helped the revolution in sexual standards," Morison wrote. "And it encouraged hypocrisy in politics." Like Morison, Pulitzer prize–winning author Robert Lewis Taylor wrote in 1966 that Prohibition led to "an orgiastic and prolonged era of hard drinking, immorality, racketeering, gun molls, gang wars, political corruption, bribed police and judges, poisoned booze, speakeasies, irreligion, emancipation of women to fresh vistas of imprudence . . . short skirts, saxophone-tooting . . . and decadence." The country, he claimed, went to bed sober on January 16, 1920, only to wake the next day, grab a New Year's Eve horn, and blow it for 14 years.[40]

As Prohibition historian Norman Clark wrote just a decade later, "There are today few reasons to believe that these legends . . . are more than an easy and sentimental hyperbole crafted by men whose assumptions about a democratic society had been deeply offended."[41] The assumption held by both Morison and Taylor was that democracy could be built only on the rights of individuals, not on the communitarian values of family. American history before the Roaring Twenties suggests this is untrue.

Today the relationship between individual rights and community values is debated by communitarians and liberals. As was the case in the 1920s, the communitarian-liberal debate is at the core of many of the culture wars of our own time, often carried forward by people who are unaware that there is more than one way to build a democracy. In the 1920s the balance of opinion was shifting in favor of the liberal emphasis on individual rights, partly because there were new avenues of individual creative expression: radio, film, jazz, and automobiles, among them. Along with these new modes of self-expression was the age-old American tradition of drinking. Stifling an individual's right to enjoy alcohol as a means of entertainment and self-expression was out of step with the liberal era that was emerging at the time. Prohibition laws were like laws against gambling, adultery, and homosexuality. They were crafted to protect a society built on family values. All are unpopular in a society built on individual rights and self-expression.[42]

CHAPTER 3

JESUS'S ATHLETES

While Billy Sunday was one of the most popular Prohibitionists of all time, his anti-alcohol efforts were but one component of his career. He was the most famous preacher of the first half of the twentieth century. Because of his status as America's leading revivalist and his own bombastic style, the press covered virtually every public pronouncement he made. For example, on March 12, 1920, as Warren Harding and several other candidates began campaigning for the presidency, the New York *Times* blared the headline "Billy Sunday Receptive: Would Take Republican Nomination for President—Chooses Cabinet."[1] He told a reporter covering his revival crusade in Syracuse that if elected, his cabinet would include Herbert Hoover as postmaster general, Judge Kennesaw Mountain Landis (soon to be baseball commissioner) as attorney general, and as secretary of state either Henry Cabot Lodge or Ma Sunday, his wife.

Sunday was a Roaring Twenties icon. He stood in a stream of American revivalism that extended from George Whitefield in the eighteenth century, to Charles Finney and Dwight Moody in the nineteenth, and on to Billy Graham during the second half of the twentieth. More outrageous than any big-time preacher before or since, Sunday had a passion for religion like that of Graham with the politically incorrect delivery of Rush Limbaugh. He could have single-handedly made religion a major phenomenon rivaling baseball and boxing, but he did not have to work alone. Rather, a host of imitators wanted to be just like him, packing coliseums, harvesting souls and dollars while campaigning tirelessly for Prohibition and other political causes.

Two months after joking about the presidential nomination, Sunday threw his support more seriously behind Leonard Wood. Always given to hyperbole, Sunday commended the former Army general for being as "resolute as Washington, as patient as Lincoln, as up to the minute as Theodore Roosevelt, and 100 per cent American."[2] The latter was a reference to Wood's support for the anticommunist Red Scare raids in 1919 that were aimed at deporting immigrants suspected of communist activities. Critics charged that in his zeal to keep the nation safe from Reds, Attorney General A. Mitchell Palmer violated the rights of many who had been accused of no crime. The controversy surrounding the raids and the hundreds of arrests and deportations that resulted may have contributed to Wood's losing the nomination to Harding. Sunday's support for Wood notwithstanding, Harding won over delegates at the June convention, after which the stalwart Republican Sunday sent his congratulations and pledge of support, saying "You are the Republican nominee, and I am an American Republican." Lest Harding be flattered by this endorsement, Sunday added, "General Wood was my first choice and I worked for his nomination. You were my second choice."[3]

Unlike televangelist Pat Robertson in 1988, Sunday never actually sought the Republican nomination, his quip about doing so notwithstanding. He was, however, as outspoken and partisan in politics as any leader of the Christian Right of our own time. The fact that his entire letter of congratulations to Harding was reprinted on page two of the New York *Times* attests not only to Sunday's popularity but also to the fact that a spokesperson in religion was considered a significant political observer, as well, even an avowed fundamentalist such as Sunday. As was the case with entertainment and sports personalities — Babe Ruth or Charlie Chaplin, for example — Sunday was a media star, and the sport of religion was no less likely to get public coverage than the major leagues, Broadway, or the burgeoning new film industry.

SUNDAY'S BACKGROUND

Billy Sunday was born in 1862 in Ames, Iowa. His father, William, was in the Union Army when Billy was born. He had instructed his wife, Mary Jane, to name the child William Ashley, should it be a boy. William Sr. never saw his son, dying of pneumonia a month after the boy's birth. Mary Jane remarried in 1864, but Billy did not get along with his stepfather and was sent to an orphanage when he was 12. The stepfather subsequently ran off, leaving Billy's mother alone again. After two years in the orphanage, Billy lived briefly with his grandfather back in Ames, then at the age of 14 moved to Nevada, Iowa, on his own. After a brief stint working at a hotel, he became the stable boy for the one-time lieutenant governor of Iowa, Colonel John Scott. The Scott family took the young Sunday into their home and sent him to high school. Although Sunday received two more years of schooling, there is no record of his having graduated.[4]

While in high school, Sunday exhibited athletic prowess, first as a runner, then as a baseball player. His reputation spread from Nevada to other small towns in central Iowa. He was recruited by the fire brigade team in Marshalltown, 30 miles away, where he also joined the local baseball team. When the team won the state championship, Sunday's play gained the notice of professional scouts, and he was signed to a contract by the Chicago Whitestockings, the forerunner to today's Cubs. These were the fledgling years of Major League Baseball, with the National League less than a decade old. Owners sought to build stable teams with quality players, but they had no system for finding talent. Scouting and player acquisition were more happenstance than design. Sunday's good fortune was that Marshalltown was the hometown of Cap Anson, player-manager for the Whitestockings. Members of the Anson family saw Sunday play and passed along his name to Cap.

Sunday's first contract guaranteed him a healthy salary of $60 a month. From 1883 until 1890 he played outfield in professional baseball for the Whitestockings, Pittsburgh Alleghenys, and Philadelphia Phillies and had a lifetime batting average of .248 with a career best .291 in 50 games for the Whitestockings in 1887. Usually a weak hitter, Sunday was a renowned base stealer, totaling 84 in his final season, in which he split 117 games between Pittsburgh and Philadelphia. He claimed to have stolen 95 bases one season, which may be true. The statistic was not kept until his fourth season in the majors and was not officially recognized by the league until 1898.

Sunday experienced an evangelical conversion in 1886 under the influence of Helen (Nell) Thompson, who would become his wife two years later. The couple met through her little brother, who was the batboy for the Whitestockings. Nell's father was not pleased that his daughter was dating a ballplayer, especially an unconverted one. Sunday attended services with Nell and her family, but his conversion took place at a revivalist street ministry. As Sunday liked to tell the story, he and his buddies got "tanked up" and were sitting outside a saloon when a street preacher invited them to a local mission. Sunday liked what he heard that day and returned several more times before going forward for conversion. He then joined Nell's church, Jefferson Park Presbyterian, and remarked later in life, "She was Presbyterian, so I am Presbyterian. If she had been Catholic, I would have been a Catholic—because I was hot on the trail of Nell."[5] When they wed, the Chicago newspaper carried a small article titled "Sunday Takes a Wife" and reported that "the clever little center fielder of the Pittsburg base ball team [Sunday had been traded] was married yesterday to Miss Helena [sic] Thompson." Billy's best man was Chicago second baseman Fred Pfeffer. Chicago was playing Detroit that day, and the Sundays adjourned from the home where their small ceremony took place to the ballpark where they took in the game. The Chicago team owner gave them box seats, and they were congratulated by well-wishers throughout the game. The couple then left for Indianapolis, where Billy rejoined his Pittsburgh teammates on a road trip.[6]

Over the next few years Sunday began working in the Young Men's Christian Association (YMCA) in the off season while also taking Bible classes. By 1890 he faced a professional crisis as he continued his career with Philadelphia. Sensing God's call to the ministry, and feeling encouraged in that direction by the leader of his local YMCA, he asked for and was granted his release from the Phillies. The Cincinnati team immediately offered him $500 per month to continue playing, but he took a full-time position with the YMCA for $83 a month instead. Before long Sunday came to be called the "John the Baptist" for revivalist J. Wilber Chapman, serving as part of Chapman's support and advance team. Billed as the ex-ballplayer turned preacher, Sunday would speak in a town before Chapman's arrival, preparing the way for the famous evangelist.[7] At one YMCA meeting in 1895, the reporter covering Sunday's preliminary service remarked, "Whatever success he had on the diamond dims in comparison with his effectiveness before a grand-stand of young men brought together not to watch and cheer players, but to bend their attention to the earnest, wise words and strong appeals of the athletic young Christian orator."[8]

In 1895 Sunday began to accept invitations to preach his own revivals. Although not a requirement for traveling revival preachers, in 1903 he sought ordination in the Presbyterian church. As his reputation grew during the first decade of the twentieth century, so did the size of the towns and cities where he held revivals. Before 1907, the largest were about 25,000. He held his first revival in a city of 100,000 in Spokane, Washington, in 1909. By 1917, however, the average size of the cities where he held revivals was 1.7 million. At the height of his fame from 1909 to 1918, Sunday was almost exclusively a revivalist to major urban centers and was one of the most famous people in America. In 1915, when he preached his first Washington, D.C., revival, he was received at the White House by President Woodrow Wilson and taken to lunch by Secretary of State William Jennings Bryan, a fellow Presbyterian evangelical.

For the first five years of his solo ministry, Sunday preached primarily in tents, but after 1900 townsfolk began to erect wooden tabernacles, usually accommodating about a quarter of the town's population. Later in his career, after shifting his focus to large urban centers, such structures were built to accommodate crowds of 15,000 to 20,000. The most elaborate of these was erected for his New York campaign of 1917. The tabernacle sat 20,000 and had within it a post office, hospital, meeting rooms for ushers and other revival staff, a room where Sunday could relax and pray, and a bookstore where people could purchase Christian literature.

The New York revival marked the peak of Sunday's career. Coming as it did just as America entered World War I, Sunday mixed in patriotic fervor, appeals for Liberty Bonds to raise funds for the war effort, condemnation of the German kaiser, and gospel preaching as he thrilled throngs of New Yorkers for three months. Dignitaries, politicians, and big businessmen supported and befriended Sunday, recognizing the benefit of standing in the good graces of America's leading preacher. He wielded considerable political clout and was a walking, talking advertisement for America's democratic capitalism.

Early in the New York campaign Sunday was honored with a large luncheon at the home of John D. Rockefeller Jr., which was attended by Major General Leonard Wood and former president Theodore Roosevelt. The New York *Times* covered the revival with 10 to 20 articles per week and estimated that more than 98,000 people went forward for conversion. At the closing service Rockefeller told the crowd that the work Sunday had done in New York was just the start. Sunday and his team, Rockefeller said, "have set in motion great forces which will go on for years and years."[9] The New York revival was the first time Rockefeller had seen Sunday in operation. He wrote Sunday privately, saying that while he had supported the evangelist for some time based on what he read and heard, "Now I believe in you because of the work which I have seen you do and because of what I know you to be."[10]

Sunday was so popular by the time of the New York revival that Frank Spell-man of the United States Circus Corporation invited him to join the show for the summer. This was a logical offer, given that Sunday's revivals had circus qual-ities. Many in the throngs that attended his campaigns were there as much for the entertainment value as for the religion. In a time before movie theaters, radio, and television, revivals provided entertainment much like public lectures, plays, music concerts, and circuses. Spellman offered Sunday $14,000 per week, $2,000 per sermon, for as long as Sunday wanted. "This may seem a sordid proposition," Spellman wrote accurately, "but underlying it is a great deal of common sense and humanity. . . . Where will you find a more prolific field, in which to hunt the devil." Sunday wrote back saying he received many offers he had to turn down, and this was one of them. As he told Spellman's people, "Mr. Spellman means all right but does not quite understand."[11] What Spellman failed to comprehend was that although Sunday got rich off preaching, he geared his antics toward winning souls, not just making money. He wanted to entertain people into the kingdom of God; joining the circus would have been too much a spectacle even for Billy Sunday. Moreover, Sunday ran his own show or, more accurately, Ma Sunday ran it. He did not need Spellman's or anyone else's promotional efforts.

In Sunday's mind, preaching was more like athletics than circus work. The same nervous energy he had used to steal bases he put into saving souls. De-scribing the hyperactivity that often kept him from sleeping well, he once said, "The blood in my brain works like a trip hammer." Just as athletes often replay games in their minds while trying to wind down after a big contest, Sunday con-tinued, "When I lie down I go over every sermon I preach. I preach it all over."[12] His preaching was every bit as athletic as his ball playing had been, and news-paper reporters often went to lengths to describe the physical aspects of his performances. In 1928 a St. Louis *Globe-Democrat* reporter called Sunday, then 66, an "Orator-Gymnast" and said that Sunday's final antic of a particular ser-mon was like that of "an inspired collegian just as the halfback made a touch-down in the last second of play."[13]

A typical Sunday revival lasted four to six weeks and was preceded by elab-orate preparation, most notably the building of the tabernacle. Sunday arrived only after months and sometimes years of groundwork undertaken by volun-teers. Thousands of people in the city's churches anticipated the event in much the same way they looked forward to the circus or in our own time to a major professional sporting event or college football bowl game. To kick off the revival, a delegation of supporters, leading residents, church groups, and local marching bands would meet Sunday at the train station on Friday. He would be placed in the backseat of a convertible sedan and paraded down one of the city's busiest sections waving to the crowd that came out to meet him, as the bands played and the entourage marched along behind.

After the grand welcome, the revival itself would commence on Sunday. Billy did not usually give an invitation for people to come forward for conversion until the second week, by which time there was so much pent-up spiritual energy that folks poured into the tabernacle aisles and proceeded to the platform where they would shake Sunday's hand, then pray with a revival volunteer from a local church. Coming forward for conversion became known as hitting the sawdust trail or simply trail hitting. The term originated from a story of lumbermen deliberately leaking sawdust from a gunny sack so they could find their way through the forest and back to their home. The aisle of the tabernacle was the sawdust trail leading home to Jesus. Because the platform from which Sunday preached was elevated, he would step through a trapdoor so he could stand roughly at the level of the people coming forward to shake his hand. He was once timed at 57 handshakes per minute. Sunday did not consider a revival successful unless 10 to 20 percent of a city's population hit the trail over the course of the campaign.

Sunday's revivals were supported by the wealthiest and most famous industrialists of the era, including J. P. Morgan, John Wanamaker, Henry Clay Frick, Cyrus McCormick, and the aforementioned Rockefeller. Although these businessmen were often personally pious, they also recognized that friendship with Sunday was good advertising. Moreover, Sunday promoted tirelessly the tenets of free market capitalism, much as Christian Right activists in the Republican Party today. Sunday may never have said that capitalism was outlined in the Old Testament, as Jerry Falwell used to claim, but he probably believed it. Sunday's evangelistic organization was a model of efficiency that big businessmen appreciated, and he was an exemplar of the entrepreneurial spirit, much of which was organized and promoted by his wife, Nell.

After 1908 the nation's most influential magazines, such as *Nation* and *Collier's*, ran feature stories on the evangelist. *Collier's* even asked Sunday to pick the magazine's all-star professional baseball team for 1911 and again in 1913. Sunday named Ty Cobb the best player ever, musing that he was to baseball what

Thomas Jefferson was to the Declaration of Independence. In the conclusion of the 1913 article, Sunday confessed that picking the team had stoked the old competitive fires. "I'd like to lead off for you fellows," he wrote. He said he still had his old uniform and "wouldn't trade it for the best diamond in Tiffany's shop."[14]

That Sunday was a former Major League Baseball player contributed to his success, as the *Collier's* article reveals. Professional and college sports were growing phenomena in the early twentieth century and would explode in popularity in the 1920s. Baseball and boxing led the way, with college football close behind. The advent of radio contributed to the sports craze as broadcasts brought the thrill of the game into homes and local establishments. Religion in America mirrored and in some ways contributed to the rise of athletics. In the late nineteenth century the YMCA that Sunday worked for aided in the growth of what historians call muscular Christianity, a form of the faith that put an emphasis on the manly and heroic. "Come on boys," Sunday liked to shout from the platform of his tabernacles. "You've got a real chance to show your manhood." He would then challenge the men to hit the sawdust trail and take a stand for Jesus and against liquor.

Reformers of the Progressive Era, whether religious or not, often provided their own version of this "masculinity." They viewed immigration, the women's movement, and big business as threats to the common man that created "a masculinity crisis" or "feminization of culture." The word "masculine" was not commonly used until the 1890s, when reformers began to prefer it over the word "manly." One of the major proponents of masculinity was Theodore Roosevelt, who was a walking testament for how exercise and adventure could transform one from a sickly boy into a man's man. In rebuking Christian pacifism at the outset of World War I, Roosevelt pointed out that when Jesus encountered the money changers, "the Saviour armed himself with a scourge of cords and drove [them] out of the temple."[15] In 1925 advertising mogul Bruce Barton wrote a popular biography of Jesus called *The Man Nobody Knows*. Debunking the notion of a "sissified" and "weakling" Jesus, Barton wrote, "[His] muscles were so strong that when He drove the money changers out, nobody dared oppose him!"[16] The Boy Scouts began in 1910 as a significant outgrowth of the emphasis on masculinity or what has been called a movement for "passionate manhood." Roosevelt threatened to resign as honorary vice president of the Boy Scouts in 1915 if pacifists were not expelled.[17]

As a baseball player then media star preacher, Sunday came to exemplify the strong, athletic, manly Christian, but he certainly had his share of detractors. Skeptical journalists wrote critical exposés especially after Sunday's fame led to wealth. The cost of his revivals to the cities where they were held fed the skepticism. In addition to the critics, he was attacked literally by the occasional lunatic, giving Sunday the opportunity to demonstrate his manhood physically. In Springfield, Illinois, in 1909 a former patient at the local mental hospital approached the platform of the tabernacle with a whip, exclaiming "I have a commission from God to horsewhip you." After being struck twice, Sunday shouted back, "Well, I have a commission from God to knock the tar out of you."[18] Unfortunately, Sunday sprained his ankle when he dove off the platform and had to preach the rest of the revival on crutches. Being a manly fighter of the devil had its risks.

At his Atlanta revival in 1917, a large man named Will H. Beuterbaugh climbed onto the platform, lunged at Sunday, and grazed the evangelist's face with a glancing blow. Sunday responded with a few good jabs of his own before onlookers tackled his attacker. Sunday's own account was consistent with that of Atlanta reporters: "He shot one across that grazed the side of my face. Then I sent an upper-cut to his jaw and we clinched."[19] As Beuterbaugh was subdued spectators yelled, "Lynch him," and the crowd may have, had the police not whisked him off to jail. Sunday was afforded police protection for the remainder of the revival, and the police also launched an investigation into who had tried to choke the mayor during the chaos that followed Beuterbaugh's attack. A cartoonist for the Atlanta *Constitution* reproduced the scene showing Beuterbaugh and Sunday squaring off like prizefighters, Sunday landing a blow while Beuterbaugh's misses its mark.[20]

Like the 1909 assailant, Beuterbaugh had also spent time in an insane asylum. Reporters assumed that he was not only crazy but also offended by the anti-German rhetoric Sunday spewed during World War I. Sunday was himself of German extraction. The family name had been Sonntag before Billy's immigrant grandparents anglicized it after coming to America in the mid-nineteenth century. Any kinship Sunday felt with Germany was long past by the time the war started, and he enthusiastically joined the chorus of anti-German sentiment that swept the English-speaking world. Sunday liked to say that if one turned over Hell, "Made in Germany" would be seen stamped on the bottom. Beuterbaugh climbed onto the stage right after Sunday had said that

America would prevail over Germany because "God is with us. He wouldn't be with a dirty bunch that would stand aside and allow a Turk to outrage a woman."[21] As the investigation developed, however, police uncovered a 40-page pacifist manuscript Beuterbaugh had written in which he called on true Christians to stop supporting war. His motivation for attacking Sunday may have had less to do with Beuterbaugh's German-sounding name than with his view that Sunday was a militarist and therefore unfit as a Christian leader. Attacking someone is an odd way to make a pacifist point, but Beuterbaugh was, after all, a former psychiatric patient.

Sunday had detractors and supporters in both the progressive and conservative camps, but progressives and theological liberals were most likely to criticize him because he was essentially conservative theologically, politically, and socially. That said, there were times when he could sound progressive. For example, he railed against churches leaving the downtown areas for the suburbs. "The downtown church [has become] a passing proposition [and] there is a breach between the masses and the church." He lambasted churches for selling their downtown property at enormous profit, then deserting urban dwellers in need. Given the growing urban blight in industrial America, Sunday asked whether this was the time when the generals in the army of God should be announcing retreat in the war against sin in the cities. The retreat to the suburbs resulted in cushy churches where "a hireling ministry" preached sermons that made the saloon owners and other shady downtown businessmen feel okay about themselves. Sunday called these types of sermons "showers of spiritual cocaine," a comment strikingly similar to Karl Marx's claim that "religion is the opiate of the masses."[22]

When preaching this sort of message just before World War I, Sunday sounded like a Social Gospel preacher. Led by theologian Walter Rauschenbusch and preacher Washington Gladden, advocates of the Social Gospel had been saying since the 1880s that Christianity should offer not only salvation for individual souls but redemption of corporate society as well. Most fundamentalists opposed the Social Gospel because it shifted the emphasis away from individual salvation toward social service, and in reality Sunday was no Social Gospeler. Social Gospel advocates believed that the structures of society needed drastic change. The government needed to regulate big business more heavily, taxes needed to be gauged progressively so that those who had the highest incomes paid the highest percentage, and so forth.

Even though Sunday talked about "fighting saints" and "progressive Christianity," he did not mean progressive in the political or even Social Gospel sense. Rather, he meant that downtown churches should aggressively battle personal sin and save individual sinners, especially urban drunks and other ne'er-do-wells. Sunday wanted little legal change in American society because he believed that "We are citizens of the greatest government on earth and we will admit it."[23] Rather than legislation, Americans needed a change of heart. When he called for fair wages for industrial workers, for example, his remedy was to convince individual business owners to be more just, not to coerce them with a minimum wage law. He spoke vigorously against abortion, citing statistics that one-third of all American pregnancies were terminated. His point was not just that innocent fetal life was being snuffed out but also that rich women were opting out of their God-given responsibility of motherhood so they could "spend their time touring in their automobiles and out at the golf links and drinking wine and playing cards and cruising yachts with their miserable hands red with blood."[24] Abortion was hardly the issue it is today, so Sunday spent much more time warning men and women against the sins of smoking, swearing, drinking, gambling, theatergoing, fornication, and telling dirty jokes. A man could smoke and be a Christian, he liked to say, "but he will be a mighty dirty one."[25] He also warned against the theater, billiard halls, and other dens of iniquity.

Sunday was also conservative, indeed nativist, on the issue of immigration. From 1890 to 1920 immigration in America shifted from mostly northern European Protestants to southern and eastern Europeans who were often Roman Catholic or Jewish. By World War I, as immigrants congregated in urban slums and took industrial jobs, many white Anglo-Saxon Protestants grew alarmed by the changes in the fabric of the culture. Sunday's awareness of the shift started when he was working at the YMCA in Chicago in the 1890s. As he grew up in Iowa, the immigrants he knew were like his own grandparents — German or Scandinavian Protestants who had come to the Midwest to farm. In Chicago, by contrast, Sunday encountered ethnic immigrants who were poor, unemployed Catholics often addicted to alcohol. These were thought of as the "new immigrants," in contrast to "old stock" Americans like Sunday. He was one of many preachers, politicians, and business leaders who linked the new immigration to poverty, the liquor trade, and vice. "Look at the brewers," he liked to say. "What are the names? No Americans, thank God!"[26] He also quoted statistics showing that the majority of criminals were immigrants. While viewed as reactionary later, such sentiment was mainstream in an America whose power structures were still dominated by Anglo-Protestants. This sort of nativism resulted in the Immigration Act of 1924, which categorized immigration ethnically and limited the inflow of each group to 2 percent of the population the group had in 1890.

The anti-Catholic side of Sunday's nativism was tame compared to many Protestants. Even during the presidential election of 1928, when the Catholic candidate Al Smith won the Democratic nomination for president, Sunday attempted to steer clear of anti-Catholicism. This was because Sunday was an urban revivalist. When he went to the nation's largest cities, there was always a significant contingent of Catholics in places of power from whom he needed cooperation. He liked to say "I am a Roman Catholic on divorce," and he often told his converts that if they wanted to join a Catholic church, "I'll help you if I can." In Boston he urged Catholics, like Protestants, to come forward and sign decision cards attesting to their conversion, promising "We'll see that the priests get them."[27]

SUNDAY AND THE ROARING TWENTIES

Sunday was actually past his prime before the Roaring Twenties began, but neither he nor anyone else knew it. His recent biographers chart a postwar decline in the size of his revivals and the size of the cities where he held them. Still, thousands showed up to hear him denounce all that the decade stood for. When Samuel Hopkins Adams's book *Flaming Youth* became all the rage in its exposé of the lives of the decade's swinging young people, their petting parties, and bathtub gin, Sunday responded that the excess passion should be paddled out of them in the family garage. On divorce he allowed only one just cause, adultery, and said he would never perform the wedding ceremony for a divorced man or woman. This was especially troublesome when his youngest son dated a divorcée. "I am disappointed in Paul going with a divorced woman with a child too," he wrote in a letter to Ma. "I am absolutely opposed to his marrying a divorced woman. . . . Such actions shut my mouth in preaching for it will become known and people will laugh at me," he wrote before suggesting that he would have to quit the ministry if his son failed to break off the relationship.[28] As we will see later, Paul was a saint compared to his two brothers, and Sunday should have been thankful if dating a divorced woman was the worst they would do.

Ma Sunday was also a strong personality. Billy's equal, she served as agent and business partner, traveling with him once the children were grown. She set the agenda for Billy's career, and he accorded her and women in general great respect. Within the bounds of the gender complementarian position that ruled the day, the man was the head of the household, but Sunday always told men to give women a fair deal, and he often did so with great humor. He liked to tell men to give their wives flowers while they were still alive rather than just covering them with flowers after they had been worked to death. "Hand her a $5 bill once in a while," he would say. Keep her happy because happiness does more to ward off gray hair and wrinkles than all the rouge or makeup a woman could buy. Turning only slightly more serious, he said that a lot of men would not have amounted to a hill of beans without a little woman "nagging him on to greater things." In an era where some women challenged Victorian gender roles, Sunday held fast to the older ideals. Echoing the nineteenth-century notion that women were more moral than men, he said in 1928, "Woman has always been found in the forefront, in the center of everything good and noble. If she is in the mire, you bet your life some brute of a man has pushed her there."[29] The message was clear: Women were morally superior to men, but weaker.

Ma Sunday wrote regular columns for various press services, newspapers, and magazines. Readers sent in their questions, asking her opinion on social, moral, and theological issues. In one of these a woman told Ma how her working outside the home had destroyed her marriage. Her good-for-nothing husband had come to rely on her income, growing ever lazier himself. The woman, therefore, quit her job and went off to live with her parents for a few months, hoping her husband would come to his senses, get back to work, and act more responsibly. Instead, he interpreted her departure as an indication that she wanted a divorce, and the couple split up for good. The woman took her story as clear indication that women should not work outside the home, and she prevailed on Ma to agree. "Don't you think that my experience is another proof that women ought not to work for themselves after they marry?" the woman asked. Ma replied, "No," and went on to explain that there was nothing wrong with a woman working outside the home. If a man and a woman had sufficient love and devotion, their marriage is bound to succeed whether the wife works or not. If the couple does not have sufficient forbearance, then the marriage will not be successful, Ma wrote.[30]

Although she favored the right of a woman to work outside the home, Ma Sunday was not a women's rights advocate, nor one to tolerate flappers and other women asserting their independence. In one of her columns she emphasized that child rearing remained a woman's "primal mission." Reprising the Victorian view of woman's moral superiority, Ma said that the health of society itself rested on her success in nurturing children. Billy agreed. He often held separate special meetings for men, women, and youth. In the men's meetings he stressed muscular Christianity. In his women's meetings he often let them off the hook for the worst evil in the world by blaming it on men. Then he would emphasize the woman's God-given role as mother to teach the youth how to live morally. To prepare for that role, women needed to cultivate godliness, which meant avoiding the dancehall. He would then imitate a dance known as the black bottom. Shimmying on one foot, he would lift the other as high as his podium, while his audience roared with laughter. In 1928 he told one audience of women that he did not object to the rouge, lipstick, or even the bobbed hair of the era, but the skimpy clothes indicated an abominably low standard of morality.[31]

Unfortunately, for all Billy and Ma's efforts to shape morally sound youths, their own children were troubled. Billy and Ma had a daughter and three sons—Helen, George, Billy, and Paul. Helen attended college, married, and had a son of her own. She suffered from a degenerative disease doctors could not identify, although the symptoms seem akin to multiple sclerosis. She also experienced periodic bouts of depression and died of pneumonia at the age of 42. Helen's tragic difficulties, of course, were not of her own making. George's and Billy Jr.'s were.

After working for his father's revivals as a young man, George headed west and landed in California, where he started a real estate business with money his dad loaned him. In 1923 newspapers reported that he had been found unconscious in his home with a hose from a gas jet in his mouth, an attempted suicide. Within a few hours George announced to local reporters that it was not him but his little brother Billy Jr. who had been injured in the "accident." Various stories emerged concerning who the police had actually found injured that day. The Sunday brothers and some of their friends denied there had been a suicide attempt.

Both brothers drank heavily, caroused with women, and divorced and remarried multiple times.[32] Billy Jr.'s second wife sued for divorce in 1929 on grounds of extreme cruelty. The couple had been married little more than a year. She claimed that Billy Jr. frequently left her alone or sent her off on trips by herself. He also failed to show up for dinner parties when they invited guests to their home. The reason for his long absences became clear when he married a woman in Mexico little more than a month after his wife filed, long before the American divorce was finalized. Ten months later Billy Jr.'s estranged American wife announced she was engaged to her attorney. The wedding was scheduled for September 20, 1930, the same day her and Billy Jr.'s divorce was to be finalized.[33]

George's life continued to spiral downward in the 1920s as he suffered from alcoholism and drug addiction. Two months after Billy Jr.'s wife filed for divorce, George's wife and a private investigator she had hired caught him with a Hollywood model. Before the police arrived to arrest him for criminal infidelity, he fled in an overdue rental car. When police apprehended him in Santa Cruz, they added grand theft auto to the sex charge. George wrote a check for his bail, which subsequently bounced, adding a third charge. He jumped bail and headed for the Midwest. He was spotted in Winona Lake, Indiana, where his parents kept their home, but he eluded police until March 1930, when he was arrested for drunk and disorderly conduct after a policeman saw him weaving unsteadily down a Chicago street. He claimed to be Leonard Johnson, but he had identification in his pocket showing he was George Sunday. California authorities were in the process of having George extradited when all charges were dropped, his father's influence to the rescue. Meanwhile, at his divorce trial, the judge asked his wife rhetorically, "[George] didn't follow the example of his father very closely eh?" To which she replied, "I should say not."[34]

In 1933, roughly a year after the death of the Sunday daughter, Ma was in San Francisco, where George was living with his second wife, the Hollywood model. In the midst of a domestic quarrel, George assaulted his wife, kicked his mother out of the house, then jumped out of a fourth-story window in another suicide attempt. His wife told police that George had threatened to drown himself and had called a cab to take him to the waterfront for that purpose. Growing impatient, she surmised, he leapt from the window instead. In the hospital with a broken jaw, he claimed in a handwritten note that he had not been drinking and that he had merely lost his balance and fallen out of the window accidentally while trying to water some plants. He died a few days later at the age of 40.[35]

These family troubles bedeviled Sunday for the final 15 years of his life, aging him prematurely. He often appeared tired and haggard with dark circles under his eyes, and he was convinced that people in hotels and other public places were staring at him because of the shame his sons brought on his name. In addition to periodic embarrassment, he believed his sons' waywardness had spiritual dimensions. In the wake of one of the scandals, he wrote to Ma, "I wonder what next the devil will frame upon me to try and break me down."[36]

MANLY CHRISTIANITY AND THE AIRWAVES

Because he exemplified what it meant to be a Roaring Twenties preacher, Sunday had a host of imitators, one of whom was Paul Rader. In one sense Rader emulated Sunday with his tabernacle revivals and manly, athletic preaching. In his use of radio, however, Rader was more innovative than Sunday and might be the most overlooked religious figure of the decade. Rader merged the old-fashioned revivalist tradition with twentieth-century technology. More than any other figure of the 1920s, he was significant for getting in on the ground floor of radio, as were several figures we encounter in the chapters to follow. Rader was a pioneer in this respect.

In September 1926 Rader appeared on the front page of the Philadelphia *Inquirer* standing on one leg, right fist thrust in the air, a pose not unlike a prize-fighter following a victorious knockout. The article covering Rader's Philadelphia crusade mentioned that the evangelist had recently been photographed with former heavyweight champ Jim Jeffries, with whom Rader shared a "remarkable similarity in build and feature." The headline read "Evangelist Warns Nation Faces Ruin by Reckless Youth," referring to his sermon the day before in which Rader had warned of America's materialism and moral degeneration.[37]

Speaking at Philadelphia's famous sports venue known as the Arena, Rader told his audience: "I have deliberately come to this home of prize fighting because it is our purpose to get close to the people of Philadelphia and particularly the young people. We could have had a cathedral had we wanted it, but that would have tied us too closely with a church."[38] Rader said he had not come to the city to talk about politics and would have no criticism of the mayor, who greeted Rader at city hall, or of the governor. Rather, he had come to offer individual salvation as the remedy for the nation's ills. To distinguish himself from other, less substantive Sunday impersonators, Rader said he was no "fly-by-night evangelist; no will-o-the wisp." Rather, "I have a large church of my own in Chicago, but the Word drives me on to these occasional evangelistic campaigns. We are not coming here to make money. We are not seeking sensational exploitation. We only want Philadelphia to hear and to heed the words of the Master."[39]

Rader may have been separating himself somewhat from Sunday's sensationalism, but in many ways he was like Sunday. Athletically, Rader was a former college football player and semiprofessional boxer. He served as a sparring partner for Bob Fitzsimmons, the first boxer to win world championships in three weight divisions, then for Jeffries when the old champ attempted a comeback. Boxing promoters had persuaded Jeffries to come out of retirement as the "Great White Hope" who might dethrone the black champion, Jack Johnson. Later, Rader and his supporters claimed that when Jeffries lost to Johnson in 1909, promoters turned to Rader as the next White Hope. Rader claimed to have fought Johnson in an exhibition a few years later, earning enough money to start an investment career on Wall Street.

Rader had been raised in a conservative Protestant home with a Methodist preacher for a father, but he drifted into liberal Christianity while in college and by his own estimation became puffed up with intellectual pride upon his graduation. He adopted modern ideas such as Darwinian evolution and critical views of the Bible and became a liberal Congregational minister, serving churches in cities on both coasts even as he occasionally left the ministry for boxing and other pursuits. In 1912, as he experienced Wall Street success, Rader felt the call of God again and reconverted to the conservative faith of his upbringing. He gave up business immediately and commenced preaching, but this time as a revivalist, much like Sunday. After Rader had early success as an evangelist, the congregation at the historic Moody Memorial Church in Chicago called him as pastor. Moody Memorial was named for the famous nineteenth-century revivalist Dwight L. Moody, one of the most important preachers in American history. Rader persuaded the congregation to build a 5,000-seat tabernacle where he operated a perpetual revival. He stayed at Moody Memorial until 1921.

After another brief stint as a traveling revivalist, Rader returned to his adopted home and founded the Chicago Gospel Tabernacle in 1922.[40] The tabernacle became another revival center, not a church in the conventional sense. Rader even avoided having Sunday morning services because he did not want to compete with area churches. Rather, the tabernacle served as an evangelistic resource, and its services fit the roaring mood of the decade. Streetcars brought masses of people to the Barry Street location, where they disembarked and hurried over to the tabernacle much as they would to Wrigley Field, which had been built just eight years earlier. The similarity was not lost on those who attended. In describing meetings at the Gospel Tabernacle, one regular said, "It was like going to the ball park."[41] Indeed, people often attended their own churches on Sunday morning, sack lunch in tow, then headed by streetcar over to the tabernacle for Sunday afternoon and evening services. The tabernacle eventually opened its own cafeteria that served patrons like the concession stands at Wrigley. If the atmosphere was like a ballpark, the services resembled vaudeville productions, with traveling preachers such as Billy Sunday making guest appearances and a regular array of cantatas, pageants, and musicals performed by choirs and bands. By the time Rader visited Philadelphia four years after founding the Chicago Gospel Tabernacle, he was a well-known fundamentalist revivalist in the muscular Christianity strain Sunday had promoted for decades.

Fundamentalists such as Sunday, Rader, and others were often of two minds regarding both their nation and the culture of the Roaring Twenties. Much like Christian Right figures today, they extolled America as God's chosen nation while condemning the rampant materialism and moral permissiveness. In short, they could not decide if the nation was Zion or Babylon. Rader's 1926 revival in Philadelphia was conducted in the context of the city's and nation's sesquicentennial celebration of the Declaration of Independence. He traveled to the city specifically to preach the gospel in the shadow of Independence Hall and the Liberty Bell. It was both an evangelistic crusade and a celebration of America

Two months after Rader's revival in the city, Philadelphia hosted the Dempsey-Tunney heavyweight championship boxing match. An estimated 135,000 people attended, the most ever to witness a sporting event in the United States. Unlike Sunday and Rader, some ministers saw prizefights as the epitome of degradation. For them, boxing was worldly and uncivilized, a brutal bloodlust. As the bout approached, Methodists, Presbyterians, and Baptists in Philadelphia all passed resolutions opposing the city's hosting the fight. Philadelphia's leading fundamentalist, Clarence Macartney of the city's Arch Street Presbyterian Church, spearheaded the opposition. In a departure from the masculine, sports-promoting themes of Rader and Sunday,

Macartney viewed boxing as debauched. He developed an imaginary dialogue among the nation's founders concerning the fight. In Macartney's drama, Washington, Franklin, Jefferson, Adams, and Witherspoon (the latter included because he was a Presbyterian Calvinist) come to Philadelphia for the sesquicentennial celebration but stumble into the Tunney-Dempsey fight instead. There they are aghast at the barbarism and agree with Macartney that the enormous attendance was "an alarming demonstration of the recrudescence of paganism in the life of the world today. . . . Thrilling as the spectacle must have been, overwhelming as the throngs were," Macartney continued, "the sum and total effect is bad and only bad." The presence of cabinet members, governors, and other public officials only made matters worse. The whole affair was in Macartney's view "a shaming throw-back to the brutality of the Roman arena."[42] After 10 rounds in pouring rain, Tunney defeated Dempsey to become the heavyweight champion. They fought a rematch the next year in Chicago in a fight marked by the famous "long count." When Dempsey knocked down Tunney in the seventh round, the referee's count was, according to many, suspiciously slow, allowing the champ to get up and continue the fight, eventually winning again.

The contrast between Macartney's and Rader's views of boxing reveals a bifurcated fundamentalism. Macartney and others distanced themselves from some forms of popular entertainment; Rader and others used the popularity of sport to advance the gospel. Rader covered Macartney's denunciation of the first fight in his magazine—ironic given that Rader often used athletics in tandem with the gospel. Back when he was at Moody Memorial, he once appeared in the church's publication Good News in a suit and tie and the three-point stance of a football lineman. The photo was part of an advertisement for the Thanksgiving morning men's meeting.[43] Later Radar integrated athletic manliness into the program of his Chicago Gospel Tabernacle. A Rader pamphlet boasted that the congregation of the tabernacle was heavily male. "That fact is explained by the manliness of the preacher," the pamphlet said. "A strong, fearless, virile man, like Paul Rader, is sure to attract men."[44] In June 1928 Rader's magazine World Wide Christian Courier carried an article entitled "Athletics and Christians? Sure—at the Tabernacle." The article began with the question "Is physical exercise essential in spiritual life?" and answered with a resounding "yes." "Because exercise is vitally important, we give it a part in our Christian activities," the article continued.[45]

The same issue drew a contrast between the "Flaming Youth" of the Roaring Twenties and the "Youth Aflame" (for Jesus) of the Chicago Tabernacle.[46] Early in the decade Rader had made light of "flaming youth," claiming that flappers were inadvertently doing mission work by driving men into the ministry. "Better a hungry heathen with a club than a thirsty flapper with a lipstick," Rader joked.[47] He also believed that young men fled liberal Presbyterian seminaries where the verities of Christian faith were being questioned "because real manly young men will not follow a banner with question marks on it." This was a reflection of his own manly decision to leave liberalism and return to the fundamentalist faith of his father. Manly young preachers, Rader claimed, were heading to the fundamentalist Bible institutes in increasing numbers. Liberalism was for sissies.[48]

Perhaps even more indicative of this love-hate relationship fundamentalists had with 1920s culture was that Rader was virtually the first regular religious radio broadcaster, using the same medium that brought nightclub jazz and juke-joint blues into the homes of America. For him and other religious figures we will encounter later, modern media could be used for great ill or for good. As Rader put it, "There's nothing in the Bible that tells the world to come to the Church; but there's everything in the Bible that tells the Church to go to the world! Radio takes the Gospel to the unchurched. That's why I'm using it!"[49]

Radio began in America with a 1920 Pittsburgh broadcast to a handful of area listeners who had receiving sets. Less than two years later Rader did his first broadcast, getting in on the ground floor of a very significant movement. That year the number of radios owned by Americans jumped from 60,000 to 1.5 million. Soon both fundamentalist and liberal preachers were on the air in every major city in the nation. Radio did for 1920s evangelism what television would do later. Preachers reached more people and enlivened the gospel with entertaining drama and music. After a few years of sporadic broadcasting, in 1925 Rader launched a regular show on major station WHT in Chicago. The Chicago Gospel Tabernacle broadcast 14 hours of programming every Sunday, carrying music, preaching, and segments aimed especially at men, women, or children. For kids, Rader developed the Radio Rangers and Aerial Girls, fundamentalist versions of Boy Scouts and Girl Scouts. In an era before regulation and crowded frequencies, listeners from the East Coast to the Rocky Mountains tuned in to Rader's broadcasts.[50] Letters, and money, poured in from around the country. As if to prove Rader's point that a medium such as radio could be redeemed, one woman told of tuning her radio in search of jazz music for a Sunday night dance party. Instead she found the Gospel Tabernacle broadcast. Taken with the message, she knelt in prayer and became a Christian. When her guests arrived later they listened to Rader preach the gospel rather than Louis Armstrong play jazz.[51]

The call letters WHT stood for William H. (Big Bill) Thompson, the Chicago mayor who started the city's municipal station WBU in 1922 and recruited Rader to help fill programming slots. In 1925 Thompson was out of office when he founded the new station WHT, partly to set himself up for the mayoral election of 1927, when he hoped to get back into office. As was the case in 1922, Rader stepped up to Big Bill's challenge and developed his all-day Sunday broadcast. The new station took to the airwaves on a Saturday in April, with Rader providing the invocation. The next day Rader's Sunday broadcast made its debut. The preacher and the Chicago machine politician would continue their friendship for the rest of their lives.[52]

Although Rader maintained that radio ministry could not take the place of the church, he was surely on the cutting edge of techno-spiritual innovation when he offered the first over-the-airwaves communion service in early 1927. Having told his listeners to prepare their own bread and wine (grape juice, actually), the service took place on February 6. The following year Rader claimed that the Bible foretold the radio. Job 38:35, he explained, says "Canst thou send lightnings that they may go, and say unto thee: 'Here we are?'" "The word 'lightnings,'" he then explained, "surely means nothing more than the radio waves which today carry the messages of men to all corners of the earth." Rader also believed that the Bible foretold the invention of the automobile, the vacuum tube, and the discovery of the circulation of blood. During the battles between religion and science in the 1920s, Rader was famous for offering to pay $1,000 to anyone who could show where science contradicted the Bible.[53]

In August 1928 Rader appeared with Billy Sunday in Winona Lake, Indiana, for a big service that was made into a Movietone. Movietone was the latest technological development, which allowed audio and visual to be recorded on the same film. By that time, there had been more than a decade of religious silent film production undertaken by Protestant denominations, Roman Catholic churches, and the Religious Motion Picture Foundation. Sunday advocated both religious and some secular films as a potentially wholesome alternative to the saloon.[54] In this instance he and Rader had a chance to put a new filmmaking innovation into the service of evangelism, and Winona Lake was just the place to make a religious talkie. The picturesque town on the shore of the lake for which it is named was the site of annual Bible conferences, summer camps, girls' and boys' Bible schools, and a host of other evangelical activities. The Sundays had purchased property there in the first decade of the century and made Winona Lake their home when they were not on the road.

Rader preached a sermon entitled "Tuning Up Your Faith" in the morning to 10,000 people gathered in the Billy Sunday Tabernacle. Sunday and Rader both preached in an afternoon service held in the outdoor amphitheater where the Movietone equipment had been set up under a beautiful blue sky. Sunday preached at length, then Rader followed with a shorter sermon. Sunday's long-time music director, Homer Rodeheaver, led the crowd and a 600-voice choir in singing hymns and patriotic songs. The Winona Band and Orchestra and the Depauw University choir from Greencastle, Indiana, also performed. The Movietone was made by the Fox News Company, named for its founder, William Fox.[55]

✦

Sunday, Rader, and other fundamentalists preaching a muscular and athletic brand of Christianity believed they were well positioned to continue Protestant dominance over America. Looking back, they possessed a level of influence conservative Christians would not experience again until the rise of the Christian Right in the 1980s. When fundamentalism did reemerge, Radar was there in spirit. Charles Fuller, who converted under Rader's preaching, became one of the leading religious radio personalities of the mid-twentieth century and was instrumental in the conversion of Jerry Falwell. Falwell became the leader of the Moral Majority, the first significant organization of the Christian Right. But fundamentalism experienced a steep decline in cultural influence in between Radar and Falwell. That decline started when fundamentalists fought and lost battles with the modernists, or liberals, in the northern Protestant denominations. A key question during the twenties was not only whether Protestants would continue to dominate America but also which group of Protestants would emerge victorious in these battles.

CHAPTER 4

"SHALL THE FUNDAMENTALISTS WIN?"

While fundamentalist preachers such as Billy Sunday could still pack stadiums, by the 1920s there had emerged a very different brand of Protestantism that sought to rout fundamentalists from the cultural field of play. Modernist Protestants, or liberals as they were also called, were led by renowned New York preacher Harry Emerson Fosdick, one of the most influential Protestants of the first half of the century. Fosdick and other liberals believed that in the face of scientific progress, Protestantism could either adjust or die. What started as theological skirmishes in the 1890s had by the 1920s turned into a full-scale culture war known as the fundamentalist-modernist controversy. Even the name "fundamentalist" emerged from this contest. In 1920 a New York Baptist preacher named Curtis Lee Laws defined a fundamentalist as someone "who was ready to do battle royal for the Fundamentals [of the faith]."

Historian George Marsden has suggested that the culture wars between today's conservatives and progressives developed during the fundamentalist-modernist controversy. The chasm dividing the two groups disappeared during the middle third of the twentieth century, when fundamentalists dropped out of sight and the rest of America came together for the great crusade against fascism that was World War II and then the Cold War crusade against communism. In the 1950s a group of historians known as the consensus school predicted that ever-increasing agreement among diverse factions of Americans would be the hallmark of the age. In the 1960s, however, the chasm began to appear once again as the nation divided over Vietnam, civil rights, and youthful rebellion against traditional morality. Then, in the 1980s, a resurgent fundamentalism arose to battle the progressive culture that had become dominant in the previous two decades, and the culture wars were on again.

When critics of the public fundamentalism of the 1980s charged that the Christian Right wanted to take America back to the 1920s, they were half right. Indeed, Jerry Falwell, Pat Robertson, and other leaders of the Christian Right were appropriating a public brand of militant fundamentalism that for the media had been out of sight and out of mind since just after the Scopes trial of 1925. But these secular critics of fundamentalism in the 1980s were loath to acknowledge that the liberal side, too, found its genesis in the 1920s.

THE FUNDAMENTALIST-MODERNIST CONTROVERSY

As modernists sought to harmonize theology with modern ways of thinking, they were influenced by evolutionary science and literary criticism. Although they accepted Darwin's biological theory, their theological innovation had more to do with applying evolution in nonscientific realms, something that was all the rage in the late 1800s. In other words, modernists argued that just as species develop progressively over time in an evolutionary manner, so does religion. Christianity was a living, organic entity that had evolved from its crude, first-century form into a dynamic, modern faith of the late nineteenth century. As Henry Ward Beecher, one of the first prominent modernist preachers of the era, put it, "Why would we want to go back and talk about acorns when we have the oaks of civilization among us?"[1] For the modernists, the oak tree was nineteenth-century Christian civilization, while the acorn was the less developed faith found in the Bible.

The modernist reinterpretation of Christianity was hugely controversial because Protestants had been arguing since the days of Martin Luther in the sixteenth century that to find pure Christianity, one must return to the Bible. Modernists, by contrast, said that what one found in the Bible was merely the seed of a faith that was now blossoming before our eyes. If the Bible was no longer accepted as the authority in matters of faith, what would be? The modernist answer was that religious experience was central, but not the supernatural new birth that revivalists from George Whitefield to Billy Sunday had preached. Human beings were not radically separated from God by sin and in need of a crucified Christ to supernaturally save them from hell. Rather, everyone was a child of God by nature and capable of experiencing a natural and intuitive, even romantic, awareness of God's presence. Such an emphasis on experience reduced the need for doctrines of sin and salvation, and the emphasis on the natural made miracles such as the virgin birth of Christ and his bodily resurrection too fantastic to take literally in a modern age. Jesus was God's son, not in some literal sense, but because he embodied most fully an awareness that we are all children of God. Modernists often reduced Christ's resurrection to a mere memory and example. In other words, Jesus did not literally rise from the dead in bodily form, as both Catholicism and traditional Protestantism taught. Rather, he rose spiritually within the hearts of his believers.

Modernism came in varying forms, and it was not altogether clear just when someone crossed the line and became a modernist or liberal. From 1900 to 1920, as the two sides organized themselves for battle, the fundamentalists sought to identify that line in hopes of maintaining traditional views, which were known as evangelical prior to the controversy. In 1910 a group of Presbyterian evangelicals fighting off the inroads of modernism within their denomination identified what they believed were the five fundamentals of the faith:

1. The inerrancy and full authority of the Bible
2. The virgin birth of Christ
3. Christ's substitutionary atonement
4. The bodily resurrection of Jesus
5. The authenticity of miracles

By 1920 the authenticity of miracles had morphed into the literal second coming of Christ. The list came to be known popularly as the five points of fundamentalism, and Curtis Lee Laws called on all fundamentalists to defend these points. The term had also been popularized through a series of pamphlets titled "The Fundamentals" published between 1910 and 1915 by two wealthy evangelical businessmen in California. "The Fundamentals" were mailed to virtually every Protestant minister, associate minister, and youth leader in America.

During the fundamentalist-modernist controversy, liberals and their media sympathizers thought of fundamentalists as backward, rural, uneducated, unsophisticated, and most of all intolerant. Fundamentalists agreed only with the last term. They were proudly intolerant of heresy, and that is what fundamentalists believed modernism was. Far from being heretics, liberals believed they were saving the Christian faith from an ignominious collapse by revising it in light of modern ways of thinking. As people became more educated, they would increasingly turn away from fundamentalism, so the modernists believed. Modern people needed an alternative to the outmoded faith of the past. Fundamentalists believed that, far from saving the faith, modernists were elitist intellectual snobs who were intentionally trying to destroy Christianity and the culture built on it. To be sure, neither side had to look far to find those who fit these stereotypes, and in a culture war, each side usually fights primarily against a caricature of the other side. History, however, is trickier. Each side had sophisticated and fair-minded spokesmen (neither side had women theologians), and each side had its share of intolerance. We can see all of this in the controversy of the mid-1920s.

THE MOSES OF MODERNISM

In 1918 three historic New York City Presbyterian churches united to form First Presbyterian, located on Fifth Avenue between Eleventh and Twelfth streets. For several months the church invited guest preachers to fill the pulpit before deciding to hire as head pastor the nearly 75-year-old George Alexander. The congregation then invited Harry Emerson Fosdick to become the church's preaching pastor. Fosdick, the former pastor of the First Baptist Church of Montclair, New Jersey, had been teaching full time at Union Theological Seminary since 1915 and had preached at First Presbyterian four times after the consolidation of the three congregations. He accepted the post and began a seven-year stint as the Baptist pastor of a Presbyterian Church.

Fosdick was born in Buffalo, New York, in 1878, the son of a public school principal. His parents were happily devoted to each other, and Harry grew up in a high-functioning home that was quite stable with the exception of the times when his mother was sick. Fosdick's mother suffered various illnesses and died in 1904, the same year Harry began his first full-time pastorate. Religiously the Fosdicks were Baptist and fairly typical in their devotion to orthodox Protestantism. Although no longer dominant in America, Calvinist orthodoxy still was prominent in the Presbyterian and Baptist denominations of Fosdick's youth. Calvinists believe that God elects some to be saved and others to be damned, and Fosdick grew up fearing that he might be in the latter group. He also felt guilty about his every misstep. He experienced conversion and baptism at the age of seven but continued to fear for his soul for years thereafter. When his family lived for a time in Lancaster, where no Baptist church existed, Fosdick attended both Presbyterian and Methodist meetings, the other two great evangelical denominations of the time. Fosdick's biographer believes that much of his liberal theology can be understood as a rejection of the Calvinist terrors of his youth and his sense that denominational labels and creeds meant little. He always deemphasized theological doctrine in favor of Christian experience and once said in a sermon, "There are no Presbyterians, Congregationalists, Episcopalians, Methodists, or Baptists—only Christians."[2]

Fosdick attended Colgate, a college of about 150 students in Hamilton, New York. After two years of excelling in oratory, debate, yearbook, school newspaper, and fraternity organizing, he was forced to take a year off when his father suffered a nervous breakdown. Back home, while caring for his father and working in a bookstore, Fosdick had plenty of time to think—and doubt. He was sincerely religious and wanted to remain so, yet he could not continue to accept the particular doctrinal verities of evangelical Protestantism. In the midst of his crisis he returned to Colgate and was influenced by one of the leading liberal thinkers of the era, William Newton Clarke, who taught at the Hamilton Seminary. About Clarke, Fosdick would later write, "[He] was really my spiritual godfather."[3]

Like other liberals or modernists of the era, Fosdick came to believe that one must remove the kernel of the gospel's truth from the husk of ancient myth that surrounded it in scripture. In short, he believed that the Bible was true but not to be taken literally. The abiding aspect of Christianity was not doctrine but an experience of God's presence within individuals that allowed them to maximize their potential as children of God. "We must distinguish between abiding experiences and changing categories," he once wrote.[4] In other words, experience trumped doctrine as the centerpiece of the Christian faith or any other religion through which one might experience God. After graduating from Colgate in 1900, Fosdick studied for a year with Clarke, then went off to Union Theological Seminary in New York City.

While at Union, Fosdick encountered urban poverty and the Protestant response to it known as the Social Gospel. During his first summer in the city, he worked with a children's ministry, then switched to a mission in the Bowery when classes began in the fall. Under the strain of his studies and his first confrontation with human deprivation, he experienced a severe and prolonged bout of depression. He left school and went to New England for a time, spent four months in a hospital in Elmira, New York, then spent six weeks convalescing in England. Not until the next September was he able to resume classes. Once back at Union, Fosdick excelled academically, studying under some of the leading liberal theologians of the day. He was ordained as a Baptist minister in 1903 and graduated summa cum laude the next year. He took his first full-time pastorate at the First Baptist Church of Montclair, where he would serve from 1904 to 1915.

During his years in Montclair, Fosdick became a renowned preacher, member of the Union Seminary faculty, and well-known author. He wrote six books during his years in New Jersey, some of which sold tens of thousands of copies and went through multiple printings for the next several decades. He had a knack for writing for a wide audience, everything from popular articles to devotionals for laypeople to serious works of theology. Among his most famous writings was a trilogy of books, the first of which he wrote while in Montclair: *The Meaning of Prayer, The Meaning of Faith,* and *The Meaning of Service.* These were highly practical books, intended to be used as devotionals for believers dealing with the same sorts of questions that troubled Fosdick. What do prayer, faith, and Christian service mean in a modern, scientific culture? Even more than preaching, Fosdick's books made him an eminent figure across the nation and in Great Britain. In 1915 Fosdick left First Baptist Montclair to join the faculty of Union full time. Three years later he accepted the call at First Presbyterian New York, or Old First, as it was affectionately known.

THE CONTROVERSY

Old First's call of the Baptist Fosdick was unusual in an age when denominational labels were still important to most people. But the church had the approval of New York's Presbyterian synod (the governing body for the state's Presbyterians), and Fosdick's acceptance was in keeping with his low view of doctrinal division. Fosdick was an immediate star in New York. Before each Sunday morning worship service, a throng of people lined up outside the church hoping to get a seat in the section of the sanctuary open to nonmembers. Frequently, overflow seats were placed on the platform behind the pulpit of the 1,100-seat auditorium. Attending a Fosdick preaching service while in New York was akin to taking in the theater on Broadway, shopping on Fifth Avenue, or going to Yankee Stadium to watch Babe Ruth play baseball. Fosdick and First Presbyterian were civic fixtures, and he was a national figure as well. In addition to preaching and lecturing multiple times each week, Fosdick continued to publish books and articles. He wrote often for popular magazines such as *Harper's* and *Reader's Digest,* and he traveled the country lecturing at colleges that awarded him a string of honorary doctorates. He might have spent the rest of his career at Old First had it not been for the fundamentalist-modernist controversy.

By the time Fosdick arrived at First Presbyterian, controversy in the denomination had been raging for more than two decades. Conservatives had issued the famous five points of fundamentalism in 1910 and by the 1920s were more determined than ever to maintain fidelity to the Presbyterian creed known as the Westminster Confession of Faith. Written during the English civil war of the 1640s, the confession had been the standard doctrinal statement of American Presbyterians since the early eighteenth century. By the 1920s, however, liberal theology had made significant inroads within the 10,000 churches and 2 million members of the Presbyterian Church U.S.A., which was essentially the Presbyterian church of the northern United States. Most people in the pews remained conservative; a growing number of the clergy and denominational leaders, however, emphasized modernist theology with its broad and tolerant form of religious experience that stood in the place of doctrinal rigor. Old First got caught in the cross-fire when the fundamentalists went after Fosdick as the most visible symbol of liberalism.

This is not to say that Fosdick was an innocent bystander who just happened to get swept into the controversy. To the contrary, he was an active participant, often as militant as the fundamentalists. He liked the fight and played a major role in bringing it to a head with his 1922 sermon "Shall the Fundamentalists Win?" Fosdick opened by pointing out that the controversy was especially heated in the Baptist and Presbyterian denominations. In that he was a Baptist serving in a Presbyterian church, he had a special interest. Fosdick couched his sermon as a plea for tolerance, but to fundamentalists it appeared anything but. He was correct in charging that the fundamentalists intended "to drive out of the evangelical churches men and women of liberal opinions." But fundamentalists saw as fighting words his insistence that the virgin birth of

Christ was merely an idiom used by biblical writers. For Fosdick, the virgin birth was "a biological miracle our modern minds cannot use." Likewise, the second coming of Christ was but "an old phrasing of expectancy" that can be replaced by the modern, progressive view that "[God's] will and principles will be worked out by God's grace in human life and institutions," not through a supernatural intervention.

Like other liberals, Fosdick believed in the progressive manifestation of Christ in the institutions of a democratic culture, especially American culture. All was progress. Music had progressed from ancient tribal drum beating to the modern symphony, architecture from the crude hut to the modern skyscraper, and art from the cave drawing to the modern painting. Moreover, Fosdick repeatedly compared biblical expressions with ancient myths from other religions. Fundamentalists could not help but read him to mean that Christianity was just one mythic expression of God's truth and that God could be found in different form in several religions. Fosdick answered his sermon's rhetorical question "Well, they are not going to do it; certainly not in this vicinity."[5]

Clarence Macartney of the Arch Street Presbyterian Church in Philadelphia answered Fosdick with a sermon of his own, "Shall Unbelief Win?" As we saw in the last chapter, Macartney cared little for boxing, but he was always ready for a theological fight. He claimed that Fosdick was responsible for thrusting the controversy onto the Presbyterian church. Such was hardly the case, but Fosdick was equally disingenuous when he called his own sermon a "frank, kindly, irenic plea for tolerance, not likely to be misunderstood except by people who persist in misunderstanding it."[6] Defending his side in like manner, Macartney characterized the fundamentalists as merely attempting to hold the line at the essentials of the faith. The virgin birth was a historical fact, Christ promised to return, and the Bible was divinely and uniquely inspired, not merely one expression among many bearing witness to God's love and grace. Overall, Macartney and the fundamentalists believed that liberalism was "a Christianity without worship, without God, and without Jesus Christ."[7]

The year after Fosdick's historic sermon, Princeton theologian J. Gresham Machen published his classic book, *Christianity and Liberalism*. The book was the most sophisticated articulation of the fundamentalist position. Machen must have had Fosdick's "plea for tolerance" in mind when he wrote that liberalism "is regarded as 'liberal' only by its friends; to its opponents it seems to involve a narrow ignoring of many relevant facts." Machen argued that liberal

Protestantism was not merely an adjustment of Christianity but a wholly different religion, all the more dangerous because liberals retained common theological terms while subtly changing their meaning. Liberals used the term "virgin birth" to mean that Christ's birth was special but not supernatural. The "second coming" meant the progressive realization of Christ's teachings within history, not that Christ would actually return to bring history to a close. Some liberals even used the term "resurrection of Christ" to mean the memory of Jesus in his followers' minds. The root of liberalism for Machen was this sort of naturalism or, as he put it, "the denial of any entrance of the creative power of God (as distinguished from the ordinary course of nature) in connection with the origin of Christianity." In the most succinct passage of his book, Machen wrote, "[I]t may appear that what the liberal theologian has retained after abandoning to the enemy one Christian doctrine after another is not Christianity at all, but a religion which is so entirely different from Christianity as to belong in a distinct category."[8]

The battle lines drawn by Fosdick's sermon and the responses of Macartney and Machen had been forming for more than a quarter century. The first heresy trials in the ecclesiastical courts of the denomination had been in the 1890s, resulting in the departure of three prominent liberal theologians: Charles A. Briggs, Henry Preserved Smith, and Arthur Cushman McGiffert. By the 1920s, liberals had sufficient numbers to mount a more serious challenge, but they were still in the minority. When Machen wrote *Christianity and Liberalism,* the fundamentalists were winning the fundamentalist-modernist controversy. Secular journalist and widely read social commentator Walter Lippmann wrote of Machen's work: "It is an admirable book . . . , the best popular argument produced by either side in the current controversy."[9] Likewise, the editor of *The Nation* wrote: "Fundamentalism is undoubtedly in the main stream of the Christian tradition while modernism represents a religious revolution as far-reaching as the Protestant Reformation."[10] Fundamentalists organized for battle and readied themselves to defend the faith. The whimper of controversy at the turn of the century had become a roar by 1922. Both Fosdick's sermon and Macartney's answer were published in periodicals, put into pamphlet form, and given wide circulation. Macartney and the Presbytery of Philadelphia then tried to persuade the national Presbyterian governing body to crack down on Fosdick. Machen's book appeared in 1923, and that year's General Assembly of the Presbyterian Church U.S.A. met in Indianapolis.

The first item of business at General Assembly meetings was the election of a moderator, who wielded considerable power. He appointed the chairs of the committees that oversaw denominational affairs and settled controversies. William Jennings Bryan was the fundamentalists' choice in 1923. He had moved from progressive politics into the fundamentalist anti-evolution crusade in 1919 and was a mere two years away from his own demise in the Scopes trial. Bryan's anti-evolution crusade made him anathema to liberals but also suspect among moderates and a few fundamentalists, such as Machen, who opposed attempts to force secular schools to follow religious doctrine. He lost the election 451 to 427 to the liberal-leaning Charles Wishart, president of the College of Wooster, in Ohio. Bryan spent the rest of the General Assembly attempting to persuade the denomination to ban the teaching of evolution in Presbyterian colleges. He believed that holding the line at evolution would remedy the theological liberalism in the denomination. "We have preachers in this audience who don't believe in the virgin birth . . . in the resurrection of Christ's body . . . in the miracles," he thundered.[11] He believed theological liberalism resulted from evolution—and vice versa, take your pick. His measure failed.

The committee handling the issue of whether Fosdick could continue as the pastor of a Presbyterian church voted 22 to 1 to leave matters to the Presbytery of New York, which at the time was investigating whether Fosdick's views were too liberal for the denomination. The one person on the committee who voted against the other 22 filed a minority report reaffirming the five fundamentals from 1910 and directing the New York Presbytery to adhere to the Westminster Confession of Faith, which would have put Fosdick at risk. When the majority and minority reports emerged from the committee, a five-hour debate ensued on the floor of the General Assembly. Macartney, Bryan, and other fundamentalists argued in favor of the minority report, and it passed 439 to 359 despite having only its author's support on the committee. Fundamentalists were ecstatic. "It was a great victory for orthodox Christianity—other churches will follow," Bryan predicted. He interpreted his defeat as moderator as providential; it freed him to join the fray on the floor fight over the Fosdick committee report.[12]

The liberals, however, redoubled their efforts and refused to accept their apparent defeat. In modern America no idea cashes out better than tolerance, and they were merely asking that the Presbyterian Church U.S.A. tolerate both camps. Henry Sloane Coffin, who pastored New York's Madison Avenue Presbyterian Church, emerged as the leader for the liberals. Before leaving Indianapolis, he told the General Assembly that any action taken against Fosdick would be action against him as well because he believed the same things. He rejected the five fundamentals of 1910 and said, "I share fully in [Fosdick's] view."[13] In June Coffin and other liberals gathered at the Auburn Theological Seminary in upstate New York (the school is now in New York City) and drafted a document known as the Auburn Affirmation, modeled in part on Coffin's views. Procedurally, liberals argued that the actions taken in 1923 as well as the five points adopted in 1910 were unconstitutional according to the bylaws of the church. A single General Assembly could not unilaterally issue theological proclamations. In effect, the 1910 General Assembly had altered the Westminster Confession of Faith by attaching to it the five fundamentals of the faith, which had then been reaffirmed by the General Assemblies of 1916 and 1923. All three actions were unconstitutional according to Presbyterian polity, the liberals argued.

Substantively, the Auburn Affirmation affirmed the inspiration of scripture, the belief that God was in Christ, that Christ was the redemption for humankind, and that he rose from the dead. Precisely because the liberals did not believe one had to take these doctrines supernaturally, as the fundamentalists insisted, the affirmation left open how one was to interpret them. "But we are united," the document stated, "in believing that these are not the only theories allowed by the Scriptures and our standards as explanations of these facts and doctrines of our religion, and that all who hold to these facts and doctrines, whatever theories they may employ to explain them, are worthy of all confidence and fellowship."[14] Over the next several months more than 150 liberals signed the document, and leaders released it to the press in January 1924.

Leading up to the 1924 General Assembly, liberals rallied around the Auburn Affirmation and Fosdick. The New York Presbytery exonerated Old First and licensed for preaching two candidates who rejected the virgin birth. Liberals then held a pre–General Assembly meeting in Detroit to plan strategy and strengthen their resolve. Fundamentalists held rallies of their own, casting the theological battle as a war for the preservation of Christian culture. "[T]he Presbyterian Church has come to the kingdom for such an hour as this," Macartney told one audience. At another meeting fundamentalists adopted their own affirmation that read, in part, "The great facts upon which the Christian revelation rests are openly questioned and rejected [by the liberals], and the very foundations of the moral order among men and nations are imperiled."[15] Rank-and-file members of the Presbyterian church read accounts of the controversy in major newspapers, but how many could actually follow the nuances of theological debate? Most members remained conservative, but unless one's own church had a flaming liberal as a preacher, or the local public school taught evolution, few middle- or working-class people had the time or inclination to get involved in a fight. Until the Scopes trial of 1925, the fundamentalist-modernist controversy looked like a preachers' row.

The 1924 General Assembly met in Grand Rapids, Michigan, and both sides were poised for battle as never before. Ironically, the assembly met in a Baptist church loaned to the Presbyterians. In tying this anomaly to Fosdick, Macartney remarked from the floor, "In as much as one of our leading Presbyterian churches is entertaining a distinguished Baptist, we are pleased to accept the hospitality of the Baptists. But hope we will not cause you as much trouble as our Baptist friend has caused us."[16] Macartney was the fundamentalists' choice as moderator. In presenting Macartney's nomination, Bryan called him "a defender of the faith . . . against the insidious attack made against the historic doctrines of the Presbyterian Church."[17] The assembly was off to a rousing start. Liberals supported Charles Erdman of Princeton Seminary. Erdman was not a liberal. Rather, he was a moderate (not modernist) in sympathy with fundamentalist theology but not their militant spirit or their insistence on doctrinal precision. At the time, leaders such as Erdman were sometimes called liberal conservatives, but the term "moderate" seems less confusing. Erdman and the others sought a compromise that would allow fundamentalists and liberals to live in peace within the denomination. Macartney won the moderator's chair in another close vote, 464 to 446.

Liberals viewed the election as a serious blow. Coffin wrote to his wife, "Here the dreaded worst has happened. On Bryan's nomination Macartney has been elected by a close majority."[18] Macartney named Bryan vice moderator and appointed a conservative as chair of every important committee, as was his prerogative as moderator. Momentarily downcast, the liberals were hardly ready to surrender, and as things turned out, the right-leaning assembly did little to advance the fundamentalist cause. No action was taken against the Auburn Affirmation or the Presbyterian leaders who signed it. Bradley Longfield, the chief historian of the Presbyterian controversy, has written that it is difficult to find reasons why the fundamentalists failed to act against the Auburn Affirmation, which was the "liberals' clearest and most aggressive declaration of faith." Even Bryan voted for no action. Coffin had a theory: "I believe the conservatives are frightened and that they shrink from extreme measures," he wrote at the time.[19] Such fright may have stemmed from an incident on the floor of the assembly. No sooner had the election of moderator taken place when a delegate from Baltimore accused the fundamentalists of playing ward politics by trying to stack committee appointments in their own favor. The Baltimore representative and a fundamentalist opponent briefly shook their fists at each other before others intervened.[20] Neither side wanted to appear guilty of inciting a riot; both sides wanted to keep peace as much as possible.

The failure to act against the Auburn Affirmation was a portent of things to come. Even while controlling nearly every important committee, the fundamentalists took very little decisive action. Although some leading fundamentalists wanted Fosdick expelled from the denomination, the assembly merely recommended that "[i]f he desires to occupy a Presbyterian pulpit for an extended time[,] he should enter our Church through the regular method and become subject to the jurisdiction and authority of the Church."[21] Liberals along with the press believed the invitation shifted matters from doctrine to constitutional polity, as if the judicial committee were merely recommending that Fosdick join the Presbyterian church. In response to this action, for example, a surprised Coffin wrote, "The General Assembly not only did not condemn Dr. Fosdick for any of his teaching but . . . graciously invited him to enter the Presbyterian ministry."[22] This was perhaps the only time during the entire fundamentalist-modernist controversy that a liberal described a fundamentalist action as gracious.

Although it did not expel Fosdick, the judicial committee wrote: "If [Fosdick] can accept the doctrinal standards of our church, as contained in the [Westminster] Confession of Faith, there should be no difficulty in receiving him. If he cannot, he ought not to continue to occupy a Presbyterian pulpit."[23] In other words, where liberals saw a gracious invitation based on constitutional order, fundamentalists actually meant that Fosdick should be required to adhere to the confessional standards of the Westminster Confession. Little wonder that while liberals saw this as a victory, so too did the fundamentalists. Bryan said that Fosdick's famous sermon "Shall the Fundamentalists Win?" had been answered "yes," and the New York *Times* reported, "Fosdick Decision Pleases Both Sides."[24] That may have been the impression when the assembly in Grand

Rapids ended, but after a few months of reports saying Fosdick had been "invited" to join the Presbyterian church and all would be well, the fundamentalists began to see they had been outmaneuvered. As fundamentalist Mark Matthews of Seattle said a few months later in the wake of such press reports, "It is a perversion of facts to say that Dr. Fosdick was invited to join the Presbyterian Church."[25]

Fosdick did not take up the General Assembly's "invitation," even though members of his church tried mightily to persuade him. From his point of view the fundamentalists were right. "The proposal of the General Assembly," he wrote a few months later, "calls for a definite creedal subscription, a solemn assumption of theological vows in terms of the Westminster Confession."[26] The way he saw things, he was being forced to either submit to the Presbyterian church or resign his post at First Presbyterian. When leaders of Old First realized that his anticreedal proclivities would never allow him to submit and join, they came up with the harebrained idea of having Fosdick officially resign as their preaching pastor but continue forever to fill the pulpit as a guest. But Fosdick had had enough. He resigned in October 1924, effective the following March. Fundamentalists had gotten rid of Fosdick, but they would not recoup other setbacks from the 1924 General Assembly meeting. Although they did not know it at the time, 1924 had been the high point of fundamentalist opportunity; and they had missed it.

The battle intensified in early 1925 as each side prepared for the springtime General Assembly. The focus of the controversy shifted, however, moving from a fundamentalist-modernist war to a break between the fundamentalists and the moderates. Fundamentalist Machen squared off with moderate conservative Erdman. Both were on the Princeton Seminary faculty, where there had been a long-running debate about how Presbyterian pastors should be trained. Machen represented the old school who believed that seminary education should be heavily doctrinal. Moderates such as Erdman believed all the same theological doctrines as Machen, but they pressed for more practical training of ministers. In short, the fundamentalists and the moderates had different views of the church's role in the world and even the nature of Christianity. Machen believed the church's primary mission was to preserve and spread the great doctrines of the faith. Erdman and the moderates believed that the church's mission was to bring people into a relationship with God through Christ. To do this, the church needed to be unified, moderates believed, and so they were willing to compromise with liberals for the sake of keeping the Presbyterian Church U.S.A. intact. Machen put the matter clearly and concisely when he said that the difference between himself and Erdman was not over this or that specific doctrine but over the importance of doctrine itself, its place in the Christian religion. When Erdman ran for moderator of the 1925 General Assembly, Machen called Erdman the liberals' candidate, but Erdman, who had the support of conservatives such as Bryan and even Billy Sunday, won.[27]

Like Bryan, Sunday was staunchly fundamentalist in his theology, but he was rarely a major player in the Presbyterian church's official policy making. He simply was not a denominational politician. During the 1924 General Assembly he was recovering from an illness at the Mayo Clinic in Minnesota. The assembly sent him a get-well telegram. While in New York for a revival campaign just a month before the 1925 General Assembly, he told reporters that modernists were "theological bootleggers." "They seemingly have no more respect for God and the Bible and the cardinal doctrines of religion than the bootleggers have for the law," he explained.[28] Sunday believed that rank-and-file Presbyterians were conservative and that the liberal preachers of the New York Presbytery were the problem. In Erdman, Sunday was supporting a theological conservative and a good man. Neither Sunday nor Bryan understood quite what was at stake for their side of the fight in taking the inclusive position that Erdman set forth.

At the 1925 General Assembly the liberals, not the fundamentalists, threatened to split the denomination. The issue had to do in part with the two ministerial candidates from New York who had been licensed even though they would not affirm the virgin birth of Christ. Fundamentalists wanted the assembly to force revocation of their preaching licenses. Liberals threatened to leave the church if this happened. In the words of historian Longfield, the liberal threat was implied but clear: "Strict doctrinal orthodoxy and a united church were no longer an option; one or the other . . . would have to go."[29] This was an about-face of sorts, as the liberals had been the party of unity. During the previous year's General Assembly, Coffin had preached a sermon in Grand Rapids saying that separation of the liberals from the fundamentalists in the Presbyterian church would be "a calamity." Moreover, the liberal party preferred to be called the "constitutionalists." In doing so, they were signaling that they were the conservatives, at least as far as procedures were concerned. When Charles Wishart made his farewell speech in 1924 and handed over the gavel to Macartney, Wishart remarked, "So far as drastic surgery is concerned, I am an extreme conserva-tive."[30] Sharing with liberals this desire to maintain unity, the moderate Erdman brokered a compromise. He recommended that the Assembly appoint a com-mission to study the causes of division and strife and report back.

After a year of study, the commission made its report at the General As-sembly meeting of 1926. Tolerance loomed large in the report. Having studied four major controversies in the history of the Presbyterian church, the com-mission concluded that tolerance of varying interpretations of core doctrines was the pattern of Presbyterian history. Moreover, where disagreement over the interpretation of core doctrines existed, the church historically emphasized the unity of spirit and common mission of advancing the gospel in the world. Most important, the commission said that it was unconstitutional by the church's bylaws for a single General Assembly to say definitively and precisely how the Westminster Confession of Faith should be interpreted. Essentially, this meant that the five fundamentals adopted by the 1910 General Assembly and later reaffirmed were nonbinding. This was the central claim of the Auburn Affirmation. The fundamentalist-dominated General Assembly of 1924 failed to take action against the affirmation; the General Assembly of 1926 essentially adopted it.

AFTERMATH

After 1926 the Presbyterian Church U.S.A. was doctrinally inclusive. Liberals had always said that this was what they wanted, and they could not understand how the fundamentalists could be so intolerant. Walter Lippmann could. In an imaginary dialogue he wrote:

> Modernist: We can at least discuss it like gentlemen, without heat, without rancor.
>
> Fundamentalist: Has it ever occurred to you that this advice is easier for you to follow than for me?
>
> Modernist: How so?
>
> Fundamentalist: Because for me an eternal plan of salvation is at stake. For you there is nothing at stake but a few tentative opinions none of which means anything to your happiness. Your request that I should be tolerant and amiable is, therefore, that I submit the foundation of my life to the

destructive effects of your skepticism, your indifference, and your good
nature. You ask me to smile and commit suicide.[31]

Lippmann believed that only the elite among modern individuals could live
with symbolism and experience alone. "For the great mass of men," he wrote,
"religious experience depends upon a complete belief in the concrete existence
[of biblical truths]." Lippmann believed that fundamentalists understood more
clearly than liberals what was at stake. As he put it: "The fundamentalist goes
to the very heart of the matter, therefore, when he insists that you have destroyed the popular foundations of religion if you make your gospel a symbolic
record of experience, and reject it as an actual record of events."[32] Liberals could
never understand this, but even if they had, it is not clear what they could have
done. They simply found the literal interpretation of much of the Bible too fantastic to believe in a modern age. While liberals came to dominate the leadership positions of the northern Protestant denominations, most rank-and-file
Presbyterians, Baptists, and Methodists proved Lippmann right. They continued believing in their private lives the literal and supernatural truths of traditional Christianity, even though their denominations no longer required such
beliefs for church membership. Liberal leaders could tolerate this sort of grassroots conservatism, but they could not tolerate leaders such as Machen who
insisted on doctrinal conformity.

In another matter of business, the 1926 Presbyterian General Assembly
blocked ratification of Machen's promotion to an important endowed chair at
Princeton. Would there really be room for fundamentalists and liberals in the
same denomination? Would fundamentalists stay if allowed? The controversy
soon shifted to Princeton Seminary where the story was repeated. The moderate conservative party once again adopted the inclusive position that tolerated
liberals and fundamentalists. Machen left Princeton in 1929 and formed Westminster Seminary in Philadelphia, then a few years later started a new denomination, the Orthodox Presbyterian Church. Fosdick's biographer caught the
irony of Machen's departure, pointing out that Fosdick thought the conservatives gave him no choice but to withdraw from Old First in 1924, but by the end
of the decade the conservatives believed the liberals gave them no choice but
to withdraw from the denomination, and so Machen left.[33]

While still the minority party, at least at the grassroots level, liberals moved
nevertheless in the same direction as a progressive modern American culture.

Their watchword was tolerance of diverse viewpoints. They would learn a few years later in the obscenity wars that they too had limits to how far tolerance should go, but a chasm was developing within Protestant America. On one side stood fundamentalists as the defenders of truth; on the other stood liberals as the defenders of tolerance.

No longer in the Presbyterian Church U.S.A., Fosdick was called to the pulpit of Park Avenue Baptist Church, part of the Northern Baptist Convention. The Northern Baptists had experienced their own chapter of the fundamentalist-modernist controversy at roughly the same time as the Presbyterians and with similar results; the liberals won. After 1925 Park Avenue Baptist had not only the most famous liberal preacher in America, Fosdick, but also the nation's wealthiest businessman. John D. Rockefeller Jr. had been largely responsible for courting Fosdick in the months when he was extricating himself from Old First and the Presbyterian controversy. At one point when Fosdick suggested flak he might receive for being pastor to America's wealthiest citizen, Rockefeller replied, "Do you think that more people will criticize you on account of my wealth, than will criticize me on account of your theology?"[34]

Part of the recruitment process was the promise that Rockefeller would build a new church edifice on Morningside Heights near Columbia University. Upon completion in 1931, Park Avenue Baptist changed locations. It had already changed identities. As part of the agreement with Fosdick, Park Avenue Baptist became the nondenominational Riverside Church, following Fosdick's anticreedal and ecumenical leanings. Still thriving today as a landmark to liberal Protestantism, the gothic skyscraper Riverside Church continues independent of denominational labels or control.

Fosdick lived another 45 years after leaving the Presbyterians, dying in 1969 at the age of 91. In 1935, from his Riverside pulpit, he preached perhaps his second most famous sermon. Always the progressive, he titled it, "The Church Must Go Beyond Modernism." In going beyond modernism, however, Fosdick also backtracked, something liberals were loath to do. For them, all was progress. Specifically, Fosdick backed away from the romantic and unrealistic optimism that denied the seriousness of sin. "Sin is real," he said emphatically. "Personal and social sin is as terribly real as our forefathers said it was, no matter how we change their way of saying so." By the time Fosdick preached this sermon, Swiss theologian Karl Barth and others were building a movement known as Neo-Orthodoxy. Neo-Orthodox theologians were products of liberalism who came to see its shortcomings. They critiqued liberalism precisely for losing sight of humankind's sinfulness and God's transcendence. In the midst of the Great Depression, it was easier to locate sin than it was to speak of progress. Moreover, when the world seemed destined for democracy in the 1920s, liberals found God present in cultural development, but with fascism sweeping across Europe in the 1930s, God was hard to find.

With his penchant for popularizing, Fosdick echoed Barth's criticism. Liberals, Fosdick said, had reduced God "to an advisory capacity, as a kind of chairman of the board of sponsors for our highly successful human enterprise." Fosdick warned that if the trend of harmonizing Christian theology with modern thought continued indefinitely, the faith would adapt itself to all sorts of ideas: nationalism, imperialism, capitalism, and racism—in his words, "harmonizing itself . . . with the prevailing status quo and the common moral judgments of our time."[35] Fosdick remained a liberal, but he feared that liberal Christianity was harmonizing itself right out of existence by losing its distinct identity and being submerged in modern culture. Machen had predicted as much back in 1923.

Two years after Fosdick's sermon criticizing modernism, Yale's H. Richard Niebuhr put the case succinctly when he described theological liberalism in this way: "A God without wrath brought men without sin into a kingdom without judgment through the ministrations of a Christ without a cross."[36] Like Fosdick, Niebuhr was a product of liberalism, and his brother Reinhold became America's most famous twentieth-century theologian. The Niebuhr brothers, Barth, and other theologians built theological careers critiquing the movement that birthed them intellectually. As H. Richard Neibuhr put it, "[T]he later liberalism increasingly identified human values with the divine, proclaimed the glad tidings of progress and hallowed man's moral efforts though they led to civil, international and class war."[37]

Critics notwithstanding, liberal Protestantism was in its heyday from 1930 to 1980. Public religion tended to be broad and amorphous, easily harmonized with liberal democracy and modern tolerance. Most everyone's faith was acceptable, as long as doctrinal peculiarities were kept out of sight. This was a far cry from the Roaring Twenties, when the doctrinal disputes of the fundamentalist-modernist controversy seemed to matter—when fundamentalists could say with a straight face that the foundations of western culture were at stake in the theological battles of the time.

During the liberal heyday, fundamentalism and even a new evangelicalism were culturally disengaged and, with the exception of Billy Graham crusades, beneath the media radar. To many, it appeared that fundamentalism was dying. Surely a remnant of a bygone era, there was little need to pay attention to fundamentalists, unless they were odd or idiotic, which many were. Fundamentalism had been defeated once and for all in the fundamentalist-modernist controversy of the 1920s, freeing America to move forward progressively—liberally. This view proved wrong, of course. We know now that while fundamentalists lost the major battles of the 1920s, they did not die out. Rather, they reorganized quietly beyond the glare of public scrutiny and lived to fight another day.[38] As George Marsden and others have suggested, the chasm that developed in the 1920s reappeared in the 1980s, as new fundamentalists emerged to lead the conservative side in another round of culture wars.

But why did things turn out the way they did in the Roaring Twenties? How did the fundamentalists go from the precipice of victory in 1924 to defeat in 1926? The answer is complex and still being unraveled by historians, but contributing to the fundamentalist demise were events from July 1925 through July 1926, the worst year in fundamentalism's entire history, even until our own time. That year fundamentalists roared—and it was not pretty. First came the Scopes trial, then controversies surrounding two high-profile fundamentalists.

CHAPTER 5

THE SCOPES TRIAL

A t the 1924 Presbyterian General Assembly meeting, William Jennings Bryan told reporters, "My religion does not interfere with my politics and my politics do not interfere with my religion. They run on parallel lines, but they never meet." Bryan did not mean this statement the way it would be understood today—that he never brought his religion into his politics. He had been stumping the nation for five years advocating state laws banning the teaching of evolution, in part because he believed evolution conflicted with the Bible. He had also attempted to get the Presbyterian Church U.S.A. to ban evolution in its schools. What Bryan really meant came in the second half of his statement: "I don't take back in politics anything I say in religion, and I don't take back in religion anything I say in politics."[1] For Bryan, separation of church and state meant that he would never ask the state to ban evolution in Presbyterian schools or assume the Presbyterian church had any power to ban evolution in public schools. But if evolution was bad for children and detrimental to religion, it should be banned by the appropriate authorities in both church and state. Such was the making of the Scopes trial of 1925.

The Scopes trial was the trial of the century, at least until O. J. Simpson in the 1990s. The event captured the attention of reporters from across the nation who came to the burgh of Dayton, Tennessee, in droves to cover the spectacle. It was truly a clash of cultures symbolizing the old versus the new, the conservative versus the liberal, and the religious versus the scientific. The trial also became a public and popular expression of the fundamentalist-modernist controversy in the northern Protestant denominations. Conservative rank-and-file Presbyterians and Baptists were often bewildered by the theological wrangling taking place at the elite levels of their denominations. Evolution, by contrast, was an issue they could get excited about. As Bryan and others framed the issue, the choice was between teaching children that they have descended from the brute or that human beings are the special creation of a loving God.

Even more than Scopes himself, Bryan became the central figure in the drama. He was an evangelical who had been for a generation one of the leading progressive politicians in the nation. To be conservative in religion and liberal in politics was not nearly as unusual in that era as it would be today. Nineteenth-century evangelicals had championed a number of social and political reforms, including the abolition of slavery, women's rights, the rights of labor, and education. As a product of this reforming tradition Bryan became the progressive Democratic candidate for president in 1896, 1900, and 1908, and subsequently the only presidential candidate in history to lose three times. He also served as Woodrow Wilson's secretary of state from 1913 to 1915.

By the 1920s evolution had become for many fundamentalists a symbol of modernism, and Bryan took up the anti-evolution cause with the same reforming zeal he had employed while stumping the nation for women's voting rights or direct election of senators. His and the movement's rallying cry was "What modernism is to the church, evolution is to the culture," and many conservative Protestants agreed. Just as modernism undercut the church's doctrinal foundation, so evolution undercut the culture's moral foundation. Bryan argued that if human beings were nothing more than animals in a highly evolved state, then the law of the jungle reigned supreme. There was no sense in telling someone that this or that action was wrong, if everything including humans had evolved naturally without a creator. Moreover, many fundamentalists believed it was impossible to reconcile evolution with the authority and infallibility of the Bible. Fundamentalists believed that Adam and Eve were created literally in the Garden of Eden, while scientists believed that human beings evolved naturally over a long period of time from lower forms of animals. Both could not be true.

Fundamentalists of the 1920s who reasoned this way, however, chose one evangelical response to evolution but not the only one. Following the publication of Charles Darwin's book *Origin of Species* in 1859, many conservative Christian thinkers worked to reconcile the new science with the old religion. Even at Princeton Seminary, a bastion of conservative Protestantism, there was openness. For example, Professor Benjamin Warfield wrote in his lecture notes:

"The upshot of the whole matter is that there is no necessary antagonism of Christianity to evolution. . . . If we condition the theory by allowing the constant oversight of God in the whole process." Warfield believed that if God started and sustained a long creation process, Christians "may hold to the modified theory of evolution and be Christians in the ordinary sense."[2]

Charles Hodge, who had preceded Warfield at Princeton, wrote a pamphlet in 1874 called "What Is Darwinism?" His answer was that Darwinism was atheism, but he made a distinction between evolution and Darwin's theory of it. The problem, Hodge argued, was that Darwin believed evolution had no purpose. It happened by random chance. If one could develop a theory of evolution that had purpose, specifically God's purpose of bringing humankind into existence in God's own image, then evolution could be acceptable. "There may be a theistic interpretation of the Darwinian theory," Hodge wrote.[3]

Hodge and Warfield were considered conservative, Calvinist, and thoroughly biblical. Warfield is even credited in part with developing a theory of the "inerrancy of scripture" that fundamentalists in the 1920s defended during the fundamentalist-modernist controversy. Yet neither Hodge nor Warfield saw any reason to insist that the six days of creation in Genesis were literal, especially given that the sun was created on the fourth day, which would have started what we now call 24-hour days. Hodge and Warfield were in the company of many other conservatives who believed that evolution could be harmonized with scripture. As Hodge argued, scripture should be read by science and science by scripture. Echoing Galileo, Hodge believed it perfectly appropriate to allow what we know from observing nature to shape how we read scripture, and vice versa.

Among scientists, the line between who accepted and who rejected Darwin is as surprising as among theologians. Darwin's chief adversary was Louis Agassiz of Harvard, who was so theologically liberal, his religious views at the time could have been considered unorthodox. On the other side, the scientist who worked hardest to give Darwin a fair hearing in the American scientific community was Asa Gray, also of Harvard. Like Hodge, Gray did not accept all aspects of Darwin's theory, but he believed that orthodox Christianity and some modified form of evolution could be harmonized. In another twist that boggles the mind today, the liberal Agassiz used science to argue in favor of racism, while the conservative Gray used the Bible to argue against it. In short, the way that we commonly think about how conservative and liberal theology play out in scientific and cultural attitudes was quite different in the late nineteenth century than it is today.

As late as 1915 in the famous *Fundamentals of the Faith,* the pamphlet series that became a rallying point for early fundamentalism, there was one article opposing evolution and another seeking harmony between religion and science.[4] By the time of the Scopes trial, however, fundamentalist voices articulating the harmony position were drowned out by those clamoring for warfare. The "warfare model" had become the dominant way of understanding the relationship between religion and science. But fundamentalists did not create this model. Rather, it was developed by two secular scholars, Andrew Dickson White and John William Draper. Beginning with an 1869 lecture entitled "The Battlefields of Science," White's ideas evolved into a two-volume work called *A History of the Warfare of Science with Theology in Christendom.* Draper's book was titled *History of Conflict Between Religion and Science.* White and Draper argued that since the time of Galileo's trial in the seventeenth century, the church had attempted to stop the forward march of modern science. This view, that conservative Christianity always battled against science, became standard in the early twentieth century and was the lens through which many interpreted the Scopes trial. In the 1980s, however, historians of science began to argue that White and Draper had been mistaken in their interpretation—that they were, in fact, "anti-Christian polemicists" who overplayed their hand. These recent historians have shown that from Galileo to the late nineteenth century, most scientists were Christians of one sort or another. In other words, the great debates of science took place among Christians, not between Christians and scientists. As historians David Lindberg and Ronald Numbers write, "[There is] mounting evidence that White read the past through battle-scarred glasses, and that he and his imitators have distorted history to serve ideological ends of their own." Specifically, White and Draper represented a scientific agenda to separate theology from science or, put another way, to get religion out of the business of interpreting science. Lindberg and Numbers continue, saying: "Although it is not difficult to find instances of conflict and controversy in the annals of Christianity and science, recent scholarship has shown the warfare metaphor to be neither useful nor tenable in describing the relationship between science and religion."[5]

The warfare model for understanding religion and science may have originated with secular social scientists, but by the 1920s fundamentalists embraced it wholeheartedly. Speaking at the historic Moody Memorial Church just months after the Scopes trial, Billy Sunday articulated a common fundamentalist belief: "Science and religion can never be reconciled."[6] Like Hodge and Warfield, Sunday was a Presbyterian conservative, but by the Roaring Twenties the warfare model reigned supreme, while the harmony that Warfield and Hodge sought was all but forgotten. Two developments are chiefly responsible for the fundamentalist acceptance of the warfare model that would dominate the Scopes trial.

The first development was the fact that evolutionary theory changed from the 1870s to the 1920s. In the scientific community during the earlier period, there was much more openness to a form of evolution that predated Darwin. Lamarckianism, as it was called, left open the possibility for purpose or design, which in turn made it easier to accept that God was directing the evolutionary process. By the 1920s, this Lamarckian interpretation had been discredited in favor of Darwin's views that chance mutations were chiefly the engine of evolution. In other words, evolution had neither design nor purpose; it just happened.

The second development took place among the fundamentalists. During World War I, many Americans came to view the fundamentalist-modernist controversy in cultural rather than theological terms. They reasoned that theological modernism had started in Germany as theologians adapted evolutionary thought to theology. German philosopher Friedrich Nietzsche merely took the next logical step, arguing that there was no meaning in the universe, only force and will. This led to the proverbial might-makes-right philosophy, which helped explain how German militarism caused the war. We know now that Germany was not solely responsible for World War I, but popular American preachers made a direct connection between the development of theological modernism and the war machine of Kaiser Wilhelm II. As evolution became the public symbol of theological modernism, fundamentalists reasoned that evolution had to be stopped, or America would end up just like Germany.[7] The fundamentalist-modernist controversy took place in two venues, therefore: within the denominations, as we saw in chapter 4, and in the anti-evolution crusade aimed at banning the teaching of evolution in the public schools. While Bryan was but one player among many in the Presbyterian controversy, and hardly the most important, he was the most famous and visible leader of the anti-evolution crusade.

WILLIAM JENNINGS BRYAN AND
THE ANTI-EVOLUTION CRUSADE

After the Scopes trial, two generations of students learned in their textbooks of William Jennings Bryan, the anti-evolution fundamentalist. Recently, a more well-rounded view has emerged. In his first run for president, Bryan represented both the Democratic Party and the People's Party, organized by populists. The populists were largely farmers who believed that the two political parties were subservient to business interests. They wanted government to intervene in the free-market economy to guarantee fair prices and wages for farmers and laborers. When Bryan was given the floor at the 1896 Democratic National Convention, he delivered one of the most famous speeches in American history, "The Cross of Gold." The speech was a call for "free coinage of silver," a plan to increase the money supply and cause inflation so that farmers could get a fair price for their produce and pay off their debts. Although the rural South and Midwest thrilled to this message, it frightened eastern big-business interests that were staunchly in favor of laissez-faire economics and the sound money policy of the gold standard. Bryan lost the election to the Republican William McKinley.

Bryan ran against McKinley again in 1900 and tried to make the Philippines the paramount issue in the election. The United States had taken over the Philippine Islands during the Spanish-American War of 1898. Bryan believed it un-Christian, unconstitutional, and undemocratic to hold people in colonial bondage against their will. This time he lost by a greater margin than in 1896. Even while losing again in 1908, Bryan continued as a spokesperson for the progressive wing of the Democratic Party, while Theodore Roosevelt represented progressive Republicans. As a progressive, Bryan championed women's right to vote, direct election of U.S. Senators (they were still being chosen by state legislatures in most states), income taxes (because they were believed to be fairer than tariffs that were paid for by working people who had to purchase goods at higher prices), and a host of other causes. Bryan's constant cry in politics was that in a democracy the people rule—the more directly, the better.

As Woodrow Wilson's secretary of state, Bryan was a staunch advocate for peace and believed that someday war would be outlawed. He served in Wilson's cabinet until 1915, when he resigned in protest over the president's handling of the famous *Lusitania* affair. When the Germans sank the passenger liner, killing 128 Americans among the 1,200 on board, Wilson sent a protest to Germany but not to Britain. To most people this seemed logical as the Germans were the ones who had sunk the ship. Bryan and a few others, however, believed that Britain was also culpable for hiding war munitions on a passenger liner. Britain also maintained a food blockade that was starving women and children in Germany. In short, Bryan sought complete neutrality, believing that both combatants in the war deserved rebuke. When Wilson protested only Germany's actions, Bryan resigned.

Bryan joined the anti-evolution movement fully in 1919, marking a change of heart he had undergone over the previous 15 years. Early in the century, preoccupied with other issues, he downplayed Darwinism's threat to society. On one occasion he remarked that while he rejected evolution, "I do not mean to find fault with you if you want to accept the theory."[8] In other words, he believed that evolution was nonsense but that if someone wanted to believe it, it was fine with him. Over time, however, he converted to the popular fundamentalist position that evolution was not only a challenge to the Bible but also detrimental to society's moral progress. Bryan saw Darwinian evolution as a "menace" because "the hypothesis . . . links man to the lower forms of life and makes him a lineal descendant of the brute." Darwinism, therefore, "is obscuring God and weakening all the virtues that rest upon the religious tie between God and man."[9] How could progressives reform culture without belief in the virtues built on the theological idea that humans were created in the image of God? How could there be a moral standard if human beings were nothing more than highly evolved animals?

Bryan grew alarmed when he read a sociological study showing that while only 15 percent of freshmen in nine selected colleges had discarded the Christian religion, nearly 45 percent of the graduates had abandoned their faith. "Is it an immaterial thing that so large a percentage of the young men who go from Christian homes into institutions of learning should go out from these institutions with the spiritual element eliminated from their lives?" Bryan asked. "What shall it profit a man if he shall gain all the learning of the schools and lose his faith in God?"[10] He became convinced that evolution caused a decline in the faith of America's youth, and so evolution had to be stopped. Moreover, he believed this theory that corrupted the belief system of college students was not even good science. Repeating a popular refrain among anti-evolutionists,

Bryan claimed that Darwin's "hypothesis" was no more than a "guess." Bryan and many fundamentalists adhered to a form of science that was Baconian. Named for the seventeenth-century philosopher of science Francis Bacon, Baconian science emphasized empirical observation and careful categorization of facts. Bryan contrasted this fact-based science with theoretical science in this way: "Science . . . to be truly science is classified knowledge; it is the explanation of facts. Tested by this definition, Darwinism is not science at all; it is guesses strung together."[11] Bryan believed he was trying to save good science from the corruptions of modern theory-driven pseudoscience, just as fundamentalists believed they were trying to save orthodox Christianity from the inroads of modernism.

THE TRIAL

Initially, the anti-evolution crusade lacked focus. This changed dramatically in 1921, after the Baptist State Board of Missions in Kentucky passed a resolution calling for a ban on the teaching of evolution in the state's public schools. The movement crystallized as a result of this specific legislative approach to the evolution problem. Fundamentalists such as William Bell Riley in Minnesota, J. Frank Norris in Texas, and John Roach Straton in New York all rallied behind the legal solution. Bryan heard about the Kentucky Baptist resolution in early 1922 and immediately adopted it as the focus of his anti-evolution efforts. Traveling to Kentucky to stump for an anti-evolution law, Bryan launched a national campaign of his own.

Over the next four years Bryan and others worked diligently to spread their message, hoping to convince legislatures to outlaw the teaching of evolution in public schools. Tennessee was one of the first states to comply. The Butler Act became law in February 1925, making it a misdemeanor offense to teach evolution in the state's schools. After the law went into effect, the American Civil Liberties Union (ACLU) ran advertisements in Tennessee newspapers offering to aid anyone who would challenge the law. ACLU lawyers believed the law was unconstitutional, so they wanted a test case to get the issue in the courts. Between Knoxville and Chattanooga, in the small town of Dayton, businessman George Rappleyea read one of the ads. He and a few others recruited John Thomas Scopes to challenge the law. Scopes taught biology and helped coach the football team at Dayton's high school. He was single, 24 years old, and living in town temporarily, so he had little to lose in violating the law. Among Rappleyea's group of supporters there were mixed motives, ranging from anti-evolution fundamentalism to the belief that the attention a "monkey trial" would bring to Dayton would boost tourism and aid business, which proved correct.

As prosecutors in Dayton prepared for Scopes's trial, Bryan offered his services even though he had not tried a case in 35 years. Through a complicated set of circumstances, and over the protest of some ACLU lawyers, Clarence Darrow became Scopes's lead defense attorney. The ACLU wanted the case to turn on Scopes's academic freedom and freedom of speech. In a grander sense, it wanted the case to turn on individual rights. Darrow, by contrast, went to Dayton to battle evangelical religion and to make a fool out of fundamentalists. He was the son of the village atheist from a small Ohio town, and he had taken his father's skepticism onto a national stage. Oddly, in 1896, when Bryan first ran for president, Darrow had run for Congress and spent more time campaigning for Bryan than for himself. Like Bryan, he lost. Whatever Bryan and Darrow shared politically had long since been submerged in their dispute over religion and science.

Darrow's most famous trial before Scopes had been the Leopold-Loeb murder case, in which he defended two Chicago teenagers who had engaged in a thrill killing just to see if they could get away with it. At the trial he urged that the young killers' lives be spared because they were not responsible for their actions. For years Darrow had been using modern social science to argue against free will. People were not free moral agents but rather were conditioned by society. If anyone should be held accountable for the actions of Leopold and Loeb, it was the violent society that raised them. (Ironically, Darrow would later be lionized erroneously as a champion of individual freedom.) Bryan had used the Leopold-Loeb case as an example of what would happen to young people if they accepted the evolutionary idea that there was no basis for right and wrong. With the presence of the fundamentalist Bryan and the antireligious Darrow, news media from across the country descended on Dayton, and the trial became something of a circus.

Built at the foot of Walden Ridge in the Cumberland Mountains, Dayton was a town of roughly 1,800 residents, the seat of Rhea County. The area's chief economic staples were strawberries and peaches. The town was considered progressive in its tax rates, roads, water plant, and city services. Typical of county-seat towns, Dayton's three-story courthouse was in the downtown square, surrounded by a grassy area with oak and maple trees. The courtroom was about 65 by 65 feet and sat just over 500 people. City fathers went to great lengths and expense to spruce up the town as the trial neared, knowing that hundreds of out-of-towners would likely come to Dayton.

As the trial approached, people across eastern Tennessee called Dayton "monkey town," and monkey jokes proliferated. The local meat market hung a sign reading "We handle all kinds of meat except monkey," and the local drugstore had one that read "Don't monkey around when you come to Dayton, but call on us." The name of the local furniture store owner was J. R. Darwin, which prompted a rumor that he had descended from Charles Darwin's family.

Scopes was well liked in Dayton, and although people generally wanted the anti-evolution law upheld as constitutional, they wished no ill on their young teacher and coach. Overall, a lighthearted air of anticipation seemed to pervade the town as the July 10 trial date drew near. In late June the local hardware store owner encountered prosecutor Ben McKenzie on the sidewalk and joked, "The judge is half monkey anyway," to which the prosecutor replied, "Now that's just the question we're going to settle next month. Don't prejudice the case." Shortly thereafter, the prosecutor explained to the reporter who overheard the street-side banter, "It is the right of our legislature to say what shall be taught our children in our schools for which we pay." This was exactly Bryan's view. For years he had been saying "The hand that writes the check rules the school." McKenzie continued, saying that Scopes had every right to go downtown, get up on a soapbox, and spout any theory he wants, but "he cannot expect us to furnish a school, pay his salary and furnish the children, too, for him to instruct in evolution. . . . Freedom of speech and freedom of thought are not involved." McKenzie also spoke of belief in God and how it oriented life in the South. "If you teach evolution to children in the formative stage of their lives before they can think for themselves, you destroy love, and man has nothing left to live for."[12]

Bryan arrived in Dayton on July 7 to much fanfare. Roughly 300 people met him at the train station, 50 of them reporters and cameramen. He joked amiably about his own "acquired characteristics," specifically his baldness and poor penmanship. In noting that reporters might have a hard time deciphering his handwritten speech when he gave them advance copies, he quipped, "Guess it'll be survival of the fittest." In a more serious vein, he claimed, "The contest between Christianity and evolution is a duel to the death. . . . [T]he two cannot

stand together. They are as antagonistic as light and darkness, as good and evil."
This is quite a contrast with his laissez-faire view early in the century. He also
mocked modern scientists who find a tooth in the sand and construct from it
a theory of origins, and he dismissed scientific attempts to judge the age of fos-
sils and rocks.[13] In his speech that evening Bryan warned that if the fundamentalists lost the case, he would head a campaign to amend the U.S. Constitution
to outlaw evolution in public schools nationwide. In simple terms, he insisted
that if the majority of people in the country believed evolution breaks down
Christianity and threatens the well-being of children, the minority should not
be allowed to use the court system to stop the majority. Bryan had prepared another speech he intended to make at the close of the trial that he hoped would
rival "The Cross of Gold." In it he intended to show that evolution was unsci-
entific and untrue.

Bryan wanted to use the trial to reinforce his majoritarian theory of government. Like Baconianism in science, majoritarianism had been a revered theory in politics through the nineteenth century. Its origins in America were
usually traced to none other than Thomas Jefferson. In his 1786 Bill for Establishing Religious Freedom in Virginia, Jefferson had written "that to compel a
man to furnish contributions of money for the propagation of opinions which
he disbelieves, is sinful and tyrannical." In Walter Lippmann's view, Bryan's logic
mirrored Jefferson's. As Lippmann put the case, Bryan asked how, "if it is wrong
to compel people to support a creed they disbelieve, it is not also wrong to compel them to support teaching which impugns the creed in which they do believe?" The people paid for the schools; the people do not believe evolution is
true; therefore the people's tax dollars should not be used for its propagation.
"Jefferson had insisted that the people should not have to pay for the teaching
of Anglicanism," Lippmann continued. "Mr. Bryan asked why they should be
made to pay for the teaching of agnosticism."[14]

This is not to deny that Bryan also fought evolution in order to protect
the teachings of the Bible. When the issue was political or legal, however, he
always maintained that because the vast majority of people believed the Bible,
the legal system could properly be used to protect its teachings, or at least be
expected not to undermine them. Evolutionists should fund their own
schools and stop expecting the majority to finance minority viewpoints. This
line of argument led Lippmann to remark in a lecture a few years after the
trial, "I am thoroughly persuaded that if Mr. Bryan at Dayton had been as

acute as his opponents, he would have conquered them in debate. Given his premises, the logic of his position was unassailable."[15]

At the outset, the defense had little interest in fighting over the validity of evolution. John Neal, one of Scopes's defense attorneys, responded to the speech Bryan had made his first night in Dayton, saying "[T]he great issue in this case is not whether evolution is true or untrue, or even whether it conflicts with religion." Rather, Neal said, the issue was whether the state of Tennessee had violated its constitution and the U.S. Constitution in passing an anti-evolution law, "thus attempting to control the mind in its struggle after truth."[16] As the trial progressed, the defense changed course and took on the very issue Neal said at the outset was not theirs: Which made the most sense, science or religion? This change of course owed largely to Darrow's presence. By the end of the trial he had come to agree with Bryan: It *was* a duel to the death.

Scopes's father came to Dayton for the trial and even met Bryan. Originally from London, the elder Scopes was a 65-year-old machinist and a liberal Christian. "I don't know anything about heaven and hell," he said in response to fundamentalist beliefs. "But I do believe what Christ taught—that God is love and love is God, and that's how I try to live." He said, moreover, that he believed he was a better Christian than those who fought over particulars. While mingling with lawyers on both sides of the issue, the elder Scopes said he could scarcely believe that anyone who read books could hold the views Bryan held. Bryan overheard the comment and came toward the elder Scopes. The younger Scopes saw Bryan coming, intervened, and introduced the men. Both shook hands cordially, but as Bryan walked out of the room, there was an awkward silence.[17]

As the press began to cover the proceedings, people across the country read articles about Bryan, Darrow, Scopes, the town of Dayton, and nearly every other aspect of the case. Like the evolution controversy itself, Bryan and Darrow were polarizing figures, and people followed the case as much for the personalities involved as for the issues. Pundits lined up on either side, with elites from northern big-city newspapers covering the rural southern fundamentalists as if they were a different species. Famed journalist H. L. Mencken of the Baltimore *Sun* newspaper and his own magazine *American Mercury* arrived in town a day after Bryan. One reporter described Mencken as a journalist "who takes particular delight in poking fun at the South." Mencken strolled up and down the street interviewing the residents of Dayton, who reportedly answered his questions graciously. The owner of the drugstore where Rappalyea had hatched the idea for the trial was particularly delighted and explained to Mencken that he always took two copies of the *American Mercury* home from his store so he and his wife wouldn't fight over it. A week later, however, the townsfolk were taking a different view. In a syndicated column the often-acerbic Mencken referred to the people of Dayton as Babbitts, morons, hillbillies, yokels, and peasants, and spoke of the "degraded nonsense which country preachers are ramming and hammering into yokel skulls." Some Daytonites held a meeting to discuss what to do about Mencken. A few suggested taking him into an alley for a good lesson in southern manners, but cooler heads advocated a committee requesting that he leave town.[18]

Many of the same folks who initially greeted Mencken with good cheer also opened their homes to the flood of reporters and spectators that overwhelmed Dayton's hotel capacity. Residents formed a greeter committee to arrange accommodations for all visitors. Dayton's civic leaders were determined that no one would be homeless during the trial.[19]

When the trial finally began, most of the first week was taken up with the question of just what it was to be about. Darrow had shifted the focus of the ACLU from the narrow question of academic freedom and freedom of speech, to the truth or falsity of evolution. He wanted to show that evolution was an undeniable scientific fact and, even more important, that there was no contradiction between evolution and modern Christianity. As for the relationship between Bryan's fundamentalism and science, that was another matter. Darrow would argue that no intelligent person could be a fundamentalist and that any thinking person could easily reconcile evolution and faith. To that end he and the defense team put together a list of expert witnesses they were prepared to call to the stand to educate the jury as to what evolution actually was and how liberal Christianity had harmonized religion and science.

The prosecution denied that expert witnesses had any constructive role to play in a court case. The issue in question as far as the prosecutors were concerned was simply whether Scopes had violated the law, something both sides agreed that he had done. Bryan told the judge that the expert witnesses should have shown up before the legislature months ago to argue against the Butler Act, but they had no place in the courtroom. As for New York City lawyers coming to Dayton to argue that the Butler Act was bad for Tennesseans, Bryan by analogy referenced New York's repeal of the Mullen-Gage Act for the enforcement of Prohibition. "Suppose the people of Tennessee had sent attorneys up there to fight that law . . . and [brought along] experts to testify how good a thing pro-hibition is to New York and the nation. I wonder if there would have been any lack of determination in the papers in speaking out against the offensiveness of such testimony."[20]

Bryan may have wanted the court to rule narrowly that the experts on evo-lution should be disallowed, but he said much more when he argued this issue before the judge. He went to great lengths to show that evolution was not only hostile to Christianity and against what the people of Tennessee wanted taught in their schools but also that it was bad science and nonsense. Moreover, he read from Darrow's defense of Loeb and Leopold to show that in that case, Darrow had held the teachings of Nietzsche and the universities that taught those ideas responsible for the murder the youths had committed. By implica-tion, Bryan suggested that the teaching of evolution would have similar effects on the children who learned the theory in school. They would learn that there was no God and therefore no moral standard, leaving them free to do as they wished.

In arguing the admissibility of expert witnesses, both sides played to the crowded courtroom and also to the press. When Bryan defended the Bible, he was met by applause and an occasional "Amen." But the defense also scored points with the audience. Attorney Dudley Malone accused Bryan of running from a fight for the first time in his life. He reminded the judge that before the trial began, Bryan had boasted that this would be a duel to the death, but now he wanted no such fight. Malone said he was having a hard time distinguish-ing Bryan the lawyer from Bryan the propagandist "who made a speech against science and for religion just now." In a line that could have come from John William Draper or Andrew Dickson White in their books advocating the war-fare between religion and science, Malone said that the same theory that made it possible for the church to prosecute and condemn Galileo was now animat-ing the prosecution in Dayton. "Are we to have our children know nothing about science except what the church says they shall know?" he asked. This was a clash not only of ideas but of two completely different ways of thinking, Malone argued. It was a clash between close-minded theology and open-minded science.

Then, returning to the question at hand, Malone argued that the defense must be allowed to call expert testimony because of the Butler Act's wording. The law made it a misdemeanor crime for a public school teacher "to teach any theory that denies the story of divine creation of man as taught in the Bible, AND to teach [students] that man is descended from a lower form of animals." Malone stressed the word "and," arguing that the state must prove not only that Scopes taught that man descended from lower forms of animals but also that he taught a theory that denied divine creation. Expert testimony, Malone argued, would show that evolution did not necessarily deny divine creation and that there was more than one theory of origins in the Bible, not just the one Bryan believed. "Is he the last word on the subject of theology?" Malone asked. In closing, Malone added that the defense was not afraid of the truth because the truth always wins. "We feel we stand with progress. We feel we stand with science. We feel we stand with intelligence. We feel we stand with fundamental freedom in America. We are not afraid."[21]

Scopes wrote years later that Malone's speech was the most dramatic part of the entire trial, indeed "the most dramatic event I have attended in my life." If the crowd's response is any indication, there were several who agreed with him. People roared and shrieked as a policeman banged his billy club so hard it split. When another officer tried to help in quelling the crowd noise, the first yelled, "I'm not trying to restore order. Hell, I'm cheering."[22]

Answering for the prosecution, McKenzie argued that any reasonable person recognized that evolution and the creation story of Genesis could not be reconciled, no matter what experts might testify.[23] Judge Raulston ruled in favor of the prosecution, prohibiting expert witnesses. Left without a case, Darrow and the defense decided on a bold gamble. They called Bryan to the stand as an expert on the Bible. Members of the prosecution wisely discouraged Bryan from accepting the challenge, but he felt goaded into taking the stand by Malone's accusation that he was running from a fight. The press had also carried such charges. Specifically, scientist Henry Fairfield Osborn had written a lengthy defense of evolution that appeared in leading newspapers around the country. Following its publication some charged that Bryan was running from the strong arguments Osborn and others put forward and that he had refused to debate them publicly. Bryan accepted the defense's challenge and agreed to go on the stand. The New York *Times* called the contest between Darrow and Bryan "the most remarkable circumstances ever known to American court procedure."[24]

Bryan took the stand July 20, fittingly the seventh day of the trial. By that time Judge Raulston had moved the proceedings outdoors to the courthouse lawn to accommodate the crowd, estimated by eyewitnesses to be about 3,000. Those standing segregated themselves into rival cheering sections, fundamentalist versus liberal, with the fundamentalists in a decided majority. Darrow peppered Bryan with questions typical of a street-corner atheist. Where did Cain get his wife? How did Jonah live for three days in the belly of a large fish? Was the story of the tower of Babel the literal explanation for how the world got its variety of languages? Darrow seemed to think that any fundamentalist who said the Bible should be taken literally had no capacity for recognizing figurative language. Bryan explained that neither he nor any other fundamentalist believed Jesus was speaking literally when he said believers were the "salt of the earth."

Repeatedly, Darrow came back to issues such as the age of the earth, attempting with varying degrees of success to get Bryan to commit himself to the widely popular belief among fundamentalists that the Earth had been created in about 4004 B.C. This view had been popularized by the Anglican archbishop James Ussher in the seventeenth century and had become standard among conservative Protestants. Bryan refused to bite, but his testimony went off the rails as Darrow pressed him to make a calculation as to the age of the Earth. Bryan replied, "I never made a calculation."

> Darrow: A calculation from what?
> Bryan: I could not say.
> Darrow: From the generations of man?
> Bryan: I would not want to say that.
> Darrow: What do you think?
> Bryan: I do not think about things I don't think about.
> Darrow: Do you think about things you do think about?
> Bryan: Well, sometimes.

The crowd roared with laughter.[25]

Darrow queried Bryan extensively on world religions. Composing himself, Bryan at one point made a lengthy and sophisticated explanation as to why he believed Christianity was superior to Confucianism. For the most part, however, Bryan expressed little interest in other religions, how many languages existed, the age of various civilizations, or the age of the Earth according to scientists. In short, he seemed completely uninformed about how one should interpret scripture in light of modern science. This was peculiar in that fundamentalist scholars such as Bryan's Presbyterian colleagues J. Gresham Machen and Charles Erdman, both of whom we met in chapter 4, were interested in these questions and had reasonable answers. Moreover, the leading conservative Presbyterian scholar, Benjamin Warfield, who had died four years before the trial, had claimed that the age of the Earth was of no theological significance. Bryan seemed to believe the same but was woefully unable to explain why.

In addition to showing that Bryan was no Bible expert, knew little about modern science, and had almost no interest in the history of civilizations, Darrow also goaded Bryan into an admission that he was not a literalist by the standards of popular fundamentalism. Bryan agreed with some fundamentalist scholars that the six days of creation in Genesis were not necessarily 24-hour days. Most fundamentalists of the type around Dayton, however, believed the days of Genesis were literal, so Darrow was able to drive a wedge between Bryan and his local supporters. Scopes himself recalled later, "The Bible literalists who came to cheer Bryan were surprised, ill content, and disappointed that Bryan gave ground."[26] Again, Bryan was puzzlingly ill prepared to stake out and defend his moderately fundamentalist position on biblical interpretation that some of his fellow Presbyterians articulated with great skill. He may have known intuitively that if he acknowledged such a position, evolution might be harmonized with conservative biblical interpretation, something some conservative biblical scholars believed but also something that was central to the defense's case.

All this is not to say that Darrow came off much better than Bryan. Harry Emerson Fosdick and other liberals may have been pleased that Bryan did so poorly, but they noticed as well that Darrow's attack was amateurish and hostile to all religion, not just fundamentalism. An official in the Congregationalist churches wrote to the ACLU: "May I express the earnest opinion that not five percent of the ministers in this liberal denomination have any sympathy with Mr. Darrow's conduct in this case." A liberal theologian at Vanderbilt University made the same point with even more force. "When Clarence Darrow is put forth as the champion of the forces of enlightenment to fight the battle for scientific knowledge, one feels almost persuaded to become a Fundamentalist," wrote Edwin Mims.[27] Fosdick's attorney brother Raymond declined to join the ACLU's efforts precisely because of Darrow, and Raymond told Harry not to attend the trial in part because neither Darrow nor Malone could be trusted.[28]

Both Darrow and Bryan found it difficult to maintain their dignity as the exchange grew more heated. As the two-hour inquisition moved along, Attorney General Tom Stewart of the prosecution repeatedly asked Judge Raulston to stop the farce. At one point, as Darrow badgered Bryan again on the age of the Earth, Stewart objected in exasperation, "What is the meaning of this harangue?" Darrow answered, "We have the purpose to prevent bigots and ignoramuses from controlling the educational system of the United States, and you know it, and that is all." With that, Bryan sprang to his feet, shook his fist at Darrow, and to roaring applause replied, "I am simply trying to protect the word of God against the greatest atheist or agnostic in the United States." At the end of the fiasco Bryan and Darrow stood opposite each other, both shaking their fists in the other's face. Bryan accused Darrow of having no purpose other than to slur the Bible. Darrow replied, "I object to your statement. I am exempting you on your fool ideas that no intelligent Christian on earth believes."[29] Taken aback by the threat of violence, Judge Raulston adjourned the court until 9:00 the following morning.

When court came into session on Tuesday, July 21, Judge Raulston ruled not only that Darrow's interrogation of Bryan would not continue but that Bryan's testimony from the day before would be expunged from the record. After some wrangling among the judge and attorneys for both sides, all agreed that the jury should be brought in and instructed to deliver a guilty verdict. Defense lawyers agreed to these terms because they wanted to lose the case. Darrow was permitted to explain to the jury that without the expert testimony that Judge Raulston had disallowed, there was no way to prove whether the law was sound. Speaking for the prosecution, Stewart then told the jurors that the defense wanted a guilty verdict. That done, the judge imposed a $100 fine, but before doing so asked Scopes if he had any reason why the court should not impose punishment. In a trembling voice, Scopes replied, "Your honor, I believe I have been convicted of violating an unjust statute. I will continue in the future, as I have in the past, to oppose the law in any way I can." Any other course of action, Scopes continued, would violate academic freedom, personal and religious freedom, and the other guarantees of the U.S. Constitution.[30] Bryan offered to pay Scopes's fine.

With no closing arguments, Bryan was denied the opportunity to present the speech he had painstakingly prepared and had hoped would be the crown jewel of his anti-evolution efforts. After a few days in Dayton working more on the oration, he took the speech on the road to Jasper and Winchester, where thousands turned out to hear him. On Sunday he was back in Dayton, where he attended church services. That afternoon he told his wife he was going to take a nap. Before heading to his room he said he had never felt better and was prepared to take the evolution fight to the nation now that his work in Tennessee was complete. A short time later Mary Bryan went to wake her husband and found he was dead of what was then called apoplexy—a stroke. When someone suggested to Darrow that Bryan had died of a broken heart, Darrow thought of Bryan's prodigious appetite and replied, "Broken heart nothing; he died of a busted belly." In Baltimore Mencken wrote, "God aimed at Darrow, missed, and hit Bryan instead." Off the record he said with glee, "We killed the son-of-bitch."[31]

A shrewd maneuver on the part of the Tennessee Supreme Court kept the Scopes trial from working its way to the U.S. Supreme Court. The appeal came forward in 1927. After two days of arguments the Tennessee justices returned a two-part ruling: First, the Butler Act was constitutional for precisely the reasons Bryan and others had argued. Scopes was an employee of the state, so the state had the right to dictate what he taught. His freedom was not being violated since as a teacher he had entered freely into a contractual relationship with the state. Second, the Tennessee court threw out Scopes's conviction on a technicality. By law the jury, not Judge Raulston, should have set the fine. The prosecutors had reminded the judge of this at the trial, but Raulston assured them it was customary in misdemeanor cases for the judge to assess the $100 minimum. After all, it was the lowest fine allowable anyway. The state supreme court seized on the error, overturned Scopes's conviction, then advised the Tennessee attorney general to seek no further prosecution—that is, to dismiss the case, which he did. ACLU lawyers could not appeal the case any further because they now had no conviction to appeal.[32]

THE LEGEND

In 1997 historian Edward Larson published *Summer for the Gods,* which won a Pulitzer Prize. The book is not only a history of the Scopes trial, it is also a history of the history of the Scopes trial. In part, Larson challenged the legend that although Bryan and the prosecution won the specific case, the trial was a colossal public relations defeat for anti-evolution and fundamentalism. Larson's graduate school mentor, Ronald Numbers, had done a study of newspaper coverage of the trial in five metropolitan areas, in different parts of the country. "I discovered not a single declaration of victory by the opponents of antievolution, in the sense of their claiming that the crusade was at an end," Numbers concluded.[33] Building on Numbers's research, Larson set out to find where the legend of fundamentalist defeat originated. He identified two events that bracketed the 30-year period from 1931 to 1960.

The first of these was a book by Frederick Lewis Allen entitled *Only Yesterday: An Informal History of the Nineteen-Twenties.* A talented journalist, Allen wrote for a depression-era audience nostalgic for the past. In doing so, he portrayed the 1920s as the decade when the old ways were left behind once and for all. In Allen's telling, complex issues such as the contest between majoritarian democracy and individual rights gave way to a tale about fundamentalism wilting before the onslaught of modern science. As Larson puts it, "Allen reduced fundamentalism to antievolutionism and antievolutionism to Bryan. Both reductions grossly oversimplified matters and forced Allen to reconstruct the story."[34] It was as if Allen were saying that it would be nice to live with the assurances of the old-time religion, but we know now that we cannot.

The more erudite defenders of the faith whom we met in chapter 4— Machen, for example—were nowhere to be found in Allen's fundamentalism. Bryan was the movement's spokesperson, and only Bryan. When he went down in flames, so did fundamentalism. Allen's use of the trial transcript was highly selective, highlighting the places where Darrow turned Bryan inside out. He ignored the passages where Bryan spoke with a degree of sophistication, and he downplayed Darrow's amateurish fixation with the year 4004 B.C. Allen claimed that Darrow got Bryan to affirm the belief that the Earth was created that year when actually Bryan allowed that the "days" of Genesis might well have been long periods of time. Allen, of course, had no way of knowing that several modernists had written privately of their embarrassment that Darrow had somehow become their spokesperson.

Allen's book was immensely popular, selling more than a million copies and shaping the way Americans viewed the Scopes trial for the next 30 years. Then, in 1960, the film *Inherit the Wind* appeared in theaters across America, further cementing the trial's antifundamentalist legend. The film was based on a 1955 play by Jerome Lawrence and Robert E. Lee. Larson identifies three ways the film differed from the actual trial. First, whereas the town of Dayton was described by a New York *Times* reporter as "half circus and half revival meeting," in the film the setting turns from circus to witch hunt.[35] In one scene, the people of Dayton parade through the streets at night singing "We'll hang Bert Cates (Scopes) from an old apple tree, our God is marching on" to the tune of "The Battle Hymn of the Republic." When they arrive at the jail where Cates is being held, someone throws a bottle that crashes against the bars inches from Cates's face. The real Scopes, of course, was never in jail, and the real people of Dayton liked him and wished him no ill. One reporter at the actual trial wrote of the many cranks and enthusiasts who came to Dayton at the outset—two blind minstrels, a racist preacher arguing that African Americans were not human, booksellers peddling *God or Gorilla* and other spurious titles, and so on. This writer pointed out repeatedly that the townspeople paid little attention to the lunatics. The people of Dayton, he wrote, "are not to be urged, as has been said, into acting otherwise than usual."[36]

Joseph Wood Krutch, who had been a correspondent at the Scopes trial, remarked after seeing the film that in the real Dayton the citizens had acquitted themselves quite well. By contrast, he wrote: "The authors of *Inherit the Wind* made it chiefly sinister, a witch hunt of the sort we are now all too familiar with. The atmosphere was so far from being sinister that it suggested a circus day."[37] Essentially, the authors of *Inherit the Wind* had adapted the story to fit the McCarthy era of the 1950s when actors, teachers, and politicians were blacklisted for alleged ties to communism.

The second alteration in the film comes in the Bryan character, known as Brady in the play and film. Played by Fredric March, Brady starts as an amiable buffoon and ends up an evil manipulator. Posing as a confidant to Cates's fiancée, Brady extracts information that he uses to bludgeon her on the witness stand. Then, during his own dramatic testimony, Drummond (Darrow) gets Brady to say that sex is the original sin. When the trial ends Brady tries pitifully to give his speech, but people mill around the courtroom ignoring him, many congratulating Drummond. Those who do listen laugh at Brady as he turns to his wife and says defeatedly, "Mother, they're laughing at me. You know I can't stand it when they laugh." Then he falls over dead of a heart attack, still in the courtroom.

The third alteration has to do with the Darrow character played by the winsome Spencer Tracy. As with the Bryan character, so, too, Drummond changes significantly from the real trial to the film, and for the better. Drummond is a hero of open-mindedness, a tolerant liberal Christian. At one point he even rebukes the Mencken character, Hornbeck, for mocking Brady's faith. "You smart aleck," Drummond says. "You have no more right to spit on his religion than you have a right to spit on my religion. Or lack of it." As we have seen, in the real trial Darrow called Bryan's faith "fool religion" several times and said no intelligent person could believe the Bible. Drummond, by contrast, believes in freedom and respects everyone's views.

When the film appeared, a reviewer in *Time* magazine wrote: "The script wildly and unjustly caricatures the fundamentalists as vicious and narrow-minded hypocrites, [and] just as wildly and unjustly idealizes their opponents, as personified by Darrow." The reviewer found fundamentalism, even as portrayed in the film, only slightly more absurd than "the shallow scientism that the picture offers as a substitute for religious faith and experience." Another reviewer said the film seemed to be calculated to make a liberal "self-satisfied with his enlightened state."[38] At a Broadway production of the play, a constitutional scholar became so disgusted he walked out and wrote later, "I ended up actually sympathizing with Bryan, even though I was and continue to be opposed to his ideas in the case, simply because the playwrights had drawn the character in such comic strip terms."[39]

THE MEANING

Larson's *Summer for the Gods* could not have been written between 1930 and 1980 for in that period the Scopes legend was taken for granted. The trial marked the decline of fundamentalism. The old religion met the new science, and the old religion lost. In other words, the view fashioned by *Only Yesterday* and *Inherit the Wind* dominated the intellectual and popular landscape in America. As one historian put the case in 1970, "No one has done more to shape the conception of the American 1920s than Frederick Lewis Allen. . . . [T]he book's most enduring bequest to later historians has been the idea that older American values, traditions, and ideals meant little or nothing to the 1920s."[40] Indeed, William Warren Sweet echoed Allen eight years after the appearance of *Only Yesterday,* writing in his popular 1939 textbook on religion in America that the Scopes trial was "fundamentalism's last stand." As for the film, Ronald Numbers has written: "*Inherit the Wind* dramatically illustrates why so many Americans continue to believe in the mythical war between science and religion."[41] In a similar vein, the late Stephen Jay Gould, Harvard paleontologist and America's leading promoter of evolution, characterized the film in this way: "John Scopes was persecuted, Darrow rose to Scopes's defense and smote the antediluvian Bryan, and the antievolution movement then dwindled or ground to at least a temporary halt. All three parts of this story are false."[42]

Before Larson could write *Summer for the Gods,* others had to chip away at the well-worn notion that fundamentalism was gone forever, that the Scopes trial and other events of the 1920s had relegated traditional religion to the private sphere where only a small number of Americans would cling to its outmoded worldview. Still, the Scopes trial to an extent represented a battle between old and new ideas. Bryan represented the majoritarian view of democracy that was part of the nineteenth century's legacy. The ACLU represented a new democratic theory based on individual rights and the autonomy of the individual that came to dominate the twentieth century. Moreover, the case was in part a battle between the old view that religion is central to American culture and the new view that religion should be private. In his gripping oration before Judge Raulston, defense lawyer Dudley Malone said, "Keep your Bible. Keep it as a consolation; keep it as your guide, but keep it where it belongs, in the world of your own conscience, in the world of your individual judgment."[43] Clearly, he was articulating the view that religion is a private matter and that science will be the arbiter of truth in the public domain. The question is this: Did the Scopes trial signify that modernism in both theology and science had triumphed over fundamentalism, and if so, could such a victory ever be reversed?

In light of the rise of the Christian Right in the 1980s, we know now that the Scopes trial was hardly fundamentalism's last stand. Rather, the trial was but one episode in a much more complex set of culture wars that erupted again two generations later. The liberals won the Roaring Twenties chapter of the story, but during the next half century fundamentalists laid the groundwork for a movement that would live to fight another day. In the period between 1930 and 1980, fundamentalists may have worked more quietly and behind the scenes, but when the 1980s arrived they were ready to reenter the fray, and their stage had already been set.

CHAPTER 6

RELIGIOUS SCANDAL RIGHT NEXT DOOR TO HOLLYWOOD

I f the Scopes trial was supposed to be fundamentalism's last stand, someone forgot to tell Aimee Semple McPherson and J. Frank Norris. Even after the trial these two complex fundamentalists acted and spoke as if their movement was in its ascendancy and poised for victory over American culture. McPherson, for example, built a fabulously modern temple in Los Angeles and had followers across the country. At times the nation's largest newspapers covered her every move in front-page articles. Whereas Billy Sunday was the religious version of a superstar sports hero, McPherson capitalized on her proximity to Hollywood and became a star of stage, screen, and the airwaves. At the same time, however, both McPherson's and Norris's scandal-ridden careers gave ample ammunition to the opponents of traditional religion. They seemed determined to live down to the caricature of fundamentalism that would become dominant in *Only Yesterday* and *Inherit the Wind.*

GOD'S FLAPPER

If any single religious figure embodied in a spiritual way the ethos of the Roaring Twenties, it was Aimee Semple McPherson. As one of her contemporaries wrote, "[The Jazz Age] was a time for petting, necking; for flasks and roadside taverns; for movie palaces and automobiles . . . and Aimee was determined to lead the parade on a grand detour to Heaven."[1] McPherson cultivated a familiarity among her followers, encouraging them to call her "Sister" or "Aimee." Two of her three principal biographers have followed this tradition, and this chapter shall as well.

Aimee was born Aimee Kennedy on a farm in Salford, near Ingersoll, Ontario, Canada, in 1890. Her father, James Kennedy, was a nominal Methodist, and her mother, Minnie Pierce, was an enthusiastic soldier in the Salvation Army. Aimee's parents experienced a strained and unusual marriage, to say the least. When they wed, James was a 50-year-old widower and Minnie was 15, younger than any of his children. Minnie had been working on the Kennedy farm when James's first wife died in March 1886. She continued to work for James, and the two were married in November. There was nothing romantic about the relationship, and there seems to have been almost no courtship. It was a marriage of convenience. He needed a woman to take care of his mentally challenged son and do chores around the farm, while she needed a place to live. Just shy of four years into the marriage, Aimee was born.[2]

Aimee was seriously religious from her earliest years. Her mother saw to that. As a girl, Aimee memorized large portions of scripture, and Minnie dedicated her only child to Christian service, believing God would use Aimee in special ways. She even embroidered on Aimee's Salvation Army sash the words "God's little child." Aimee took the religious upbringing to heart and became a dedicated and enthusiastic Salvation Army kid. As a young girl she invented a game called "Army" in which she convinced classmates to march in a line behind her as she banged a drum and waved a red flag.

Over time Aimee became more skeptical about religion, especially after having her faith shaken by an encounter with Darwin's theory of evolution. While some evangelical Protestants in Canada and the United States attempted to reconcile faith and science harmoniously, Aimee opted for the warfare model and took a stand against evolution in a letter she wrote to the local newspaper editor. She encouraged her classmates to join her. Later she presented this story as a watershed in her life, the time when she worked through her momentary uncertainty and chose religion over science. She opposed evolution actively and enthusiastically for the rest of her life.

Like so many young people, Aimee went through a period of teenage rebellion, not so much against God but against her religiously overprotective mother. In defiance she attended social dances, ice skating parties, ragtime music concerts, and plays. None of these amusements were frowned on by the churches of Ingersoll, but Minnie believed they were sinful. She simply could not accept that her daughter would engage in such activities, even if other young people did. As one of Aimee's biographers puts it, "For her part, as new horizons beckoned her daughter, Minnie clung more fiercely to the determination that her will would be accomplished in Aimee's life."[3]

On the heels of her rebellion, Aimee came to a deeper and more serious experience of faith in 1907. By this time she was a popular, fun-loving high school student, performing in dramas and speech contests. Then a Pentecostal "holy roller" meeting came to town. Having heard that the Pentecostals were themselves dramatic and that they spoke in tongues, Aimee attended out of curiosity during a few spare minutes before drama rehearsal. She was mesmerized and believed God was speaking directly to her through the Pentecostal preacher she heard that day. Shortly thereafter, while driving the horse and buggy from town back to the farm, she stopped and yielded to the spirit. She promptly quit her worldly endeavors, even dropping out of the looming Christmas play. Through December and into the new year of 1908, Aimee dedicated herself wholeheartedly to seeking the Holy Spirit. Her religious longings and her new lifestyle were so austere that even her mother worried she was going overboard. Moreover, as she dropped her social interests, so too did she neglect her studies. The principal of her school wrote to Minnie warning that Aimee was about to fail her classes.

At the time Aimee encountered Pentecostalism, it was a new form of evangelical Christianity marked by gifts of the Holy Spirit, the most important of which was speaking in tongues. The movement started in Topeka, Kansas, in 1901 when Agnus Ozman got the spirit under the preaching of Charles Parham. Soon many others experienced similar stirrings as Parham traveled about the country preaching the doctrine of tongues as a sign of being filled with the Holy Spirit. Black preacher William Seymour from Houston worked with Parham briefly before heading to Los Angeles in 1906. Dismissed from his church for speaking in tongues, Seymour moved his ministry to a dilapidated building known as the Azusa Street Mission. Here Pentecostalism exploded. Meetings took place three times a day for three years before the revival began to ebb in 1909. People from as far away as the British Isles and Australia made the pilgrimage to Azusa to be part of the movement.

The Azusa Street Revival placed Pentecostalism firmly on North America's religious landscape, and Aimee was fascinated by this new and vibrant form of

Christianity when it came to her hometown. Defying her mother, Aimee continued to attend the services. On Friday, January 31, 1908, she skipped school to attend a prayer meeting. Trapped in town by a snowstorm, she stayed at the home of a Pentecostal woman. The next day she received the baptism of the Holy Spirit and began to speak in tongues. On Sunday Minnie drove to town to fetch her daughter and spent the ride home angrily trying to persuade Aimee to leave her newfound faith. Minnie threatened to withdraw Aimee from school if she ever visited the Pentecostals again. Aimee countered: If Minnie could persuade her from the Bible that Pentecostals were in error, Aimee would leave the faith. While Aimee spent Monday in town at school, Minnie spent the entire day searching her Bible for refutation of Pentecostalism. When Aimee returned, her mother admitted that the Bible seemed to support the gifts of the spirit that Pentecostals experienced. The two tearfully embraced and sang the hymn: "Give Me that Old Time Religion."

Aimee was not only taken by the new ecstatic faith, she was also smitten with Robert Semple, the preacher who brought Pentecostalism to her little town. Nine years older than Aimee, tall, blue-eyed, and wavy haired, Semple's preaching was enhanced by his Irish accent. He had come to the United States a decade earlier. Aimee and Robert began a brief courtship and were married in August. Both were ordained the following year by William Durham, a Pentecostal leader in Chicago. With Durham they worked to spread the Pentecostal faith in various parts of the Midwest and back in Ontario. During this time the Semples felt God's call to missionary work, to China in particular. Evangelicals of all kinds were fascinated by the prospect of spreading Christianity in the world's most populous country. In 1910 the couple departed North America aboard a ship bound for the Far East. After two months of mission work, however, Semple died of dysentery on August 19. A widow, Aimee was 19 and pregnant. One month later she gave birth to a daughter, whom she named Roberta Star. Aimee's three years with Robert were pivotal. Through her relationship with him she had become a Pentecostal preacher and determined that her life's calling was to spread the gospel in all its fullness. Even after remarrying she used Semple as her middle name for the rest of her life and kept photographic reminders of him about her wherever she went.

After Semple's death Aimee returned to North America, still longing to preach God's word but unsure how she would sustain herself and her young daughter. Rather than going to her parents' home, she stayed for a time in New

York. By this time Minnie had developed the practice of leaving Aimee's father when the harvest was complete and spending the winters in New York working at Salvation Army headquarters. Aimee and her mother were reunited when Minnie came to town for the winter. Still recovering from the loss of her husband, and wondering how she might make ends meet, Aimee met Harold McPherson, a reasonably successful businessman who could provide financial stability. The two courted briefly, then eloped in 1912, in large part to get away from Minnie, who disapproved of Harold. The couple settled for a time in Chicago, where Aimee reconnected with the Pentecostal friends she and Semple had made while ministering there four years before. Back in the Pentecostal fold, Aimee once again felt the call to Christian service and before long was spending three nights a week at meetings. Sensing that she was moving away from him, Harold moved the family to Providence, Rhode Island, where he had lived as a boy. There Aimee gave birth to a son, Rolf, in March 1913.

The married life in Providence proved unhappy for Aimee as she longed to preach and spread the gospel. She interpreted a severe illness in the winter of 1913 as God's way of telling her she should leave Harold and go back into full-time ministry. In the summer of 1915 she returned to Ontario to her parents' home briefly, then set out as a traveling preacher while Minnie cared for the children. The couple reconciled when Harold received the Holy Spirit at one of Aimee's early revivals. They determined to travel together so she could preach, and they even purchased a large tent for revival meetings. Harold accompanied her for over a year, traveling all the way to Florida twice. He served as her manager and organizer with little Rolf in tow. The arrangement soon proved unsatisfactory, however, and Aimee and Harold separated again in 1917. When Harold left, Aimee contacted her mother, who had been in New York caring for the oft-ailing Roberta. Minnie and Roberta joined Aimee and Rolf on the road, and Minnie replaced Harold in managing Aimee's budding career and caring for the two children. Harold and Aimee divorced three years later, in 1921. Aimee always considered her marriage to Harold a mistake, not because it was unhappy but because it interfered with God's call to preach the gospel.

At first Sister Aimee, as she quickly became known, preached primarily on the East Coast, traveling in an automobile she called the Gospel Car, which was painted with religious slogans. In 1918, after a successful six-week revival campaign in Philadelphia, she decided to head west. With Minnie's help she sold the old Gospel Car and bought a new one, which she quickly plastered with the slogans "Jesus is coming Soon, Get Ready," and "Where will you spend Eternity?" The two women and Aimee's children set out for California, preaching and distributing gospel tracts along the way. Scholars believe this may have been the first cross-country automobile excursion undertaken by women. They arrived in Los Angeles in December, where Aimee already had meetings scheduled. She had started a newsletter called *Bridal Call* when she and Harold were campaigning in the Southeast. The newsletter bound her converts together in a loose network and served to spread the word of Aimee's revivals. Her first California meetings took place at Victoria Hall, then at a larger venue called the Temple Auditorium. Before long she had an enthusiastic Los Angeles following, and her supporters quickly donated a land lot and built a house for her. Along with her Gospel Car, she now had "the house that God built," as she called it.

Los Angeles remained McPherson's headquarters for the rest of her career, but she continued to hold revivals across the country. From 1918 to 1923 she crisscrossed the United States almost constantly, holding crusades in tents, theaters, and municipal auditoriums. She preached in cities large and small, including New York, Philadelphia, Chicago, Denver, Dallas, San Diego, and St. Louis. Her message became progressively less Pentecostal and more generically evangelical as she reached out to Baptists, Methodists, Presbyterians, and other Protestants. Even as she preached less about speaking in tongues, however, her message was no less supernatural, and before long she was engaged in a healing ministry. During her San Diego crusade in 1921 she healed people for the first time; she continued this practice throughout her career. Still, for her, Pentecostalism was less a denomination than an expression of simple Bible Christianity in all its fullness: tongues, healing, prophecy, and the like. With this approach she routinely attracted Christians from many denominations who found their faith revived and enlivened through her preaching. She held preaching credentials from the Pentecostal Assemblies of God as well as from other Protestant denominations.

So winsome was her personality, Sister Aimee sometimes appeared at nightclubs and sports arenas and was given a few minutes to make a gospel appeal. Likewise, she could walk through the red-light district of a major city and stop to pray with prostitutes. She was well known everywhere and operated in a culture that had a residual knowledge of revivalist Christianity. When she appeared at a nightclub, the band already knew a hymn and could play it from memory as she took the stage, and the people on the dance floor understood her message readily, even if they were at the club trying to escape the clutches of conservative Christianity. In short, even as the Roaring Twenties threw off traditionalism, the baseline of American culture was still, for a few more years at least, revivalist Christianity. Billy Sunday was just past the peak of his career as Aimee rose to national prominence. The many critics who mocked them and the traditional Christianity they represented were everywhere in elite circles, but those critics faced a difficult task. Skeptics were in the minority, fighting an uphill battle against religious forces that still animated the masses. But this was also post–World War I America, when the nation was on something of an emotional drunk, escaping the horrifying memories of wartime destruction and death. The public turned increasingly to entertainment as the first era of public stars appeared on radio and in film. Sister Aimee emerged as a star who embodied both the older, traditional religious culture as well as the new age of personality.

In the early 1920s some questioned whether McPherson was truly Pentecostal. The official journal of the Assemblies of God denomination debated her Pentecostal authenticity, but Aimee hardly needed a denominational structure. Her missives in *Bridal Call* had laid the groundwork for her own organization. In 1921 she and Minnie recruited a California businessman to help them incorporate the Echo Park Evangelistic Association, which funded Aimee's revivals. Aimee then renounced her Assemblies of God preaching credentials and started her own denomination called the Four Square Gospel. The organization grew out of her interpretation of the four faces of Ezekial 1:4–40. In a vision the prophet Ezekial saw a lion, ox, man, and eagle. For Aimee these represented the four sides of the gospel message. Her interpretation had been gestating for a couple of years when she preached her sermon "The Foursquare Gospel" for the first time in Oakland in July 1922. A year later she formed the Four Square Gospel Association and had roughly 1,000 signers of the first doctrinal statement, which stressed that Christ was "Savior," "Great Physician," "Baptizer of His people with the Holy Spirit," and "coming King." From this loose association of Aimee's followers grew a new Pentecostal denomination known as the International Church of the Foursquare Gospel. Today the denomination has roughly 50,000 churches and 6 million adherents, the majority of them outside the United States.

In the early 1920s, Minnie saved $5,000 and purchased a plot of land in the Echo Park section of outer Los Angeles, which became the site of the Angelus

Temple. Aimee raised the rest of the money to build the church as she preached across the country. Mimicking the burgeoning stock market craze, she sold "chairs," as opposed to shares, and told purchasers that their investment would fund a seat where an unbeliever would likely come to conversion during one of her services. She also used *Bridal Call* to raise funds, appealing directly for financial contributions for the first time. "We believe you will all want to share in the joy and privilege of erecting this Tabernacle for God," she wrote. "We have faith to believe that for every dollar given, a precious soul will be won for Christ."[4]

Angelus Temple opened to a packed house on January 1, 1923. Earlier that day a replica of the new facility won second place in its division at the Tournament of Roses Parade in Pasadena. In today's parlance it was a megachurch not unlike Rick Warren's Saddleback Church founded in 1980 farther south in Orange County. The temple was a lavish and modern domed structure that sat 5,300 people and was debt free from the start. The first year at Angelus Temple was a perpetual camp meeting as people came in droves to hear Aimee preach and to be healed. When people converted, Aimee promptly put them to work in one of the temple's many ministries. Before long Angelus Temple operated social programs for those in need, a Sunday school, children's church, nursery, *Bridal Call* magazine, a training institute for preachers and missionaries, and even a call-in number that gave the correct time.

Sister Aimee began using radio haltingly in 1922, two months before Paul Rader pioneered regular religious broadcasting from his Chicago Gospel Tabernacle. By 1924 she was fully on board with the new medium, opening her own station and hiring an experienced radio engineer named Kenneth Ormiston away from a secular station. From that time forward she stood alongside Rader as an innovative religious broadcaster, and hers became one of the most instantly recognizable voices in America. Along with radio, Aimee used all sorts of visual aids, props, footlights, and advertising gimmicks. Before the temple opened Aimee was a national preaching phenomenon, but she was better known across the country than in Los Angeles, which served primarily as her home when she was recuperating from her exhausting road schedule. She had not held a revival in Los Angeles since early 1919, right after she arrived on the West Coast. Angelus Temple changed this. Within two years she was a Los Angeles fixture along with politicians, sports figures, radio and film stars, and even other religious figures.

Among the latter was the fundamentalist Methodist preacher "Fighting Bob" Shuler, who became McPherson's fiercest critic. In 1924 he preached a series of sermons warning against "Aimeeism." He saw her brand of revivalism as doctrinally dangerous with its inclusion of tongues and healing, but he also saw in Aimeeism a cult of personality that was superficial. Here he had in mind her use of drama, props, elaborate stage sets, costuming, and music to make the gospel palpable to a modern audience. Such devices were "worldly" by fundamentalist standards, and, indeed, Aimee's dramatic productions held their own against the secular theater. This was the vaudeville era, and as one critic put it, "Angelus Temple offered the best show in town."[5] Moreover, her methods attracted stage and film stars to the temple, some of whom assisted the productions. By the time Angelus Temple opened, Sister Aimee had become something of a "divine dramatist," a title a scholar once bestowed on the eighteenth-century revivalist George Whitefield.[6]

Angelus Temple contributed to a religious boom as Los Angeles grew rapidly. Half the city's population were church members, and many others attended missions and nondenominational religious gatherings that were not officially counted. The city's church members were divided almost evenly between Protestants and Roman Catholics, and Los Angeles was already becoming a mecca for what are today called New Religious Movements. Some of these are still around, such as Christian Science, while others were fleeting and temporary spiritualist movements that ceased to exist almost the moment the founder passed from the scene.

Like Billy Sunday and most other big-time fundamentalist preachers of the Roaring Twenties, McPherson became a civic reformer and moral crusader. She lashed out against loosening morals such as drunkenness, dancing, and the end to which those two sins often led, a lack of sexual restraint. A steady stream of abused women and homeless families arrived at Angelus Temple to find at least temporary relief. When a major earthquake hit Santa Barbara in 1925, McPherson rushed to her radio station, pushed a singer off the microphone, and put out a spontaneous call for aid. By the time the local newspapers reported the event the next morning, Angelus Temple had a convoy of trucks filled with supplies and workers speeding up the coast to help out. Politically, in the wake of the Scopes trial, McPherson was a major force behind a referendum to pass an anti-evolution law in California, and she sent a telegram to William Jennings Bryan during the trial assuring him that folks at Angelus Temple were praying as he took on Darrow and Darwinism.[7]

By the mid-1920s, with Angelus Temple up and running smoothly, Sister Aimee was at the peak of her career. Along with Billy Sunday, she was one of the most famous preachers in America and a star in the kingdom of God.

THE GREAT SCANDAL

And then she was gone. On May 18, 1926, Aimee disappeared while swimming in the Pacific Ocean off Venice Beach near Santa Monica, where she had gone to rest and study. Minnie suspected that her daughter was dead and told worshippers at the temple that evening, "Aimee is with Jesus; pray for her." Presuming Aimee had drowned, deep-sea divers searched for her body, a trawler dragged the bottom of the sea with a grappling hook, and others surveyed the ocean's surface from an airplane above the water. Meanwhile, thousands of volunteers searched the beach, nearby canyons, and adjacent hills while some of Aimee's followers roamed the shoreline, mourning and holding prayer vigils. One man reported seeing Sister Aimee walking in spirit on the surface of the ocean.[8]

Almost immediately newspapers reported various theories that competed with the accidental drowning presumption. The first was that underworld crime bosses put a hit on Aimee because of her opposition to Sunday dances at a Venice Beach dance hall and more generally her crusade against amusements that crime syndicates funded. Another theory was that Aimee had been kidnapped and was being held for ransom.

For a brief few days the search focused on Bouquet Canyon after a note appeared on June 2. Scrawled in what newspapers dubbed a "woman's handwriting," the note said, "Help. They took me to a cabin in Bouquet." The kidnapping theory was bolstered further when a blind attorney in Long Beach named R. A. McKinley told Judge Carlos Hardy that two men had contacted him with a demand for $25,000 ransom. Hardy was a regular at Angelus Temple, often giving radio talks on the role of religion in crime prevention. He took McKinley's story to Aimee's mother. Convinced it was a hoax, Minnie nevertheless agreed to submit a list of questions, the answers to which only Aimee would know, in order to establish through the kidnappers that Aimee was still alive.[9] The next day, June 4, Los Angeles County Sheriff William Traeger received a letter saying

"Dear Bill: It might happen to interest you to know that Aimee Semple McPherson was kidnapped and is being held either willingly or unwillingly. I know all about it, but am afraid to peep. So be careful not to involve me. I am not revealing my identity as the gang will croak me if I squeal." The letter writer claimed that Aimee could be found in the mountains behind Santa Barbara or in a remote area along the Santa Ynez River.[10]

After three weeks of a failed search, and with rumors of kidnapping swirling through the Los Angeles community, authorities finally stopped looking for Aimee's body. Differences of opinion over what happened to her continue to this day, but all rumors of her death came to a halt on June 23, when Aimee reappeared in a hospital in Douglas, Arizona, a small town on the U.S.-Mexican border, 10 hours from Los Angeles. A taxi driver named Johnnie Anderson in Agua Prieta, a small town on the Mexican side, found Aimee covered by a blanket, pillow under head, on the front porch of a home in the town. He drove her to the hospital in Douglas, where she told of being kidnapped and held for ransom in Mexico.

From her hospital bed, Aimee told Douglas police that she had been lured to a car in Ocean Park near Venice Beach on May 18 by a woman who claimed she had a sick baby in need of Aimee's prayer. Aimee was then pushed into the vehicle by one of the woman's two male accomplices and rendered unconscious when one of her captors held over her face a washcloth soaked with a sedative solution of some sort. She awoke the next day in a shack with the woman, who went by the name Rose. One of the male accomplices was Steve. Rose and Steve told Aimee that she was being held for $500,000 ransom. During her captivity the kidnappers tried to force her to give answers to the set of questions they had received from Minnie. Aimee refused this request even though tortured with cigar burns to her fingers. Newspapers reported erroneously that her captors had also cut her hair short and threatened to cut off a scarred finger. After many days in the shack, Aimee freed herself by rolling off her cot and rubbing the ropes holding her wrists against the sharp edge of a large metal can. Her harrowing escape proceeded with a 15- to 20-mile walk through the desert before she collapsed in Agua Prieta and was found by Anderson. Aimee requested immediate protection for her daughter, Roberta, and also warned that the kidnappers had a plan to snatch movie star Mary Pickford.[11]

Minnie left immediately by train for Douglas, taking Rolf and Roberta with her. Not far behind were investigators from Los Angeles. District Attorney

(DA) Asa Keyes wanted more information about Aimee's case. Immediately skeptical, Keyes announced that he would be looking into the many inconsistencies and unusual circumstances of Aimee's alleged ordeal. "Mrs. McPherson's story of the kidnapping will be checked, step by step," he reported. Keyes mentioned specifically the $25,000 reward for Aimee's safe return that had been offered and withdrawn twice. Moreover, he also asked whether the $15,000 that had been collected at Angelus Temple for Aimee's memorial would be returned.[12] Ironically, Keyes had spoken at Angelus Temple in 1924 on the topic "The Part of the Church in Law Enforcement."

Los Angeles detectives were on the scene the day after Aimee's reappearance, as was the sheriff of Cochise County, Arizona. In vain they looked for the shack. Aimee led the editor of the Douglas *Dispatch* on an unsuccessful search and the next day offered a $500 reward for anyone who could locate the site of her captivity. On June 26 Aimee boarded a train and returned to Los Angeles. When the train stopped in Tucson, local detectives came on board with a man who positively identified Aimee as the woman he had seen on the streets of the city four weeks before.[13] This was merely the first of several Aimee sightings that would be reported over the coming months, any of which would have blown holes in her story of abduction. When she arrived back in Los Angeles, Aimee was greeted by thousands of well-wishers and curiosity seekers. In the throng were many of her women followers wearing white dresses, Aimee's signature public outfit. At the train station they spread before her a path of roses. The following day, June 27, Aimee made her first appearance in front of 7,500 people jammed into Angelus Temple.[14]

Three days later, on Wednesday, June 30, Aimee and her mother made the long train trip back to Douglas to search once again for the shack; on Friday they returned to Los Angeles, unsuccessful yet again. By that time, there were two grand juries investigating the Aimee Semple McPherson disappearance, one county and one federal. The feds got involved when U.S. Post Office inspectors alleged that someone had tampered with a letter to Minnie proving that Aimee was alive. The culprit had allegedly altered the document to make it appear that it was received after the memorial service that had raised $15,000; the letter actually had been received before the service. The implication was that Minnie or someone else associated with Angelus Temple had deliberately suppressed the fact that Aimee was alive in order to raise money off her alleged death. The letter contained a lock of hair purported to be Aimee's.[15]

The L.A. *Times* and the *Examiner* took great interest in Aimee's disappearance. This was an age of intense newspaper rivalry, and yellow (sensational) journalism abounded. Over the next six months as the two competing newspapers covered the story, letters to the editor poured in, showing the public to be about equally divided between those who believed Aimee's story and those who suspected a hoax.[16]

On July 8 McPherson made her first appearance before a grand jury that had been convened to investigate the alleged kidnapping. Accompanied by her attorney and six women from the temple, she retold her story of abduction, captivity, and escape. A detective testified that he had been told by McPherson's attending nurse in the Douglas hospital that the preacher showed no signs of having trekked 15 miles through the desert. She was not sunburned, her lips were not dry and cracked, and she seemed in need of neither food nor water. Another inconsistency District Attorney Keyes noticed was that Aimee recalled leaving her wristwatch on the dresser drawer in Ocean Park the day she went swimming off Venice Beach and subsequently disappeared; yet when she resurfaced in Douglas, Arizona, she was wearing her watch. Keyes pressed McPherson: "I seem to have observed that wrist watch in a picture which was taken of you in Douglas, five weeks after you went to the bathing beach. You are sure you did not have it with you?" To which Aimee replied coolly, "I guess the watch must have been brought to me in Douglas by my mother."[17]

Five days later Minnie Kennedy testified concerning the temple's financial conditions just prior to Aimee's disappearance. This was part of the attempt by the DA to develop plausibility for the theory that the kidnapping may have been a fundraising gimmick. Then the DA produced the mystery witness he had previously promised would cast more doubt on the Aimee kidnapping. The witness was identified and took the stand, testifying that at roughly 4:00 P.M. on the day of Sister Aimee's disappearance, he had seen a woman in a green bathing suit answering to Aimee's description near a pier five blocks from the place Aimee claimed to have been abducted. Aimee said she had been forced into the car around 2:00 or 2:30.[18]

There was another theory afloat as to why McPherson may have faked her kidnapping. On July 15 came the electrifying testimony of the deputy DA, who told the grand jury that Aimee had been seen with Kenneth Ormiston in Salinas, California, up the coast from Los Angeles, on May 29, 11 days after she had disappeared. Ormiston had resigned as Aimee's radio engineer in December

1925 and had separated from his wife at about the time of Aimee's alleged kidnapping. District Attorney Keyes had noticed that Ormiston had gone missing shortly after Aimee. Ormiston resurfaced in late May, was questioned by police and cleared of any wrongdoing, and then promptly disappeared again. Now, in the grand jury investigation, the DA claimed that Ormiston had been with Aimee after her disappearance, the implication being that the two had run off together and faked the kidnapping. By July 29 Keyes had lined up witnesses from Carmel by the Sea, a resort town about 300 miles from Los Angeles, who were prepared to identify Ormiston and "a woman resembling Mrs. McPherson." Subsequent investigation showed that Ormiston had rented a cottage in Carmel under the name George McIntyre and stayed there with a woman for at least 10 days. The press dubbed the woman "Miss X." If Miss X was Aimee, then Aimee had perjured herself before the grand jury. Asked whether he intended to pursue perjury charges, Keyes said he would go after Aimee and anyone else who had testified falsely.[19]

Enter Lorraine Wiseman-Sielaff. On September 13, from her Los Angeles jail cell, this check-bouncing seamstress claimed that Sister Aimee had offered her $5,000 to go before the grand jury claiming she, not Aimee, was Miss X. Documents revealed that Wiseman-Sielaff had been in constant contact with Aimee and had indeed received money. She claimed Aimee had paid her about $200 of the promised $5,000. Although hired to say she had been Miss X, Wiseman-Sielaff claimed she had farmed out the job to a Rachael Wells from Philadelphia, who had already appeared in Salinas swearing in an affidavit that she had been with Ormiston there. Wiseman-Sielaff had also floated the story that Miss X was her sister. (She actually had a twin sister who visited her in jail.) Wiseman-Sielaff was released from jail on $1,500 bail for the bad-check charges and promised to appear before the grand jury to tell the truth about Aimee, not the phony story of being Miss X.[20]

On September 16 Keyes ordered the arrest of McPherson, Ormiston (still missing), Minnie Kennedy, Wiseman-Sielaff, and two others. They were charged with conspiracy. In calling for their arrest, Keyes regretted having to take action against a religious figure such as Sister Aimee. "I have proceeded from the beginning with the thought in mind that Mrs. McPherson's position as the religious leader of a considerable number of people and the custodian of their Christian faith entitled her to protection from hasty or ill-considered action," he said. "It is with regret that I take action against a person so high in the religious esteem of many persons, but the community and the upright members of all religions would welcome a fair and open hearing of a situation which has become a national scandal."[21]

McPherson's arrest prompted the seating of a second grand jury inquiry, one that would last five weeks from mid-September until early November. On September 27 five witnesses appeared before a judge in a preliminary hearing. Some identified Sister Aimee as the woman who spent late May in the cottage in Carmel with Kenneth Ormiston, while others were unsure. As they testified, an estimated 5,000 people milled around either in the courthouse or on the streets outside. Twenty policemen were on hand to keep order. Near-riot conditions ensued when several hundred people hissed at Aimee as she exited the courtroom. One of the Carmel witnesses claimed that after realizing in July that the woman he saw in May might have been Sister Aimee, he drove to Los Angeles on August 3 and attended services at Angelus Temple. There, he reported, "[I] made up my mind positively that she was the woman I saw at Carmel."[22] The owner of the cottage in Carmel refused to positively identify Aimee in court, saying the woman he had seen in May wore a wide-brimmed hat hiding her face. Others reported the Carmel Miss X as having been "begoggled," a reference to her wearing glasses, probably sunglasses. The cottage owner also saw a green bathing suit on the clothesline, but he and others also failed to positively identify Aimee as the woman in Carmel.[23]

Drama abounded early in the second grand jury investigation when Minnie collapsed in court while Keyes read into the record the transcript from McPherson's first grand jury testimony telling of her ordeal in the desert. Minnie's breakdown coincided with the reading of Keyes's earlier exchange with Aimee concerning her wristwatch. The next day Aimee made a dramatic display of letting her hair down, then doing it back up into the tight bun she usually wore. All in the courtroom seemed taken aback until her attorney explained that this act was to allay allegations that Aimee had used hairpieces and had switched hairstyles to disguise herself, allegations that had arisen in conjunction with alleged sightings of her during the time she was missing and after she resurfaced in Douglas. Revealing as it did that McPherson often wore her long hair in a tight bun, this display also explained why some reports from Douglas back in June said that Aimee's hair had been "shorn" while she was in captivity. On the same day that Aimee dramatically displayed her hair, witnesses testified to seeing her enter a hotel lobby with Ormiston on the day she disappeared. The

DA also produced an alleged ransom letter that had been received at the Angelus Temple the day before Aimee resurfaced. The two-page, typed letter read in part: "We took her for two reasons—the first to wreck the damn Temple. . . . You have taken some of our girls, damn you, and given us many a jolt."[24] Prosecutors pointed out later that kidnappers typically did not send long letters typed in near-perfect grammar.

And so it went for five weeks as the prosecution attempted to establish enough evidence to move the case toward a jury trial that would determine Aimee's guilt or innocence. Keyes and his associates needed only to convince the grand jury that McPherson, her mother, Minnie Kennedy, Kenneth Ormiston, and Miss Wiseman-Sielaff should stand trial. Aimee's high-priced and well-known defense team attempted to show that she had indeed been kidnapped and had told the truth in her first grand jury testimony, in which case there was no perjury or conspiracy to obstruct justice.

The drama of the second grand jury inquiry was riveting not just because Sister Aimee was a celebrity, but all the more because she was a religious figure. As the representative of the state, District Attorney Keyes walked a fine line between upholder of justice and grand inquisitor. On the other side, Aimee and Minnie capitalized on every opportunity to play the martyr card. Even before the grand jury convened, Minnie issued a statement comparing her daughter to Old Testament figures Jeremiah and Joseph, who had suffered for their faith.[25] On September 26 Aimee led her teenage daughter, Roberta, to the microphone at the temple. Roberta began to tell the audience that she wanted to be just like her mother, then her speech became rapid and inarticulate. Finally, she broke down and began to wail repeatedly, "Why do they pull mother down? Why do they pull mother down?" before being led away as she convulsed in sobs. A reporter covering the scene wrote, "Even to skeptics who had come to see Sister McPherson in action, the woe of the child must have seemed sincere, one thing beyond doubt or questioning in the world's leading mystery."[26] Then, on October 3, Angelus Temple held a "March of Martyrs" extravaganza depicting the history of hostility to religion in conjunction with what Aimee called her own "persecution." Included in the march were characters representing Stephen, the apostle whose stoning death is recorded in the book of Acts; the apostle Paul, who is believed to have been beheaded for the faith; the medieval Joan of Arc, who was burned at the stake in the fifteenth century; and, most important, the crucified Christ. The seventh and last scene in the drama represented Aimee's own case. It included a large Bible on a chair next to a pair of scissors and a pile of mud, perhaps symbolizing the prosecution's effort to get dirt on the famous evangelist. Thousands attended the spectacle.[27]

In response to the martyr posturing of McPherson and her mother, Keyes was in a tenuous spot throughout the summer and fall as the case proceeded from the first grand jury to the second. In mid-September, even before the March of Martyrs, he rejected charges of persecution, saying "Mrs. McPherson is not and never has been made a victim of persecution in so far as the law enforcement agencies of this city and county are concerned." He also attempted to head off any argument that Aimee and Ormiston's activities behind closed doors were their own private business. "By virtue of the fact that Mrs. McPherson poses as a religious leader in the community, as a pretended guardian of Christianity and a campaigner against sin, the actions between herself and Ormiston take it out of the class of private delinquency."[28] Such a view was precisely the opposite of that which became the norm later in the century. While in the later period Americans tended to see religious matters as private unless there was something attendant to religion, such as sex or crime, that made religion public, Keyes saw it the opposite way. He was saying that the presumed sex acts between Sister Aimee and Ormiston would have been a private matter had Aimee not been a religious leader. The fact that she engaged in the public act of defending Christianity and campaigning against sin meant that her private sex life was a public issue. Religion made sex public, not the other way around. As Keyes put the case, "Aimee Semple McPherson, Kenneth G. Ormiston, Minnie Kennedy and others combined together with the object in view of perpetrating a gigantic hoax *in the name of that which the people hold sacred, namely—religion.* That such a thing is a corruption of public morale is without contradiction."[29]

Significantly, Los Angeles's most liberal newspaper, the *Record,* made the opposite case, arguing that Aimee's travails were a private matter. Her own church should decide whether she had sinned against the faith or not. "It is none of the business of other sects, or of a scoffing public," the *Record* editorialized.[30] The progressive view that sex and religion were private matters was based on the idea that what is most sacred to people should be kept private. This would become the dominant view between 1930 and 1980, but it was not during the Roaring Twenties. During that era, religion was still public precisely because it was of sacred importance to the people and was considered the glue holding together the fabric of society. Compounding the issues of sex and religion was the fact that the case took place in Los Angeles, a stone's throw from Hollywood. It was hardly an accident that Aimee chose L.A. as her base, given that she was the religious version of a movie star. Little wonder that when she resurfaced in Douglas, she told authorities that her captors also planned to kidnap Mary Pickford.

Sexual sensationalism took center stage as the case unfolded. There were occasional references in the press to the fact that Aimee was "attractive" and red-headed, but in late October the focus shifted briefly to her underwear. In the effort to track down Ormiston, who was still on the lam, authorities in New York seized a trunk that contained women's clothing, allegedly belonging to Aimee. Tags on the trunk showed it had been shipped originally from Pasadena, California, on May 6, nearly two weeks before Aimee's disappearance. The trunk went to Jackson county, Florida, then to New York, where it had been transported to the Cumberland Hotel. Authorities established that Ormiston had stayed at the Cumberland while he was in the city. Once opened, the trunk was said to contain a "dazzling display of feminine apparel" and a strand of auburn hair. New York authorities air-mailed the strand of hair to District Attorney Keyes, who compared it to locks taken from Aimee. He announced to the press, "There was such a similarity that any one could see they came from the same head."[31] Items from the trunk listed by newspapers included expensive evening gowns, shoes, a red robe, "flimsy negligees," and "gorgeous pajamas."[32] The trunk also contained love letters that Keyes alleged were written by Aimee to Ormiston while he was in New York.[33] Then a second trunk surfaced in Oakland containing more items allegedly belonging to Aimee, but this trunk cast a shadow of doubt over the state's clothing allegations because the shoes were a different size from the ones found in the New York trunk. Keyes remained confident, however, that he had plenty of evidence that the items were Aimee's. When the second trunk turned up, Aimee and her mother were spending a quiet day at, of all places, the beach.[34]

When the grand jury determined the next day that McPherson should be held over for jury trial, she suggested that the clothing and letters had been planted by her enemies, presumably the district attorney and the press. "I care not if they plant and produce 100 trunks full of *decollete* evening gowns—of all colors of the rainbow—or though they print and forge a million love letters, this does not change my position or my faith in God." Aimee expressed confidence that her followers who had heard her preach the gospel all these years could see through the charges, and she regretted that her "dear old mother" had been dragged into the case.[35]

Throughout the proceedings, from late May through November 3, when the second grand jury wrapped up its five-week inquiry, Ormiston had not been found, despite a manhunt that extended nationwide and even to a few foreign countries. In addition to spending time in New York, he had also been in Chicago. From there he had issued an October affidavit admitting that he had spent time in the cottage in Carmel as George McIntyre, but that the Miss X who had been with him was not Aimee. He refused to identify the real Miss X. On December 9 private detectives from Chicago finally tracked him down in Harrisburg, Pennsylvania. One of detectives had been tracking Ormiston for months through a dozen states. Ormiston had been living in a Harrisburg apartment for two months and working nights as a mechanic. His landlord found him to be a pleasant man who made no trouble and paid his bills regularly and in cash. With no warrant for Ormiston's arrest, the two private detectives could only persuade him to travel with them back to Chicago, which he did. His parents promptly issued a statement from their home in San Francisco saying that they stood by their son and believed the entire case had been a "gigantic conspiracy to injure the evangelist and destroy the work of her Four Square Gospel Church." They said their son had been in Carmel with another woman "for no immoral purpose" and that he would never reveal the identity of that woman, even if they put him in jail for 1,000 years.[36]

For the next week Ormiston remained in Chicago a free man, making no attempt to flee or hide. Rather, he retained a lawyer and prepared to fight extradition. District Attorney Keyes wanted him bound and returned to L.A., but since he had not yet been arrested this was impossible. Keyes arranged for a new L.A. warrant, then booked a train to Chicago to be personally present when Ormiston was arrested. The presiding judge in L.A. issued the arrest warrant on December 15, but two days later Ormiston surprised everyone by walking into the Los Angeles DA's office unannounced, saying he was "tired of waiting to be arrested in Chicago." He then sat down at an office typewriter and wrote a short statement, reading in part "Intrigue and hokum are as thick as a fog. . . . I have entered into no understanding, agreement or contract with any newspaper. I have not received one penny from any newspaper, nor will I in the future."[37] The statement was an attempt to head off charges that the press was interfering in the case. He acted as his own attorney and succeeded in getting his bail reduced from $10,000 to $2,500.

Ormiston's voluntary surrender was an embarrassment for the district attorney's office, robbing it of the chance to make a high-profile arrest. One of Keyes's assistants charged that the DA's office had been double-crossed by the detectives in Chicago, but this proved to be a small matter compared to the unraveling of the case altogether. The first signs of trouble for the prosecution appeared as early as mid-October when Aimee's lawyers established that Lorraine Wiseman-Sielaff had been legally committed to an insane asylum by a Salt Lake City court a decade earlier. Wiseman-Sielaff's testimony that McPherson had paid her either to pose as Miss X or recruit someone who would do so was key to the prosecution's case that Aimee was involved in conspiracy. Establishing that Wiseman-Sielaff was insane lent credence to the defense argument that her story was inconsistent and nonsensical. As Aimee's attorney argued, "[O]nce a court has ruled that this woman is insane the presumption is that she remains insane until a court rules that she is sane. No court has so ruled. I challenge her as a witness."[38]

True to form, Wiseman-Sielaff eventually changed her story and ran into trouble with the DA. She claimed that in the course of her conspiracy with Aimee, she had worked closely with McPherson's personal attorney, Roland Rich Woolley. Furthermore, she claimed that she and Woolley had a history that went back to their being schoolmates in Salt Lake City. Woolley, however, claimed that he had never seen Wiseman-Sielaff before she recently visited him in his office in L.A. Even more damaging was Wiseman-Sielaff's outright admission that she fabricated the Miss X angle in an effort to cut a deal granting her leniency in her arrest for writing bad checks. This was the last straw in a series of Wiseman-Sielaff gaffes and reversals. Keyes told the press in late December that it would be extremely difficult to prove conspiracy and perjury after "the collapse of testimony of the principal witness." He described Wiseman-Sielaff as a "turncoat" and a "perjurer" with "a different story everyday."[39]

Still, Keyes persisted for another 10 days into early January to try McPherson on lesser charges, even convening yet another grand jury. In preparation for the new inquiry Ormiston made a detailed public statement of his movements the previous May. He told of his time in Carmel, insisting that the Miss X who accompanied him was not Aimee. Rather, she was a nurse from Seattle. The couple went from Carmel to Santa Barbara, where they quarreled and split up.

Ormiston then left California for Denver, Chicago, New York, and various places in Pennsylvania. Keyes rejected the account and continued to believe that Aimee had run off with Ormiston and fabricated the kidnapping, but he had little with which to proceed and so dropped the charges, saying Aimee would have to be tried in the court of public opinion. All charges against McPherson, her mother, Ormiston, and Wiseman-Sielaff were dismissed. Sister Aimee went back to preaching; Minnie resumed management of Aimee's career; Ormiston got on with his life; and Wiseman-Sielaff was rearrested in San Jose on more bad check charges.[40]

AFTERMATH

In the immediate aftermath of the scandal, Sister Aimee emerged with more followers than ever,[41] which is not unusual in such scandals where courts cannot convict. Without enough evidence for conviction, the accused religious figure can claim persecution by the state and the media. Aimee and her mother played the martyr card with great fanfare during Aimee's ordeal. Moreover, the publicity a scandal brings often attracts new followers to replace the disillusioned ones, which happened, too, when J. Frank Norris went to trial for murder. The only sure death knell for a popular media-savvy preacher is conviction followed by a prison term, such as that which brought down Jim and Tammy Faye Bakker in the 1980s. Even so, Bakker's contemporary Jimmy Swaggart survived multiple sex scandals. In the face of photographic evidence of one of his visits to a seedy New Orleans hotel, Swaggart tearfully confessed his sin. He took a brief sabbatical from his ministry, returned, then was caught with another prostitute in California a few years later. Still, his ministry continued, although with a diminished television audience.

When District Attorney Keyes dropped the charges, McPherson expressed her regret that the case would not go to trial. She claimed that her preference would have been vindication wrought by a jury. More than likely, however, she worked behind the scenes to have her case dismissed. A few even speculate that she blackmailed William Randolph Hearst into pressuring Keyes. According to this theory, McPherson had dirt on Hearst, the tremendously influential owner of the Los Angeles *Herald-Examiner*. She threatened to expose Hearst over the radio, either for marital infidelity or for the wrongful death of film director Thomas Ince, who had died on Hearst's yacht, where alcohol was being served in violation of Prohibition laws. The Federal Bureau of Investigation had a file of information pertaining to the case, and agents knew Hearst was innocent of the murder. Still, Hearst wanted to avoid an exposé of his marital infidelity or violation of Prohibition laws. He was already under investigation for bootlegging in another venue. Hearst may have persuaded or even paid Keyes to drop the charges against McPherson in exchange for her agreeing to be silent on the Hearst fiasco. Given Keyes's subsequent history, it is not hard to believe he could be influenced in this way. He went to prison in 1929 after being convicted of taking bribes in an oil case. While he was on trial investigators looked into whether McPherson had paid him off during her ordeal in 1926. Nothing ever came of that investigation, and the theory that she blackmailed Hearst contains no hard evidence. Oddly, Aimee and Minnie visited Keyes while he was in prison.[42]

Sister Aimee's biographers agree that the mystery of her disappearance will never be solved conclusively. As historian Edith Blumhofer writes, "Sister's disappearance remains an historical mystery in the same way that Marilyn Monroe's death does."[43] It is possible that she was really kidnapped. There had been threats of kidnapping and acts of violence against the Angelus Temple since 1925. One man threatened her, then broke into Aimee's home and terrorized those present until being subdued by a nearby carpenter who heard the commotion. Still, as another biographer, Matthew Sutton, speculates, "In the eighty years since McPherson vanished, most Americans have assumed that she had an affair with Ormiston."[44]

Aimee's disappearance lived on in fiction long after the scandal. Upton Sinclair's novel *Oil!* (1927), Sinclair Lewis's *Elmer Gantry* (1927), and Frank Capra's film *Miracle Woman* (1931) all contain stories of a female evangelist who is basically a con artist and/or sex siren. In 1961 folk singer Pete Seeger wrote a song about Aimee, and in 1999 she appeared in a novel entitled *Jim Morrison's Adventures in the Afterlife*. There, Sister Aimee is in heaven where she splits into two personalities. Under the control of Prozac and Valium, one persona goes about doing good and acting well, while the natural Aimee is a sex-crazed party animal who hooks up with Jim Morrison, who was the lead singer for the rock group The Doors before dying of drug and alcohol addiction in 1971.[45]

The reality of McPherson's life after the scandal contains elements of both personalities in the novel. In the late 1920s and early 1930s, she attempted to cash in on her notoriety by becoming a Christian movie star. She had already written "sacred operas," and she was a religious pioneer in radio. She made

films and briefly joined a vaudeville road show. Claiming she was merely trying to "get a little word in for the Lord" and not actually the last act of a vaudeville show, she appeared at the Capitol Theater on Broadway in New York in
the fall of 1933. The entire show received bad reviews and was forthwith canceled, along with Aimee's $5,000-a-week contract.[46] She also appeared in
newsreel films that contained shots of famous celebrities from the secular
world, including Mary Pickford, Franklin Roosevelt, and Charles Lindbergh.
In the years following the scandal Aimee enhanced her sex symbol image by
bobbing (cutting short) her hair, flapper style, dropping 40 pounds, and allegedly getting a face lift.

She married a third time in 1931, eloping in Yuma, Arizona, with David
Hutton, a singer who had starred in her most recent sacred opera. The day
after their marriage before a local judge, the couple invited reporters into their
bedchamber for a radio interview. Hutton wore a robe and Aimee appeared in
a negligee. They even broadcast the sound of a kiss over the airwaves for
Aimee's followers, prompting Minnie to say "There are things that just aren't
done, and one of them is broadcasting from one's bridal boudoir."[47] The marriage was stormy; Hutton filed for divorce in 1933 after Aimee perpetuated an
embarrassing hoax. In an effort to prove that her mail was being leaked to the
press, she wrote a letter to Hutton from Paris announcing that she had given
birth to a baby boy. Sure enough, the supposed fact appeared in headlines before Hutton received the letter back home, but he used the embarrassment
that ensued as evidence of mental cruelty. Aimee countersued a few months
later claiming mental cruelty against him.[48] The hoax was merely the last straw.
In reality, Hutton had tired of being "Mr. Sister," as a Denver newspaper
dubbed him. Aimee made her Broadway debut as the divorce proceedings were
under way and while Hutton was scheduled to perform at another theater a
few blocks away.

Like so many famous people, McPherson was a complex figure. Just when
it appeared that she was determined to be the religious version of Greta Garbo
or Marlene Dietrich, in the mid-1930s Sister Aimee returned to her Pentecostal
roots, preaching the gospel and engaging in social service during the depths of
the Great Depression. Years earlier she had started the Angelus Temple Commissary to meet the needs of the poor and indigent of Los Angeles. Aimee put
it well when she said, "Let us ever strive to lighten our brothers' load and dry the
tears of a sister; race, creed and status make no difference. We are all one in the

eyes of the Lord."[49] In 1932, even as the drama of her third marriage unfolded, Aimee persuaded a Los Angeles business to donate a large warehouse where the temple expanded the social services provided by the commissary. Before long the private welfare facility was serving 2,100 meals a day and providing a variety of other services, including unemployment counseling and medical and dental care.[50]

Like other fundamentalist and evangelical preachers, Aimee believed America in the 1930s was secularizing and in need of re-Christianization. In response, she called America back to its religious roots. This effort often included praise for leaders she believed were helping America retain a Christian base, including Franklin Roosevelt. Although Roosevelt is not generally remembered as a personally pious man or devout believer, he used the language of civil religion pervasively in an effort to connect American values to a religious foundation. Even though he was on the opposite side of Prohibition, she appreciated his religious rhetoric and interpreted it as an attempt to keep America on sound footing. She continued to fight against evolution and for Prohibition while regularly criticizing the cultural separatism that increasingly dominated fundamentalism. "How much longer will red-blooded Americans, who claim to be worthy offsprings [sic] of the Pilgrims, sit still and tolerate this wholesale destruction of the faith of their fathers?" she wrote in a publication entitled America Awake![51] In 1932 she debated actor Walter Huston on Prohibition, and in 1934 she engaged in a series of debates with well-known atheist Charles Lee Smith. While many fundamentalists retreated to the sidelines of American culture, she renewed her fighting spirit and remained an activist to the end of her life.

McPherson was right in a sense when she claimed that America was moving away from religion. The Great Depression of the 1930s shifted the nation's attention to secular problems and secular solutions. Compounding the secularization was the apparent disappearance of fundamentalists from the public eye. We know now that fundamentalists were not dying out. Rather, they were working behind the scenes, in less public ways than before their apparent defeat in the Scopes trial and the fundamentalist-modernist controversy.[52] For her part, Aimee was as public and famous as ever, as were a handful of other important religious figures from the Roaring Twenties. They continued to lay a foundation for the reemergence of evangelical religion in the public square that would take place in the 1980s. Still, by the mid-1930s, revivalist Protestantism was no longer as central to culture as politics, sports, and entertainment. Aimee and other religious leaders of the 1930s understood this, at least intuitively, hence her call for America to awake and return to its roots.

During the last decade and a half of her life, it is difficult to say whether Sister Aimee ever found peace. After business clashes with her mother, one of which included a fistfight, she and Minnie went their separate ways. Then Aimee split with her daughter, Roberta, who had been groomed as her successor. This painful experience left Aimee's son, Rolf, as heir apparent to the Angelus Temple and the Foursquare Gospel denomination. He led the movement until his retirement in 1988; he died in 2009 at the age of 96.

In addition to family squabbles, for Aimee the 1930s were punctuated by legal wrangling between her and a rival woman evangelist she had hired, between Roberta's and her lawyers, and between her and some of her alienated followers in the Foursquare Gospel movement. The latter concerned both theological and property disputes. Aimee experienced multiple nervous breakdowns and other physical maladies. In many ways her final years were as troubled as ever. She died on September 26, 1944, in Oakland, where she had gone for a revival—the site of her first Foursquare Gospel sermon 22 years before. She had contracted a tropical fever in Mexico shortly before the Oakland crusade and was taking medication. She was also taking the sedative Seconal to help her sleep. Although there were rumors of suicide, the coroner ruled the death accidental, stemming from an overdose of Seconal combined with a previously undiagnosed liver ailment. One theory is that she took Seconal, which can cause forgetfulness, forgot how many she had taken, and took more.

McPherson's funeral was delayed for almost two weeks. On Sunday, October 8, her body lay in state most of the day in Angelus Temple. An estimated 50,000 mourners paid their respects. The next day, Aimee's fifty-fourth birthday, the temple was jammed with 6,000 mourners and thousands more outside. More than 75 policemen were on hand to keep order. She had purchased a plot in the famous Forest Lawn cemetery in Glendale, resting place for the rich and famous. There she was buried in a 1,350-pound bronze coffin in a marble vault guarded by two life-size statues of angels. As pallbearers carried her casket to its resting place, they walked up a hill lined on one side with 25 ministers holding American flags and on the other with 25 holding the flag of the International Church of the Foursquare Gospel. Men and women wept, some falling to the ground in sorrow.[53] This time Sister Aimee was not coming back.

CHAPTER 7

MURDER TRIAL
IN TEXAS

As the first grand jury convened to hear evidence concerning Aimee Semple McPherson's alleged kidnapping, the Reverend J. Frank Norris of Texas shot and killed an unarmed man in his office at the First Baptist Church of Fort Worth. Norris's subsequent trial for murder came on the heels of the Scopes trial and McPherson's great disappearance. As yet another national scandal unfolded, things seemed to be going from bad to worse for fundamentalists. These events further cemented the losses they incurred from 1924 through 1926 during the fundamentalist-modernist controversy.

Norris was a well-known preacher and perhaps the most influential fundamentalist in the South. He was born in 1877 in Dadeville, Alabama. Like McPherson's mother, Minnie Kennedy, Norris's mother, Mary, also dreamed that her child would do something great for God, dedicating him to the ministry at an early age. Norris's father was an abusive alcoholic. Poor and with few prospects for success in Alabama, the family followed the pattern of many nineteenth-century Americans; they headed west, settling on a farm near Hubbard in the Hill County region of central Texas. Norris became one of the two most famous people to come from Hubbard. The other was Hall of Fame baseball player Tris Speaker, who was born the year after Norris.[1]

Norris's first violent experience came at an early age. In 1891 his father, Warner, ran afoul of some local outlaws, who came to the Norris farm and shot him. Young Frank ran to aid his father, and the gang opened fire on him as well. The shooter, John Shaw, claimed that Frank had charged him with a knife. This claim cannot be substantiated with certainty, but Shaw was sentenced to three years in prison for shooting Warner while the charges were dropped for shooting Frank. Ironically, Norris's injuries were far more serious than his father's. He spent several days in critical condition, then gangrene set in, which took months of recovery. The boy convalesced for more than a year before fully recuperating.

Norris attended Baylor University in Waco, Texas, 30 miles from his home, graduating in 1903. He then attended Southern Baptist Theological Seminary in Louisville, Kentucky, taking his theological degree in 1905. He distinguished himself as an outstanding student at both schools and commenced full-time work as a Baptist preacher in 1905 at the McKinney Avenue Baptist Church in Dallas. Starting with 15 parishioners in a dilapidated building, Norris was wildly successful. Within three years McKinney Avenue Baptist had over 1,000 members and a new building. (In the 1980s the church Norris built became Dallas's Hard Rock Café. It was torn down in 2008.) After a brief stint as a religious newspaper publisher, Norris took the reins of First Baptist Fort Worth in 1909, where he spent the rest of his career.

Norris's method of church growth consisted of precipitating a split in order to run off any opposition. Then he would recruit new members to replace those who had left. First Baptist Fort Worth had been known as the church of the cattle kings before Norris arrived, but during his first three years there some of the most influential members departed. Norris replaced them with masses of working-class people he referred to as "folks from the forks of the creek." Norris attracted people with sensationalized sermons. On the heels of the 1912 presidential race in which Theodore Roosevelt failed in his comeback bid, Norris preached a sermon entitled "If Jim Jeffries, the Chicago Cubs, and Theodore Roosevelt Can't Come Back, Who Can?" While Norris knew that the aging Great White Hope Jeffries had been bludgeoned by Jack Johnson, he could not have known that more than a century after their last championship in 1908, the Cubs World Series drought would continue. On another occasion, following a heartbreaking loss for the Fort Worth industrial league baseball team, Norris hung a sign outside his church reading "Why Dallas Beat Fort Worth in Baseball." People packed the church that night and heard Norris preach a basic revivalist sermon with no mention of the baseball teams.

Norris's first brush with the law came in 1912. He had accused city officials of lax enforcement of laws against prostitution and gambling in a crime-ridden section of Fort Worth known as Hell's Half Acre. When he opened a tent revival there, the mayor had Norris cited for code violations and ordered the tent removed. In February First Baptist Church burned to the ground, and Norris blamed his enemies, although not naming any names. Norris produced a stack of threatening letters he allegedly had received. The investigation, however, focused on Norris, the theory being that he had torched his own church and forged the letters himself. On March 1 he was indicted for perjury for his grand jury testimony about the letters. The next day his home burned to the ground. The local newspaper asked skeptically, "How the residence was set afire without arousing the family or awakening the night watchman is the question that thousands of citizens are asking one another."[2] The newspaper also questioned whether there really was a conspiracy against Norris, as he claimed. On March 28 Norris was indicted for arson in the burning of his church and home. In a three-week trial in April Norris was acquitted of perjury for allegedly lying about the letters. Although he could not prove who wrote them, neither could the prosecutor prove that Norris had typed them himself. The arson trial was postponed for a year and a half before Norris was acquitted of that charge, as well.

Norris possessed an uncanny knack for turning bad publicity and controversy to his own advantage. Throughout the rest of the second decade of the century he built First Baptist into a southwestern religious empire. By 1920 the church sat more than 5,000 people, and the choir often had 700 voices. His burgeoning downtown empire included a recreation complex complete with gymnasium and pool, and he founded a school called Bible Baptist Seminary and a newspaper called the *Searchlight,* which changed its name to the *Fundamentalist* in 1927.

After World War I Norris moved into national fundamentalist circles that included William Bell Riley of Minneapolis, John Roach Straton of New York, William Jennings Bryan, Billy Sunday, Aimee Semple McPherson's Los Angeles nemesis Fighting Bob Shuler, and to a lesser extent J. Gresham Machen. As a tongues-speaking Pentecostal, McPherson stood apart from this group theologically and organizationally while supporting many of the same social and cultural causes. As the fundamentalist-modernist controversy heated up, Norris took the lead in the southern theater of the war on liberal theology. In this role, he squared off with the moderate leaders of the Southern Baptist Convention (SBC), accusing them of everything from believing evolution to endorsing communism; he also made accusations in his newspaper against his alma mater, Baylor. Texas Baptist leaders responded with "A Statement and A Pledge," a document signed by more than 30 of the state's most influential Baptist leaders. The statement registered "[o]ur emphatic disapproval upon, and our most earnest condemnation on the method and spirit of this destructive reactionary movement . . . ruthlessly carried on by the *Searchlight* of Fort Worth."[3] One of the authors of the statement then wrote and distributed a pamphlet called "The Fruits of Norrisism." As a result of these and other controversies, Norris was ousted from the Baptist General Convention of Texas and ostensibly from the SBC, as well. He responded by forming his own fundamentalist denomination and for years by holding revivals in the same city as the SBC's annual meeting, usually in a venue next door or across the street from the convention. Oddly, for all Norris's efforts against liberalism, there were actually few in the South and almost none in the SBC who really were liberals. His efforts to portray orthodox and conservative denominational leaders as liberals resulted in some of his most spurious charges.

As Norris's reputation grew he held revivals across the country and in Great Britain, usually in the largest fundamentalist churches. He preached at the Spurgeon Tabernacle in London, and during the 1920s he appeared at least yearly at the largest New York churches, First Baptist and Calvary. Norris, in turn, invited the highest-profile fundamentalists to preach at First Baptist, and most obliged. William Jennings Bryan, for example, spoke at Norris's church in 1924 and 1925, the latter as part of the World's Christian Fundamentals Association meeting that was held at First Baptist. Founded in 1919 by William Bell Riley, the association was the first national organization of fundamentalists. In conjunction with his appearance at the Fort Worth meeting in 1925, Bryan encouraged Norris to come to Dayton for the Scopes trial. Although he was unable to attend, Norris sent his stenographer to record the trial so testimony could be reproduced verbatim in the *Searchlight*. Norris then attempted to capitalize on the publicity of the trial and Bryan's subsequent death by reprinting what he claimed was "Bryan's Last Letter" and by publishing a book marketed as the "Only Authentic Book on the Dayton Trial." By the mid-1920s Norris had been a fixture in Fort Worth for 15 years and was well known nationally. Although not nearly as famous as Billy Sunday and Aimee Semple McPherson, Norris exploded onto the national scene in the summer of 1926 as a result of his trial for murder.

THE MURDER TRIAL

During the summer that year Norris was once again enmeshed in controversy with city politicians in Fort Worth, in particular the mayor, H. C. Meacham, and the city manager, H. B. Carr, both Roman Catholic. Norris believed it his duty to protect Fort Worth from the domination of Catholics no less than he believed it necessary to protect Baptists from liberal theology. He also fashioned himself a watchdog of corruption in high places. In his dispute with the mayor, he combined anti-Catholicism with civic-minded reform. It was an ideal battle for Norris.

When the city arranged to purchase a piece of property from the St. Ignatius School, Norris saw Catholic conspiracy. He charged that the city had overvalued the property then arranged to buy it at the inflated price in order to funnel city funds to the Catholic church. He also charged that the city intended to cut a new street in order to aid both the church and the school. Norris wove these charges into an alleged plot by L. B. Haughey, the manager of Meacham Dry Goods, a local store owned by the mayor. Norris claimed that six First Baptist members who worked at the store were fired because of their association with him. At the July 11 service Norris invited the six to the platform to tell their stories. Two told of being given the choice of leaving Norris's church or losing their jobs. Norris then launched into his attack, claiming that City Manager Carr was "the missing link" and Meacham was not "fit to be mayor of a hog pen." (He may have actually meant that Meacham *was* fit for such work.[4])

The article covering the July 11 service appeared in the *Searchlight* on Friday of that week. The next day Norris went to his office at the church, where he received a phone call from D. E. Chipps. Chipps had come to Texas from Virginia two decades before and established himself in the lumber business. Well known around town, he was a prominent member of Fort Worth's wealthy elite. He also supported the mayor, and he was Catholic. Chipps had probably been drinking when he threatened that if Norris did not lay off the mayor, he was going to do something about it. What Norris said in reply is not known, but it is reasonably clear that his response contained no acquiescence or compromise because sometime later Chipps appeared at Norris's door and challenged him to a fight. According to Norris, Chipps threatened repeatedly, "I'm going to kill you for what you said in your sermons, damn you." Norris tried to escort Chipps out of the church, but when they reached the door, Chipps repeated his threat. Then, according to another person in the church, Chipps followed Norris back toward the pastor's office saying "Let's go to it." In response, Norris pulled the night watchman's revolver from his desk drawer and figuratively said "goodbye Mr. Chipps." Norris then calmly called the police and his wife, Lillian, saying "I've just killed me a man." Three of the four shots fired hit the unarmed lumberman, and the weapon was empty of bullets when police arrived. Norris was arrested and charged with murder.[5]

Released after church members posted his $10,000 bail, the following morning Norris preached to a packed auditorium and an overflow crowd of several hundred people outside the sanctuary. His sermon text was Romans 8 and included the verses "There is therefore now no condemnation to them which are in Christ Jesus" as well as "And we know that all things work together for good to them that love God, to them who are the called according to his purpose." He was not his usual bombastic self, however. Subdued and chastened, he seemed to grasp the magnitude of having killed a man just 50 feet from the pulpit less than 24 hours earlier.[6] A headline on the front page of the Charlotte, North Carolina *Observer* typified the national coverage Norris was about to receive. The headline read: "Thousands Hear Pastor Preach." On the same page appeared a story on Aimee Semple McPherson titled "Mrs. M'Pherson Likens Herself to Mighty Oak."[7] For a time in July stories covering the Norris and McPherson grand juries appeared on the front pages of newspapers across the country.

Within a few days Norris went back on the offensive. *Searchlight* staffer and First Baptist church member J. J. Mickle charged that Chipps had been part of a plot to kill Norris. Refusing to elaborate, Mickle promised that the whole story would come out at the proper time. Norris's supporters claimed that someone had seen two men accompanying Chipps as he approached First Baptist on the day of the shooting. Allegedly, the three had come to kill Norris, but two backed out, leaving Chipps to face Norris alone. Given that Chipps was unarmed, it seems implausible that his intent was murder, but the conspiracy theory helped set the stage for Norris's plea of self-defense. The police chief dismissed the rumor of a Chipps conspiracy as being without foundation. Those supporting Chipps argued there was a pool of blood far from Norris's office door, evidence that the man had not been threatening Norris in the pastor's study but was actually leaving the building when Norris shot him and dragged the body back into the office.

The district attorney's office convened a grand jury to determine whether Norris should be indicted for murder. Norris issued a statement to the press demanding that he be indicted so that he could clear his name in a trial. Like McPherson, he claimed he wanted to be exonerated by a jury and therefore feared being "no billed." Appearing before the grand jury, he tearfully recounted Chipps's killing, but the tears turned to anger when he reiterated the conspiracy against him. Saying that Chipps and the others intended to kill him, he claimed, "I beat them to it. . . . I had to defend myself." When questioned by reporters, Mayor Meacham said that charges of a conspiracy were "silly."[8]

Norris was indicted on July 29, with his trial set to begin November 1. During the first week of October, attorneys for the two sides began to negotiate the details of the trial. They established a jury pool of 500 men and developed the witness lists. Mrs. Norris was slated as a witness for the defense, as was the switchboard operator at a local hotel who was believed to have heard Chipps's phone call to Norris before the shooting. The star witness on the defense list, however, was Norris himself, who planned to take the stand. Everything was ready, and reporters from 30 newspapers from all over the country descended on Fort Worth for the trial. This was not quite the coverage that Scopes received in Dayton little more than a year before, but it was significant nevertheless. Norris's trial was set to begin two days before a grand jury indicted Aimee Semple McPherson for conspiracy.

The week before Norris's scheduled trial, the defense began to waver, with the attorneys saying they were not sure they would be ready. The trial opened on November 1 nevertheless. Even though the judge barred spectators, the courtroom was nearly filled with prospective jurors, witnesses, and reporters from across the country, including one from the Associated Press. Many had their manual typewriters with them, and there were telegraph wires strewn across the floor to transmit reports of the trial to the outside world. The court turned away scores of people, many of whom milled around outside.

On the first day, Norris's attorneys asked for a change of venue, claiming it was impossible to seat an unbiased jury in Fort Worth. The defense made the conspiracy theory official, naming Mayor Meacham, City Manager Carr, and Meacham Dry Goods store manager Haughey, along with the secretary of the local Knights of Columbus as lead conspirators. Defense attorneys told the judge they were prepared to show that this conspiracy against Norris existed because "of the defendant's religious opposition to the faith of Roman Catholicism" and that Norris had "incurred the individual ill-will, great prejudice and hatred of a major portion, if not all of the members of the Roman Catholic Church and Knights of Columbus."9 The defense said that none of the 6,000 Roman Catholics in the county could adjudicate the case fairly.

Bolstering the conspiracy theory, Norris's attorneys called Meacham to the stand in order to establish that he had agreed to pay $15,000 for private lawyers to assist the prosecution in the case. Norris's lead attorney asked Meacham if he had called a meeting of city leaders to plan "how to get rid of Norris." Meacham acknowledged that there had been a recent meeting of the city council to discuss a tax issue, but he said the only discussion of Norris concerned his recent attack on the city leaders. Defense attorneys then probed the firing of the First Baptist Church members who worked at Meacham Dry Goods. Meacham told how his store manager, Haughey, had questioned the six, asking them if they believed the things Norris said about the mayor and telling the workers that if they did, they could not continue working at Meacham's store. The mayor insisted, however, that most of the First Baptist members stayed on anyway. Several other witnesses were called to express their views as to whether Norris could get a fair trial in Tarrant County. The prosecution, of course, denied that there was a Roman Catholic conspiracy against Norris. Instead, the state accused Norris of using his change-of-venue petition to stir up religious intolerance against any faith other than his own.

After presenting their motions for and against a change of venue, attorneys for the two sides agreed to move the trial to Austin, nearly 200 miles to the south. The trial there was set for January 1927. During the pretrial preparations and the change-of-venue hearing, Norris continued with business as usual. He attempted to rent a municipal auditorium in San Antonio in mid-November in order to hold a revival that would compete with the annual meeting of the Baptist General Convention of Texas, which had expelled Norris and his church in 1924. When Baptist state leaders threatened to move the convention to Waco or Dallas, however, the mayor of San Antonio canceled Norris's reservation and assured the Baptists they would not have to worry about the rabble-rousing preacher's presence in the city during the convention.

Norris's trial began on January 14, 1927. The prosecution called but six witnesses and took less than a day before resting its case. The prosecution's star witness was Roxie Parker, who was described as "a gentlewoman of the old southern school." She had come forward with her story a few months after the shooting. She testified that she had gone to Norris's office on July 17 to speak with the preacher about a piece of property she thought Norris might be interested in purchasing. As she approached Norris's study, she saw Chipps leaving and heard him say "I'll come back." She claimed she could see Norris with a gun in the study behind Chipps. "Dr. Norris shot," she recalled. "The man staggered. I turned and left. It seemed to me I heard two or three more shots." She then ran from the building, where her daughter was waiting for her in an automobile, and the two sped away from the scene. By putting Parker on the stand, the prosecution tried to establish that Chipps had not been threatening Norris when shot but was attempting to leave.

During cross examination Parker admitted to defense attorneys that she and her now-deceased husband had both been married and divorced before marrying each other. What exactly was to be made of this was left to the jury, but the implication was that she was morally disreputable, perhaps not the gentile southern belle she portrayed herself to be. A few days later defense lawyers called witnesses who testified that they were just outside the church when they heard the shots. They entered the building and raced up the stairs to Norris's study. They never saw Roxie Parker.[10]

Other than Norris himself, the key defense testimony came from L. H. Nutt, a local banker who served as the Sunday school superintendent and on the church's finance committee. The defense presented Nutt as the only eyewitness to the shooting, essentially saying that Parker's story was unbelievable. Nutt testified that he was having a conference with Norris in the pastor's study when Chipps arrived. Chipps entered without knocking and proceeded to warn Norris to lay off Meacham. Chipps and Norris engaged in a heated exchange before Norris asked Chipps to leave. Norris stood and attempted to escort Chipps to the anteroom, told the lumberman he wanted no more trouble with him, and bade him farewell. As Norris headed back toward his desk, however, Chipps followed the preacher back into the study, saying "I'll kill you; let's go to it." Chipps then reached for his hip pocket, Nutt said, and at that time the shots rang out. Chipps doubled over and appeared to be trying to pick up a small brown object before he fell to the floor. The object was never found. Because Nutt was looking at Chipps with Norris behind, Nutt did not actually see Norris fire the weapon, but when he turned around the pistol was lying on Norris's desk.

Testifying the same day as Nutt was a second key witness for the defense, a former Fort Worth policeman. He told the court he had gone to First Baptist around noon the day before the shooting, warning Norris that Chipps had made threats against the pastor. This witness also recounted having arrested Chipps months before on a charge of drunkenness and disorderly conduct.[11]

The defense called 30 more witnesses. Some testified that Chipps had said many times in the days leading up to the shooting that if Norris did not lay off the mayor, he was going to kill the preacher. One witness said he asked Chipps, "Are you serious? Are you really going to kill Norris?" to which Chipps replied that he was. Many of the witnesses reported that Chipps used liquor "habitually" and was often belligerent and violent when he was drinking. One witness claimed Chipps was drunk and armed with a pistol on one of the occasions when he threatened Norris. An owner of a local barber shop and three of his barbers all said Chipps had come in around 11:30 a.m. the day of the shooting and had obviously been drinking. One of them put Chipps's intoxication level at "about 50 percent" that day.[12]

On the third day of the trial two women testified to hearing Chipps threaten to attack Norris on the day of the shooting. A former employee of Meacham Dry Goods told the jury that she overheard a conversation between Chipps and Meacham outside the store in which Chipps told the mayor, "I'm going over to stop Norris or kill him," after which Meacham shook Chipps's hand and said, "If you need me, call me." The second woman was a telephone operator at the Westbrook Hotel. She told of two conversations on the day of the shooting, one between Chipps and Meacham and the other between Chipps and Norris. She was not allowed to testify about the Meacham conversation, but she told the court she heard Chipps say to Norris over the phone, "It's none of your damn business who [I am], but [I'm] coming over there to talk things over."[13]

The next day Norris took the stand in his own defense, but before he could testify he and the jurors were briefly dismissed from the courtroom so the attorneys could argue a defense motion before the judge. The defense wanted the judge to instruct prosecutors to refrain from mentioning Norris's previous indictments and trials on perjury and arson stemming from the 1912 burning of his church. The defense also insisted there should be no mention of reports of Norris having had a gun on occasions other than the Chipps shooting. The prosecution agreed to these motions, and the trial resumed with Norris taking the stand the next day, Friday, January 21. When he did, he sobbed with regret for having killed Chipps, insisting nevertheless that he had to do it. Then he told the same story Nutt had told a week before. Norris denied that he knew Roxie Parker and said he had never had a conference with her, refuting her claim that she had come to his office to continue negotiations about property. Following Norris's testimony, however, the prosecution produced a surprise witness who said he saw a woman run out of the church, jump into a car, and speed away, an account that corroborated Parker's claim to having been an eyewitness to the shooting.[14]

In closing arguments the lead prosecutor portrayed Norris as a violent and dangerous sensationalist who should be executed for slaying Chipps. Chipps, the prosecutor claimed, went to Norris's office with no intent of harming the preacher, yet Norris responded by shooting an unarmed man in cold blood. The jury did not buy that interpretation of the facts.

On January 25, after 16 days of proceedings, jurors took less than two hours and only two ballots to acquit Norris of murder. Norris's acquittal came two weeks and one day after the Los Angeles prosecutor dismissed all charges against Aimee Semple McPherson. When the decision was read in the courtroom, supporters pressed in around Norris with congratulations, only to be warned by the judge that they would be held in contempt if they continued to celebrate in court. When the verdict was read, Chipps's 16-year-old son remarked audibly, "I'm sorry for mother; it will hurt her."[15]

AFTERMATH

On the night of his acquittal Norris returned triumphant to Fort Worth and was greeted at his church by a packed house. Like McPherson's, Norris's career hardly missed a beat. However difficult the trial was for him personally, he seemed to thrive on the publicity. In the year following the shooting, First Baptist Church added 2,000 members, bringing its total to roughly 6,000. The church would double in size over the next 15 years. Less than two years after the trial, Norris played a major role in the presidential election of 1928, as he fought to maintain Prohibition and keep a Catholic from becoming president.

In 1929 First Baptist Fort Worth was destroyed by fire for a second time. Judged by witnesses to be one of the most spectacular conflagrations the city had ever witnessed, it took the city's entire firefighting force to extinguish the blaze. Investigators found several tubs and a five-gallon gasoline can in the charred remains of the immense sanctuary and four-story Sunday school building. As was the case in 1912, this was clearly arson, but Norris was not a suspect this time; he was in Austin when the fire occurred. The damage to the $1 million church was estimated at $200,000 to $300,000.[16] Rebuilding was difficult due to the onset of the Great Depression, and by the mid-1930s Norris's empire was strapped for cash.

In 1934 Temple Baptist Church in Detroit, Michigan, invited Norris for a revival meeting. Shortly thereafter the congregation called Norris as its pastor. He accepted but retained leadership of First Baptist Fort Worth as well. For the next 16 years he pastored both churches, shuttling back and forth by plane and appointing lieutenants in each city to administer church affairs in his absence. The new church meant increased revenues to fund some of his operations in Fort Worth as well as increased exposure in the Midwest and more church members under his influence. By the 1940s the combined membership of First Baptist and Temple was reported to be 25,000 people, allowing Norris to boast that he had more church members under his pastoral care than any preacher in America.

Like McPherson in the 1930s, Norris was an early supporter of Franklin Delano Roosevelt, but by 1934 had turned radically against the New Deal and even speculated that the president might be the beast of prophecy, something akin to being the antichrist. In the 1940s Norris turned to anticommunism as his primary political battle. Rather than charging that his Southern Baptist opponents were liberals, he accused them of being soft on communism, if not outright pinkos. This turn put him in the good company of the pope, so he quit his anti-Catholicism. Explaining that just as Winston Churchill aligned with the Soviet Union to stop Hitler, he was now aligning with Catholics to stop Stalin. "The world is on fire, and I'll take my stand with the Catholics before I will with Joe Stalin and his cutthroats and criminals," he told an audience in 1947.[17] He had traded one anti for another, but for him the choices were always either/or. That same year Norris and a small delegation of fundamentalists gained an audience with Pope Pius XII, whom Norris referred to as "the last Gibraltar in Europe against Communism."

Norris's change of heart toward Catholicism put him at odds not only with most of his fundamentalist allies but also with his moderate enemies in the Southern Baptist Convention. While Norris visited the pope and praised President Harry Truman's anticommunist policies, the president of the SBC said Truman's recent letter exchange with Pope Pius made it appear that the United States was "an ally of clerical totalitarianism." Moderate Southern Baptist leaders opposed Truman's naming an ambassador to the Vatican because they believed the appointment was a violation of the separation of church and state, something Baptists were known to defend. Norris responded that preachers who attacked Truman were "doing the bidding of Stalin. . . . They talk of [Truman] lining up with the pope. But they are lining up with the Communist regime in Moscow." He thought the church-state issue was a red herring and told reporters, "The issue for America in the world is not the union of state and church but whether we will have a church or no church, state or no state, God or no God."[18]

Although joining heartily in antimodernism, anti-Catholicism, anticommunism, and the typical anti-black racism of his day, there was one anti Norris steered clear of. While many fundamentalists in the 1920s and 1930s became anti-Semitic, Norris never did, and he broke with one of his prominent allies, Gerald L. K. Smith, over this issue. Smith was a well-known fundamentalist anticommunist and former associate of Louisiana governor Huey Long. Norris scheduled Smith for a revival at First Baptist billed as "A Mammoth Christian America Rally" in 1947. The event was a big success, and the two began planning a second Smith visit. That fall, however, Smith wrote an article arguing that Jesus had not been Jewish. Already growing suspicious about Smith's racism, this was the last straw for Norris, especially given his efforts at the same time to rally support for the creation of modern Israel. Norris wrote a public denunciation of Smith in his newspaper, known now as the *Fundamentalist.* In the article Norris compared Smith's antics to those of Hitler and Goebbels. Smith responded in a letter, writing "I suggest that in your anxiety to please some of these hooked nose kikes that curse the name of Jesus Christ that you go a little easier on some of your brethren in Christ."[19]

Norris thrived throughout the 1930s and 1940s, but just as Aimee Semple McPherson would forever be that lady preacher who ran off with her radio guy, so Norris was always the preacher who shot and killed a man in his church office. Although there was doubt about whether McPherson actually had an affair with Kenneth Ormiston, Norris's killing Chipps was without question. Nevertheless, Norris fought back against those who used his scandal against him. In 1947, when columnist Ralph McGill of the Atlanta *Journal Constitution* called Norris a "pistol toting divine," Norris sued the newspaper. The incident stemmed from a near riot Norris set off at that year's Southern Baptist Convention annual meeting held in St. Louis.

Norris attended the preconvention pastors' conference in order to harangue SBC president Louis Newton, pastor of the Druid Hills Baptist Church in Atlanta. Norris often accused Newton of being a theological liberal and a communist sympathizer, especially after Newton's visit to the Soviet Union. At the pastors' conference, Norris rose from his seat in the middle of Newton's report on his Russia trip and began reading from a list of 13 questions he demanded Newton answer. Newton responded by spontaneously leading 1,000 pastors in the hymn "How Firm a Foundation." Norris joined in and even tried to lead another verse after most of those present had quit singing. There followed several more minutes of shouting before order was restored. In the midst of the disturbance someone called the police, but by the time officers arrived Norris had ceased his antics.[20]

The disruption received national coverage in newspapers and magazines, and the *Journal Constitution* paid particular attention because Newton was from Atlanta. In response to Norris's lawsuit, the *Journal Constitution* printed a retraction.[21] *Time* magazine also covered Norris's performance in St. Louis, and Norris sued the magazine for $20,000. It is unclear whatever became of that suit.

Norris was involved in six trials. He lost only one. In 1940 one of his fundamentalist allies sued him for libel. Norris's friends often became his enemies, and this was one of those occasions. R. E. White was the editor of *Amazing Grace,* a fundamentalist newspaper in San Antonio, and was also part of the Fundamental Baptist Missionary Fellowship, which Norris had started years before. When Norris and others sought to move the organization to Chicago, White opposed them, touching off a fundamentalist newspaper war in Texas. Norris used the *Fundamentalist* to criticize White, and whatever he said resulted in the lawsuit. The initial settlement in 1940 was $15,000 in actual damages and $10,000 for malicious intent, but over the next five years it appears that Norris's lawyers were able to whittle the actual payment down to $2,000.[22]

Norris's continued infamy in the 1930s and 1940s, most of which stemmed from his bizarre behavior, seemed to fit the growing public profile of fundamentalism as a fringe movement. The days seemed long past when Walter Lippmann and *Nation* magazine found J. Gresham Machen's defense of conservative

Protestantism more cogent than the liberal theology of the Presbyterian church's progressive leaders. Increasingly, after the 1920s, fundamentalists seemed either to disappear or withdraw to the margins of culture, and that year in the middle of the decade was largely responsible. From the Scopes trial in July 1925 through Aimee Semple McPherson's first grand jury and Norris's killing Chipps, both in July 1926, fundamentalism experienced a tough year. Like McPherson, Norris was a product of the Roaring Twenties. Already in his early forties when the decade began, he found his niche as religion roared along with everything else in American culture. Both religious figures benefited immensely as the criteria for fame in America shifted from character to personality. While McPherson played the role of religious flapper, Norris took the muscular Christianity of Billy Sunday to new heights, and depths. Coming on the heels of the Scopes trial, the legal travails of Norris and McPherson unfolded at the same time the fundamentalists suffered major setbacks in the fundamentalist-modernist controversy in the Presbyterian church. All these events helped keep religion center stage in American culture, but some asked whether this was a good thing.

When fundamentalism reappeared as a public force in the 1980s, Norris was there, in spirit at least. The first major organization of the Christian Right of our own time was the Moral Majority, founded in 1979 and exploding onto the political scene during Ronald Reagan's campaign for the presidency the next year. Moral Majority founder Jerry Falwell was a graduate of Baptist Bible College in Springfield, Missouri, a college founded by men who had been Norris associates in the 1940s. As Falwell put it, "In my own personal life, I have been greatly influenced by [Norris's] ministry, as men trained by him were instrumental in leading me to Christ and training me for the ministry."[23]

CHAPTER 8

BLACK HERESY

lthough their careers and movements peaked in the 1930s and 1940s, Daddy Grace and Father Divine were products of the 1920s. The Roaring Twenties made innovation possible on a number of fronts. From blues and jazz to flappers, the norms of society were in flux. In this climate, Grace and Divine became jazzmen preachers in an age of religious ferment that also celebrated the stardom of Billy Sunday, Aimee Semple McPherson, and the shenanigans of J. Frank Norris. For the most part African American religion was segregated from white society, but black people participated in the religious ferment and the cult of personality no less than whites.

At the time of the Scopes trial and the McPherson and Norris scandals, one of America's most notorious black prophets was just starting his career, launching his first revivals in the South in an effort to spread his distinct style of black religion. Much as Sister Aimee had done during her early career, this preacher, too, traveled in a car plastered with gospel slogans. When he entered a city members of his evangelistic team drove through the streets shouting over a loudspeaker "Daddy Grace is in town. Come one and all, and listen to the man of God."[1]

Daddy Grace was born Marcelino Manuel da Graca in 1881 in the Cape Verde Islands, off the coast of West Africa. Under Portuguese rule since the sixteenth century, the islands had played a significant part in the slave trade. Over time, as slavery ended, a thriving population of free Africans developed there. Catholicism was the dominant faith under the Portuguese, yet because of a chronic shortage of priests there was ample lay involvement, which led to religious innovation. African tribal faiths often mixed with Christianity to produce distinctive styles of worship and ecstatic religious experiences. Alongside Catholics, the Cape Verdes also had a smattering of Protestants, and by 1900 some were members of the early Pentecostal movement that we encountered in chapter 6.

In the early nineteenth century, American merchants recruited free laborers in the Cape Verdes to work in the New England whaling industry, which started a migration pattern from the islands to New Bedford, Massachusetts. By late century New Bedford had become home to roughly 2,000 residents of Cape Verdean descent. The first immigrant members of the da Graca family arrived in New Bedford in 1902. Marcelino was in his early twenties when he came over a few years later. For the next several years he worked at various jobs to make ends meet. His biographer writes that the period from his arrival until 1920 or so is "mostly a jigsaw puzzle with the majority of pieces missing."[2] He picked cranberries, a staple of summer employment for the black Portuguese population of New Bedford, and served as a cook, then medicine salesman, and for a time apparently operated a grocery store. He married in 1913, had two children over the next few years, then divorced in 1920. He also traveled during this period to Boston, Baltimore, Los Angeles, and Mexico. Like many immigrants he anglicized his name, changing it to Charles Grace.

Approaching the age of 40, in 1921 Grace was ordained as a minister and elected as a bishop in the Rock of the Apostolic Faith Church, a fledgling Pentecostal denomination. In December, however, he opened the New Bedford House of Prayer, which had no denominational affiliation. Some evidence suggests that this was actually the second House of Prayer he started, the first being in West Wareham in 1919. After founding the New Bedford House, Grace started his standard mode of operation, holding services every night of the week and incorporating lively music with a variety of instruments. Grace's theology was much like Aimee Semple McPherson's early Pentecostalism: He spoke in tongues and practiced faith healing. In one respect, however, Grace's career was something of the reverse of hers. Whereas McPherson began as a traveling preacher and eventually settled at Angelus Temple, Grace founded the New Bedford House of Prayer but within two years was traveling about, founding other churches. He never settled permanently in one location but instead started many Houses of Prayer and oversaw their operation like a chief executive of a Pentecostal franchised corporation.

In 1926, a month before McPherson disappeared and two months before Norris shot and killed D. E. Chipps, Grace held a tent revival in Savannah, Georgia. He was an immediate success in the South, and newspapers ran stories of his preaching and healing. "[T]he people of the city are astonished to see the blind get their sight through prayer," reported the Savannah *Tribune*.[3] In addition to his unusual services, Grace wore long flowing black hair and a pointed beard. He kept the long hair for the rest of his life and also grew fingernails two to four inches long. As Grace drew crowds and attention from the press, local pastors in Savannah challenged his authenticity and persuaded the local newspaper and the police to move against him. He was arrested for disorderly conduct, and a Seventh-day Adventist pastor named J. W. Manns offered $25 to anyone who could prove a healing. Manns then wrote an editorial warning against false prophets and began preaching sermons such as "Is the Fake Healing of Bishop Grace of God, or the Devil?" Grace responded by placing advertisements in the newspaper that were made to look like articles, and before long the two preachers were engaged in a war of words. Sometimes the dueling preachers' newspaper columns appeared side by side. In his ads, Grace pointed out that despite the discrimination against him, his revival continued to flourish. Grace's series of meetings concluded successfully in Savannah, and he moved on to Charlotte, North Carolina.

On July 1 the Charlotte *Observer* issued the headline "'Healer' Stirs Negro Frenzy." The quotation marks around "Healer" were evidence of the white reporter's skepticism, as were the quotation marks around "Faith Man" in a headline a week later. The racist analysis included a reference to "darkies" and a "babbling mass" that followed Grace through the streets shouting "Jesus." Grace held a tent revival in the Brooklyn area of Charlotte and was quoted in the *Observer* as saying "I am de true—ain't dat right honeys?" The Charlotte revival included the same demonstrations of healing that occurred in Savannah. The lame, sick, and infirm lined up and came forward like trail hitters at a Billy Sunday crusade; one emaciated man lay on a stretcher at the foot of the stage, hoping for Grace's healing touch. Although attendees were predominately black, there were "not a few whites" as well, newspapers reported.[4]

In North Carolina, Grace was hailed as the "black Christ," a portent of spiritual superstardom soon to come. Follower Ed Black recalled more than three decades later that Grace seemed different from any man he had ever known. One day Black asked Grace bluntly, "Ain't you Jesus?" Grace answered, "Look upon me and what you see then that is what I am."[5] While in Charlotte, Grace founded a House of Prayer that would be prominent for the rest of his career. He then moved across the state, encountering both wild support and stern opposition. In Seversville he held a mass river baptism. A man who could not swim strayed too far from shore and began to struggle. Grace tried to save him, but the man slipped away and drowned. Grace left town, which made it appear that he was running from trouble. In fact, his hasty departure was the result of his father's sudden death back home in New Bedford. Returning to his revival work following the funeral, Grace traveled into Virginia and was arrested in Newport News, charged with holding an integrated meeting.

By the time Grace returned to the South in 1927, he was known as Daddy Grace. This was not a unique term for a black leader; there are other examples of African and African American religious figures being called "Daddy" by their flock. When asked why his followers called him by this name, Grace referenced the apostle Paul calling Timothy his "son" and said, "I am a father to them in the Gospel and they are my children. . . . No matter how old they are, whether they are men or women, it makes no difference, they are all my babies; that is the way I feel."[6] The vast majority of Grace's "children" in the various Houses of Prayer were African American, but he did not consider himself "negro" or black. He was of both African and Portuguese descent. Even more important, he grew up outside the segregated American racial structure. At times he bristled when newspapers referred to him as a "negro" preacher. "These papers call me a 'Negro,'" he once complained to a reporter. "I am not a Negro, and no Negro in this country can do what I am doing. . . . I am a colorless man. I am a colorless bishop. Sometimes I am Black, sometimes I am white. I preach to all races." On another occasion, when asked if he was white, he replied, "I say I do not consider myself either white, Black, blue or red. It is whatever you take me and say, I am satisfied." When his questioner pressed, "What do you say?" Grace replied, "I do not say."[7]

For a decade after 1926, Grace made the Hampton Roads region of Virginia his quasi headquarters. He established Houses of Prayer in Newport News, Norfolk, and other cities and collectively his movement took the official name United House of Prayer for All People. The New Bedford, Massachusetts house continued as well, and the Augusta, Georgia house grew to be one of the largest. By the 1950s there were Houses of Prayer stretching from New England to Florida. Although the movement centered on Daddy Grace, most individual worship services took place in his absence. As Houses of Prayer spread across far-flung regions of the country, Grace could visit each house only occasionally.

The front of a House of Prayer sanctuary consisted of a raised platform called the "holy mountain." On the mountain stood an elaborate chair Daddy Grace occupied when he was present at a service. The chair had the plush trappings of a throne, and behind it were pictures of Daddy and some of the buildings he came to own over the years. Even when Grace was in town, services usually started without him, then he would make a dramatic entrance surrounded by bodyguards. He would stroll down the center aisle, take his seat on the throne, and observe the service from this high perch while being fanned by female attendants. When he felt moved by the spirit, he preached, occasionally engaging in unusual exegesis. He once said that he preached faith not religion, then gave the etymology of the word "religion." "The 're' before 'ligion' means a great number, and stood for the devils that Jesus cast out of the men of his day. Religion, then, is the return of the very things that were destroyed by God."[8]

Often Grace did not preach at all but merely sat on his throne and watched over his flock. As he aged, he increasingly left the preaching to church elders, and when he was not in attendance they often read letters he had written to the congregation. Whether Grace was present or not, worshippers would "come to the mountain" as they felt led, engaging in ecstatic worship: crying, falling to the floor, speaking in tongues, and the like. There also developed the practice of "walking the benches," jumping from seat to seat across the auditorium as the music blared. Houses of Prayer all had Grace Concert Bands consisting of a choir, horn section, and other instruments. One of the most famous of Grace's worship forms was the fire hose baptismal ceremony. Hundreds of followers would gather in the streets for a festival of preaching and music followed by a mass baptism in the fast-flowing water from hoses attached to neighborhood fire hydrants. Baptismal candidates dressed in white, and some experienced the street ritual multiple times. Newspapers covered the baptisms and carried photographs of new House of Prayer members experiencing this unusual rite of passage.

Grace not only healed people in House of Prayer services, but he also claimed that items he touched had healing power. This led to the development of products that were manufactured and marketed up and down the East Coast. Starting with "miracle-working handkerchiefs," the movement eventually developed cookies, creams, powders, shoe polish, coffee, Daddy Grace Allwater Soap, Grace Royal Vitamins, and stationery. Not all the products were supposed to have special healing power; many were just useful, and their sale helped fund the ministry.

Initially, Grace relied on donations to keep his ministry afloat. Often when he arrived at a House of Prayer or a street baptism his followers would shower him with bills or press them into his hands. By the time he reached the mountain he might have hundreds or even a few thousand dollars on his person. Among the enumerated General Council Rules for Houses of Prayer, Rule 48 stipulated that each house must raise money to buy a car for Grace. Rule 50 said that there would be a contest among houses to see which could raise the most money. The winner secured an elaborate banquet with Grace that would be paid for by the losers.[9]

As the movement grew, Grace became extremely wealthy due in part to his own business acumen. Early on he claimed that all property belonged to the House of Prayer and not to him, but over time he became the owner of the entire empire. In the 1930s he began to invest in high-end real estate, purchasing hotel buildings in New York and other cities, historic mansions, and other extravagant homes that remained at his disposal. Purchasing high-visibility and extremely expensive homes became Grace's favorite hobby. He employed a team of lawyers and accountants to execute the land deals, and in each locale the pastor of an individual House of Prayer was in charge of stores, apartments, and other holdings. Eventually, the House of Prayer developed funeral insurance, and Grace often loaned money at low interest rates to various houses and their members. Still, Grace was solely in charge of the church's finances and probably the only one who knew what exactly the church owned. His biographer believes the vast real estate purchases served as investment and publicity. As she writes, "[I]t was a point of pride for House of Prayer members nationwide to know that they were part of a church that owned glamorous buildings."[10] Generous offerings, a ritual of worship for House of Prayer members, supplied a ready cash flow for the movement.

Predictably, the financial structure of the church led to a series of lawsuits following Grace's death in 1960. The movement and its finances were so concentrated in his person that his followers had no idea who should take charge of the ministry or its vast wealth. Moreover, the Internal Revenue Service stepped in with a claim that Grace was $5.9 million in tax arrears. The next year the government adjusted the amount downward to \$1.9 million which had to be paid before family members or the House of Prayer could divide up what Grace left.[11] A judge appointed two lawyers to sort out what belonged to Grace personally and what belonged to the church. The whole movement had been rumored to be worth between \$16 million and \$25 million. The lawyers determined that only \$700,000 belonged to Grace personally—essentially, his mansion and apartment building in New Bedford, an estate in Cuba, properties in North Carolina, and an apartment building in Los Angeles. The rest belonged to the House of Prayer. The division of the property between Grace's family and the church resulted in numerous lawsuits over who controlled the House of Prayer once he died.

DADDY GRACE CONTROVERSY

Daddy Grace became a famous and controversial figure, though not always for the right reasons. Like Aimee Semple McPherson and J. Frank Norris, Grace too survived a serious trial, and like them he seemed capable of turning even the worst publicity to his own good. In 1932 Grace took one of his followers, Minnie Lee Campbell, by car from Brooklyn, New York, to his home in Philadelphia, to Washington, D.C., where they stayed at a House of Prayer guest house, then on to Baltimore, where Grace had arranged a job for Campbell playing piano at the House of Prayer there. She stayed for several months playing piano without event. Grace and Campbell agreed on this much of the story, but Campbell had a different version after she gave birth to a baby boy in July 1933 and named Grace as the father.

Campbell claimed that on the first car trip from Brooklyn to Philadelphia, Grace stopped the vehicle in New Jersey and raped her. Then, while staying in Washington just before going to Baltimore, he pressured her into having sex with him again. On the basis of Campbell's story, Grace was charged with violation of the Mann Act, a federal law that makes it a crime to transport someone across state lines for illicit purposes. The public took keen interest in the case, especially given that Grace was considered a black man and a preacher who had gotten rich off religion. The trial took place in March 1934 in New York. Grace himself testified that he had been asked by Minnie Lee Campbell's sister to preside over a House of Prayer case in which Minnie Lee was accused of being in a lesbian relationship with two other women. (It was not unusual for House of Prayer members to be tried for violations of the moral standards of the church.) Grace found the three women guilty of moral turpitude and ordered them to stop their relationship and cease living together. He then took Campbell with him to Philadelphia. He denied keeping her there for a number of weeks, testifying rather that after a day he took her to Washington, then Baltimore. In Washington, they stayed in separate rooms on opposite ends of the House of Prayer guest house. The only route from her room to his was through the dining area. There were several people in the dining area attending to an ill elderly woman, and none of them saw Campbell come through on the night in question.

There were 21 other witnesses at the trial, and their stories often conflicted. Some testified that Campbell had been in a sexual relationship with another House of Prayer minister, and one man even claimed he had paid Campbell for sex, contradicting her account that Grace was her only partner. Grace's biographer believes the memory of minute details on the part of several witnesses makes it likely they were coached, which raises the question as to whether there was a conspiracy of House of Prayer believers to secure a not-guilty verdict. The jury did not have to determine whether they believed Grace was the father of Campbell's child, nor that he had actually had sex with her. The Mann Act outlaws the transportation of an individual for sexual purposes. If the jury believed that Grace's intentions in taking Campbell to Philadelphia and Baltimore were sexual, that was enough. The jury decided he had, and Grace was convicted and sentenced to a year in the federal penitentiary. He was released on bail pending appeal.[12]

A few months after his March conviction, another court determined in a paternity case that Grace was not the father of Campbell's child. Then, in November, Grace's conviction was thrown out when the appeals court ruled that the case had been filed in the wrong jurisdiction. The appeals judge also noted that Campbell's car rape story was "highly incredible." The federal magistrate could have refiled the case in the proper district but never did, probably because Campbell's story had fallen apart in the paternity trial.[13]

While we will never know whether Grace was guilty of sexual impropriety with Minnie Lee Campbell, he had that preacherly knack for turning negative publicity into his own good fortune. In between his conviction and appeal Grace preached, "I'm convicted! Convicted! Tried in the courts of the United States and convicted!" "Why then do you follow me," he asked his Norfolk followers. "I'll tell you. Every Christian church is led by a convicted man, a man convicted as I was by the courts of the land. Was Jesus Christ not convicted?"[14] As Grace's biographer puts it, "[T]he Mann Act case created an important moment in House of Prayer history. The moment when followers took a leap of faith. Their faith in Grace transcended worldly accusations."[15] Such was the case for McPherson during her grand jury investigation and for Norris during his murder trial.

Daddy Grace survived and thrived, hitting his peak of popularity in the late 1930s and into the 1940s. Even as fundamentalism seemed in eclipse after the 1920s, flamboyant figures such as Norris, McPherson, and Grace attracted attention, in part because the secular press believed they were holdouts in an age where no serious person could believe what they preached. They were newsworthy because they were relics of a bygone era. With his shoulder-length curly hair, expensive suits, jewelry, automobiles, and mansions, Grace was looked on by critics as a religious huckster getting rich off the donations of gullible and simpleminded followers. Moreover, African American Pentecostal and Baptist preachers viewed him as a heretic, especially in light of his alleged statement: "If you sin against God, Grace can save you, but if you sin against Grace, God cannot save you." The quote appeared in a 1944 book about African American religious figures, and it is unclear whether Grace ever said this or merely allowed some of his followers to say and believe it. Softer but perhaps more typical were the views of a woman House of Prayer member who wrote, "[Daddy Grace] is my life, health, strength, and my salvation. . . . The more Satan oppresses me the more Daddy blesses me." A Bible lesson that appeared in House of Prayer literature once referred to Grace as "Sweet Daddy Grace Emmanuel, the present God," but Grace himself was vague and equivocal on the issue of his divinity. On one occasion in 1938 he said to a reporter, "Do I look like God? I don't regard myself as God." On other occasions when asked if he was God, he replied, "Some people say that I am,"[16] a phrase remarkably similar to Jesus's question to his disciples, "Who do people say that I am?"

FATHER DIVINE

Daddy Grace may have compared his Mann Act conviction to Christ's, and he sometimes implied that he might be God, but his statements were never as strong as those of George Baker. Baker was born sometime after the Civil War, perhaps between 1877 and 1883. It is hard to say precisely the year of his birth because of a lack of records and the contradictory statements he made as an adult. We are also unsure where he was born and raised, although it was most likely in the so-called Black Belt region of the American Southeast. He may have come from one of the Sea Islands off the coast of South Carolina and Georgia, where African culture, language, and tradition survived more strongly than anywhere else in the United States.

In 1906 Baker met Samuel Morris. Having read in I Corinthians 3 the words "Know ye not that you are the temple of God and that the Spirit of God dwells in you," Morris understood this to mean that he was God. He took to crashing black worship services in Baltimore, where he would walk to the podium and declare, "I am the Father Eternal."[17] This usually led to his physical expulsion. On one of these occasions Morris was befriended by Baker, and the two took up with a third individual named John Hickerson, who was one of Morris's followers. From 1907 to 1912 Morris, Baker, and Hickerson teamed up as a trinity. Morris was "Father Jehovia," Baker "the Messenger," and Hickerson "Saint John Divine Bishop." The threesome broke up in 1912 when Saint John headed off to New York City to found a church, and Baker headed back to the South as a traveling preacher. There, Baker first claimed that he was divine, much as Morris had done in Baltimore.

Many women in Georgia and South Carolina left their husbands, families, and churches to follow this divine figure. On at least two occasions authorities charged Baker with insanity, and he spent time in both jail and a mental institution, but his friendship with a visiting scholar at Valdosta State College in Georgia and the scholar's lawyer friend helped him win his freedom each time. Baker left the South in 1915 and headed for New York with a small but loyal band of followers. After three years in Brooklyn he purchased property in Sayville on Long Island and settled his flock there in 1919. That same year he married a woman named Peninniah. Her name was likely a variant taken from I Samuel 1:1–2, where the name Peninnah means "precious stone." The biblical Peninnah was one of the two wives of Elkanah, whose other wife was Hannah, the mother of Samuel. Peninniah would be Baker's partner in ministry throughout the rest of her life. When they purchased the property together, he used the name Major J. Divine, the "J" standing for "Jealous." The "Messenger" was now Major Jealous Divine, a name derived in part from a handful of Old Testament passages, such as Exodus 20:5, "For I, the Lord your God, am a jealous God," and Exodus 34:14,

"For the Lord, whose name is Jealous, is a jealous God." To his followers he became known simply as Father Divine. George Baker was no more.

The ministry grew on Long Island throughout the 1920s. Divine continued to attract African Americans for whom he was able to find good jobs as domestic servants. His home became a meeting place where the congregation
enjoyed Sunday banquets that evolved into lavish ritual feasts. By the end of
the decade hundreds met together, requiring police traffic control to accommodate the flow of people out of Harlem and Brooklyn and into Divine's suburban neighborhood. The numbers increased after the stock market crash of
1929 and the onset of the Great Depression, as more and more people came to
share in the banquets provided by Divine and his followers. Along with typically
spiritual matters, Divine taught hard work, self-reliance, and social responsibility. Those arriving from the city saw signs that read "Be of one accord, drive
slowly," and "Notice—Smoking—Intoxicating Liquors—Profane Language—
Strictly Prohibited."[18] In the mid-1920s a handful of educated whites joined the
community, making Divine's congregation one of the few integrated bodies in
New York or elsewhere in the United States. That Divine chose banquets as
the centerpiece of his ministry is especially significant, given the prohibition
against integrated dining that he encountered in his early ministry in the South.
He seems to have chosen the intimacy of the meal intentionally to foster racial
equality. As he put it, "We charge nothing. Anyone, man, woman, child, regardless of race, color or creed, can come here naked and we will clothe them,
hungry and we will feed them."[19]

As Divine's ministry grew, he encountered increasing resistance. Not only
were his claims to divinity heretical by orthodox standards of African American
Protestantism, but his social ministry was an affront to both conservative black
churches and the so-called black cults, both of which paid more attention to
otherworldly concerns than to the issues of poverty and racism that animated
much of Divine's ministry. Sectarian groups proliferated in the black community of New York City during the 1920s. Some were storefront Pentecostal
churches, while others were called cults because they centered in the highly
idiosyncratic teachings of one leader. The cults often promised everything from
instant resolution of difficult interpersonal problems to spiritual contact with
dead relatives. In the mid-1920s only about 39 percent of Harlem's churches
were storefront upstarts. By 1930 that figure was 75 percent.[20] Such groups proliferated in the face of grinding poverty brought on by the depression. In the

context of this religious ferment, Father Divine found his niche, but as was the case with Daddy Grace, preachers closer to the mainstream of black Protestantism tended to see him as a blasphemous heretic, his concern for racial equality notwithstanding. Ironically, as mainstream black preachers debated him publicly through the press, Father Divine's ministry gained a degree of legitimacy, enhancing his stature.

A more immediate problem for Father Divine began in the early 1930s. The influx of African Americans into suburban Long Island bothered white neighbors, and authorities became suspicious of Divine. They wondered how he paid for the elaborate banquets and his other expensive activities. In response to complaints and financial questions, the Suffolk County district attorney employed two attractive black women to infiltrate the movement. In the course of their covert investigation they sought to eavesdrop on Divine's conversations and even feigned seduction in order to entice him into giving them information. Not only was no information forthcoming, the two found Divine to be incorruptible. The next step was to move against Divine on the issue of disturbing the peace.

Like Daddy Grace and McPherson, Divine emphasized vibrant and ecstatic worship at his Long Island banquets. Many were healed of various afflictions at these meetings, although Father Divine neither engaged in overt faith healing nor claimed special power. As the community in Long Island grew, the worship services often lasted long into the night, prompting frequent noise complaints from neighbors. In November 1931 the Long Island police clashed with Divine's followers, and the confrontation turned tense and momentarily violent. An assistant district attorney crashed through the back door of Divine's home and was knocked unconscious by a roundhouse from one of Divine's men. With deputies, firemen, and deputized citizens all at the ready, Divine and the DA negotiated a surrender. Divine instructed 80 followers to accept arrest, board buses, and head off to jail peacefully. Fifty-five of the 80 paid the $5 fine and were released. As one put it, "If singing the praises of God is disorderly conduct, then I plead guilty."[21] Divine and the others, however, decided to contest the charges.

On November 21, as legal measures proceeded, more than 600 residents of Sayville met to discuss ways of ridding their community of Divine. The attendance of about 40 of Divine's followers ensured that the meeting would be tense and confrontational. Concerns ranged from the decline in property values that resulted from the influx of blacks into Sayville, to the fact that white women were joining Divine's movement. One such woman was a former governess to the children of a leading state Republican. Authorities had her committed to a state asylum to be treated for "religious mania." As the white residents hissed and booed, a California lawyer whom Divine had authorized to speak at the meeting told them that if it was the will of the community, the group would leave Long Island.[22]

As had been the case back when he was first arrested in Georgia, Father Divine once again attracted the legal support of a fine lawyer. This time assistance came in the form of James C. Thomas, a former assistant United States Attorney who sent a message that he would represent Divine and seek a permanent injunction prohibiting the residents of Sayville from interfering with the worship services in Heaven, which was the name Divine had given his home.[23] Despite Thomas's efforts, Divine was convicted. During the trial several witnesses said they had never heard Divine claim that he was God. At least two said they believed he was, regardless of whether he claimed divinity. A Boston University student testified, "I believe that the same as everybody who has God in them, Divine is the perfected expression of God." Once again race mixing and the presence of white women in Divine's congregation came to the fore. Divine's white female secretary was grilled particularly hard by the DA, then the judge had the DA interrogate her privately to determine whether she was underage. During the case the judge himself questioned Divine's followers whenever he determined the DA was not vigilant enough. Then the judge instructed the jurors to keep in mind that the issue at stake was neither Divine's religious beliefs nor those of his followers. Rather, the issue was whether Divine used religion as a cloak to cover a crime. "There may be those who believe this defendant is God," the judge added. "There are undoubtedly many who believe he is not God, and those who do not believe he is God are entitled to have their rights protected the same as those who believe he is God."[24] On June 4 Divine was sentenced to a year in jail and fined $500.

During sentencing the judge made a series of disparaging remarks, pointing out that Divine's real name was George Baker and that he was not from Providence, Rhode Island, as Divine had claimed, but from the South. The judge also mentioned hearsay evidence that Divine took the income of his followers and used it for his own gain. The judge concluded, "I have information that this man is not a moral man but immoral. I believe that he is not a useful member of society but a menace to society." Four days later the judge died of a heart attack.[25] According to one report, Divine responded, "I hated to do it," but the statement cannot be confirmed.

Divine was released on bail while awaiting appeal. In January 1933 the conviction was overturned and the original trial court ordered to repay Divine's fines. Still, the ordeal of 1932 transformed Divine into a martyr within the black community of New York City. In the months between his arrest and trial he preached to overflow crowds in Harlem, requiring police escorts through throngs of people crowded outside the hall where he was scheduled to speak. Clearly, the time had come for him to move out of Sayville and into the city. In 1933 Divine and Peninniah, now known as Mother Divine, moved the headquarters of the ministry to Harlem, where they rented an apartment building they called Number One Heaven.

It was no accident that both Divine and Daddy Grace ended up in Harlem. Around the turn of the twentieth century, investors built Harlem as a planned neighborhood for whites. Anticipating economic growth, they overbuilt and could not fill their apartment buildings. Out of necessity, the developers welcomed black people to rent in Harlem, and the area began a slow transformation that accelerated during the Great Migration, which began during World War I. The Great Migration saw African Americans from the rural South move to the urban North to take industrial jobs, many of them in New York. Divine himself had been part of this migration in 1915 when he moved to Brooklyn before going to Long Island. Many African Americans coming from the South ended up in Harlem, which paved the way for the Harlem Renaissance.

Also known at the time as the New Negro movement, the Harlem Renaissance was an integral part of the Roaring Twenties. This was a remarkable period of development for African American culture, and the movement marked the first time in American history that mainstream white institutions took note of African American artistic endeavors. In particular, major presses began to publish the works of black writers. James Weldon Johnson, Claude McKay, and Jean Toomer were among the early renowned black authors of the Harlem Renaissance, followed quickly by Langston Hughes and Zora Neale Hurston. The movement also contributed to the development of jazz and blues music, and Harlem contained some of the most exciting nightlife in the nation. Whites and blacks were drawn to the Apollo Theater and clubs such as the Savoy that featured a burgeoning group of musicians that included Bessie Smith, Louis

Armstrong, and Duke Ellington. Ellington began performing at Harlem's famed Cotton Club in 1927. By the mid-1930s, however, the Harlem Renaissance was spent, due in part to the Great Depression. Nevertheless, Harlem remained the most important African American population center in the nation and as such attracted the attention of both Divine and Grace.

Divine's overall ministry became known as the Peace Mission, and he taught members a form of communal economics that allowed them to thrive even during the depression. Instructed to reject credit and therefore debt, they paid cash for everything, and no one was to accept charity of any kind. On at least one occasion a woman who wished to join the Peace Mission was first required to pay back government relief money she had received almost five years before. Only when she presented a receipt for the $148.80 was she allowed to join.[26] Although such repayment may appear to be legalistic, it was consistent with the restitution that Peace Mission members made for old debts and thefts. The history of the mission is replete with stories of unsuspecting people receiving restitution from former employees converted by Father Divine. One man contacted a railroad company in Georgia, confessing that he rode the rails 40 years before. "Enclosed find 66 cents for the two rides," the man wrote. Another woman sent $3 to the drugstore proprietor she had worked for 16 years earlier, writing "I took candy & Icecream, and ate it while on the job. . . . I had no intention of ever paying for these things, but since Father Divine, God Almighty has entered into my heart, not only mine but also 22 million of us. He has absolutely changed our minds and bodies."[27]

Father Divine taught his followers to live upstanding lives free from drugs, alcohol, cigarettes, and sexual immorality. Peace Mission centers often policed their communities vigilante style, running off thugs and drug dealers. In the year following the establishment of a Peace Mission in Los Angeles, the chief of police reported that arrests in the area declined by 2,600. In New York another police leader said he wished everyone in Harlem would join the Peace Mission, and city officials once estimated that Divine had saved New York millions in welfare payments.

Peace Mission members most committed to the cause were known as angels. They shared all goods with each other and lived in community. Others, known as children, kept their private property but contributed generously and often paid rent to live in one of the Peace Mission centers. Father Divine declined outside contributions and frequently turned down speaking engagements worth thousands of dollars. The movement sustained itself through the contributions of its members. Angels and children who ran either their own or Peace Mission businesses sold the goods they produced at fair prices, not at the highest price the goods could fetch in an open market. While Divine owned practically nothing personally, the Peace Mission through the cooperation of its members operated a variety of businesses—shops, groceries, dry cleaning operations, barbershops, apartment buildings, and even farming collectives. Members were expected to be celibate even within marriage, largely because their earthly bodies were considered representations of the spiritual. Rather than indulging the flesh, members were taught to keep their bodies pure in order to keep their spirits undefiled.

By the mid-1930s, Divine's Peace mission operated Number One Heaven and a variety of businesses in Harlem as well as a farming cooperative in Ulster County, New York, modeled on the early Christian community recorded in the book of Acts. As had been the case in Sayville, the presence of about 2,000 Peace Mission members at the cooperative caused a stir. A minor annoyance was the practice of taking spiritual names. The new names caused record-keeping problems with authorities. For example, the public school system of Ulster County announced in 1938 that schoolchildren would not be allowed to use their heavenly names on school records. The judge handling the dispute explained, "Imagine what will happen to the discipline in a school where a teacher is required to address a boy as 'Great Bear' or a girl as 'Bright Beautiful.'"[28] On another occasion an immigrant woman from Barbados declined U.S. citizenship when the judge refused to allow her to sign government documents with her heavenly name "Love Nut." Two other followers were denied the right to vote because they insisted on signing their names "John the Baptist" and "Love and Do Right."[29]

DADDY GRACE VERSUS FATHER DIVINE

In 1938 Father Divine's Peace Mission ministry collided with Daddy Grace's United House of Prayer for All People. The encounter resulted from Grace's calculated effort to take down a rival.

The year before, Divine and the Peace Mission experienced several controversies that seemed to signal that the movement might be ripe for a fall. There was a violent encounter at Peace Mission headquarters in April, when three men arrived during a late-night worship meeting and served Father Divine with a civil suit alleging he had defrauded one of his members of $2,000. In several instances disgruntled Peace Mission members tried to recoup the money they had given to the organization. The process servers walked to the pulpit as Father Divine was preaching and slapped the papers on his chest. A fight ensued, and one of the men serving the suit was stabbed with an ice pick. Divine fled and was found a few days later hiding behind a furnace in the basement of a house in Milford, Connecticut. By 3:00 the morning following his arrest, about 500 of his followers had gathered in a peaceful protest outside his jail cell.[30]

Authorities eventually cleared Divine of all charges, but there was more trouble that year. Just a few days after the riot at Number One Heaven, one of the residence dorms at the Ulster County commune burned. Some angels had to leap from windows to escape, landing on the ground in singed nightgowns. The riot and the fire compounded an ongoing property dispute between Divine and one of his followers who went by the name Faithful Mary. While Divine was in hiding in Connecticut, she seized control of the property the two had quarreled over, denounced Divine publicly, and took some of his followers out of the Peace Mission into her rival movement. She then publicly accused Divine of sexual misconduct and racketeering. Then in May a former member named Verinda Brown won a court decision against Divine for return of money she and her husband had given to the Peace Mission. Divine appealed, and the matter bogged down in the courts for years, but other former members, emboldened by Brown's apparent victory, also sued Divine for return of donations. Divine's movement suffered further when John the Revelator, a key leader, was found guilty of violating the Mann Act for seducing the 17-year-old daughter of two Peace Mission members and transporting the girl from Denver to California. Later two other members were found guilty of child neglect when one of their children died of tuberculosis.[31]

On the heels of this very bad year for Father Divine, Daddy Grace came to town and heard that the building that housed Peace Mission headquarters might be for sale. While Divine and his followers referred to the building as Number One Heaven, the New York *Times* called it a "ramshackle tenement." The building was owned by a New York bank and was rented in the name of one of Divine's followers, Blessed Purin Heart. When Grace learned that the bank was interested in selling the property, he instructed one of his business associates to arrange to purchase it for $20,000, to be paid in full within one month. Hoping the bank would let Divine's followers stay in the building, Purin Heart countered with an offer of $16,000. Grace announced publicly that he intended to open in Harlem the northern headquarters for the United House of Prayer for All People. The advisor who executed the purchase for Grace told reporters, "God is dethroned. Divine has usurped his place. God is still in heaven."[32] Grace told the Peace Mission residents that they were welcome to stay if they wanted to experience a real work of God. As for Divine, Grace told reporters, "I will not drive him out of Harlem. . . . I will just let him stay. Poor fellow. . . . I will give him peace and pity."[33]

If Grace thought the purchase of one building out from under Father Divine would undo the Peace Mission, he was sadly mistaken. At the time Peace Mission members owned 3 apartment buildings, 9 houses, several meeting halls that contained dormitories, 25 restaurants, 6 groceries, 10 barbershops, 10 cleaning stores, and a couple dozen huckster wagons from which were sold clams, oysters, and fresh vegetables. They also owned a coal business that ran trucks from mines in Pennsylvania into Harlem.[34] Out in Ulster County the Peace Mission ran a 75-acre farm cooperative, which was about to become much larger.

Divine countered the notion that he had been bought out by Grace by saying the building had actually been sold "according to my instructions." In a public statement he said, "I had instructed those of my followers who had asked my advice, to have the owners to sell the building if they desired to, for we have aplenty, aplenty of buildings."[35] He reiterated three times that the building's sale had been according to his will, sounding less convincing each time. A few weeks later, after Grace paid off the note, one of Divine's followers told reporters the building was too small for the Peace Mission anyway. This came amid rumors that Divine was thinking about building a skyscraper.[36] Grace and some of his followers held a House of Prayer–style worship service in mid-June to celebrate the opening of their new Harlem headquarters.

Not to be outdone, in late July Divine purchased the Krum Elbow estate, which stood across the Hudson River from President Franklin Roosevelt's Hyde Park. The new estate enhanced the Peace Mission's Ulster County properties and included 500 acres of orchards and vineyards and more than 25 buildings. A week later, in early August, Divine's followers purchased a 50-room mansion on Madison Avenue at the edge of Harlem that was to serve as Divine's private residence. In both cases Divine and his followers claimed that he did not own these properties personally but rather his followers did. One of Divine's white assistants arranged the mansion purchase. When Father Divine showed up for an inspection of the property, the seller was astounded to see that a black man was buying the home. "I'm Father Divine, peace," Divine told the owner, who then showed him the property. Although the Peace Mission experienced problems in 1937, 1938 became a year of expansion. Grace's February purchase of Number One Heaven notwithstanding, by summer Father Divine's movement rolled on to new heights. In light of the Krum Elbow and Madison Avenue purchases, the New York *Times* ran a story in August entitled "The Divine Movement Waxes," which recounted the astounding acquisitions that had taken place over the previous few years.[37]

In 1940 Father Divine incorporated the Peace Mission, largely to protect assets from members who wanted to leave the movement and take their investment with them. The formalization marked a departure from Father Divine's former preference for loose organization and little hierarchy. The bylaws made him the unquestioned and absolute leader of the movement. The impetus for this momentous shift was Verinda Brown's suit in 1937, which was finally resolved with her being awarded the $7,000 she had invested in the Peace Mission. By 1942 Father Divine faced the choice of paying up or going to prison. Instead, he left New York altogether and moved with several hundred of his closest followers to Philadelphia. Largely abandoning the sort of populist and utopian reform he had led in Harlem and Ulster County, Father Divine became increasingly conservative in the final decades of his life. Like J. Frank Norris and other white fundamentalists, he turned his attention to fighting those he believed were subversive to America, communists and labor unions in particular. Like many white conservatives, he often equated the two. In 1951, in a statement that could have been uttered by Norris, Father Divine responded to strikes that he believed threatened the Korean War effort by saying "I will not tolerate it, strikes, and such as that, to try to retard the advancement of our defense . . . and I know it is Communistic . . . inspired by atheism and Nazism and other isms that spell division, to undermine the foundations of our government, of which we all revere."[38]

Divine's biographer believes the anticommunist crusade gave Father Divine a sense late in life that he was still on the cutting edge of something radical when in fact the Peace Mission movement had lost its energy and its reason for existence. As the postwar economic boom made the depression but a memory, the Promised Land cooperative of Ulster County and the other communal living centers became less appealing. With the exception of a core in Philadelphia, Newark, and Harlem, most Peace Mission centers and their businesses shut down.

In 1946 Father Divine appeared in a Philadelphia Peace Mission service with a 21-year old Canadian woman and announced that they had married. Her name was Sweet Angel. Peninniah, Mother Divine, had died in 1937, but no one was quite sure what had happened to her, and all were afraid to ask. Father Divine had never made her death public because he had taught his followers that they would not experience death. "If you die, you are not of me," he said often.[39] In announcing his marriage to Sweet Angel, Father Divine said that she and Mother Divine were one and the same. "Mrs. Divine presently, as you see her, is the reproduction and reincarnation of the spirit and the nature and the characteristics of Mother Divine."[40] This reincarnation was hard to swallow given that Sweet Angel was thin, white, and attractive whereas Peninniah had been a large black woman a head taller than Father Divine and much heavier. Over the next two decades the young Sweet Angel cum Mother Divine II matured into a steady leader as Father Divine prepared her to succeed him. In the mid-1950s a follower donated the 32-room Woodmont Estate outside Philadelphia. Overlooking more than 70 acres of gardens, Woodmont was a beautiful and lavish setting in which to live out retirement. After 1955, Father Divine made few public appearances, and his prolonged periods of seclusion often prompted rumors that he had died. He finally did in 1965, not long after passage of the Voting Rights Act, one of the crowning achievements of the civil rights movement. He was too old and spent to play any role, but he believed his spirit was one with the message of equality and integration that Martin Luther King, Jr. and other civil rights leaders preached. Of course King and his followers were orthodox Christians in contrast to Divine and Grace.

THE MEANING OF GRACE AND DIVINE

As African Americans were uprooted from their sense of place in the rural South, they became open to new forms of religion, such as those offered by Grace and Divine. In many ways innovation has always been a significant part of black Protestantism. Scholars of black religion in America highlight the ways in which experiences in Africa prepared slaves in colonial America for revivalism in the eighteenth-century Great Awakening. African religions tended to be mystical, experiential, and ecstatic. When revivals swept the colonies from the 1740s to the 1760s, many slaves responded to the message that God's Holy Spirit would fill one immediately in the experience of being born again. The result was the nearly complete conversion of African American slaves to revivalistic Protestantism by the 1830s. Just as Protestantism changed African Americans, however, they also modified Protestantism, and black religion became a distinct type of American Christianity. When southern blacks migrated to the cities after 1915, they were well prepared for new experiences, and their uprootedness often left them searching for a cultural anchor. Because of segregation, black worshippers turned to black preachers for a sense of religious assurance.

As the lines of segregation hardened, African American religion traveled along a separate track from that of the whites we have seen in this book. Early Pentecostalism provided the closest example of a truly integrated faith, and McPherson's movement always had a smattering of black believers. By the 1920s, however, even Pentecostalism was conforming to the cultural pattern of segregation. When we combine the historical development of a distinctly African American type of religion, entrenched segregation of the 1920s, and the displacement that African Americans experienced in the Great Migration to northern urban centers, we can better understand two things:

1. Why so many African Americans were attracted to the ministries of Daddy Grace and Father Divine.
2. Why African American religion, whether orthodox or heretical, traveled on a separate track from white religion during the Roaring Twenties.

This pattern of largely separate religion for whites and blacks persists into our own time and manifests itself in our own culture wars. While white Protestants of the Roaring Twenties fought the fundamentalist-modernist controversy that we saw in chapter 4, many black Protestants were following the likes of Daddy Grace and Father Divine, engaging in highly experimental forms of religion that existed on the boundary between orthodox Christianity and Christian heresy. White fundamentalists such as Billy Sunday, J. Frank Norris,

J. Gresham Machen, and William Jennings Bryan paid almost no attention to black religion. At the same time, they viewed the much milder innovations of liberals such as Harry Emerson Fosdick as a monumental threat to the faith. Black religion was the sole American institution independent of white control. Because these separate and different religious tracks persist into our own time, not many African American people of faith have joined the culture wars fought by the white Christian Right. White fundamentalists and evangelicals are overwhelmingly Republican, while black evangelicals, like African Americans in general, tend to be Democrats.

In our own religiously segregated culture black religion continues to be highly experimental and experiential. Largely free from the concerns that occupy much of white Protestantism, black religion focuses on individual experience, political freedom, social justice, and equality—the same concerns that animated Father Divine and Daddy Grace. Black religion today ranges from the orthodox Protestant perspective of T. D. Jakes, who like Grace is known as Bishop, to Louis Farrakhan and the Nation of Islam, which is considered unorthodox by Christians and Muslims alike—a double heresy, so to speak.

Throughout the twentieth century the marginalization that segregation caused for African Americans had the salutary effect of leaving black religious figures more free to experiment and to avoid white culture war. Nowhere was this more significant than in the leading religious issues of the 1920s: Prohibition, the fundamentalist-modernist controversy, and the Scopes trial. Black believers and black religious leaders supported abstinence from alcohol, opposed liberal theology, and opposed evolution, yet they played almost no part in those controversies. Few joined the predominately white, Anglo-Saxon Prohibition movement; almost none participated in the fundamentalist-modernist controversy; and there was not a single black spokesperson at the Scopes trial. Likewise, African Americans played no part in Protestant efforts to censor salacious literature in the obscenity wars that are the subject of the next chapter or in the religiously contentious presidential election of 1928. As we have seen, however, African American religious leaders, such as Daddy Grace and Father Divine, participated fully in bombast and scandal on a scale that rivaled Aimee Semple McPherson and J. Frank Norris. Black believers were very much a part of the public religion of the 1920s, but when it came to white culture war, they either took a pass or were not allowed to participate.

CHAPTER 9

CENSORSHIP AND THE OBSCENITY WARS

One of the fascinating aspects of the culture wars of the Roaring Twenties was the way in which fundamentalist and liberal Protestants aligned and realigned. They fought against each other over evolution in public schools and over theology in Protestant denominations, but they joined together in the Prohibition movement and so, too, did they align themselves on the same side of the obscenity wars. As was the case with Prohibition, Protestant efforts to censor salacious literature were motivated not so much by a desire to control people's private lives but by the belief that a democratic society needed strong families. Censorship was intended to protect the Victorian family, the place where individuals learned how to live responsibly in a free society.

In April 1926 H. L. Mencken was arrested on Boston Common for selling a copy of his magazine, *American Mercury.* The magazine carried an article entitled "Hatrack," an excerpt from Herbert Asbury's forthcoming book *Up from Methodism.* "Hatrack" was the allegedly true story of a prostitute who plied her trade in two cemeteries in Farmington, Missouri, where Asbury grew up. Townsfolk nicknamed her "Fanny Fewclothes" or Hatrack, the latter because she was as skinny as a hat rack. She attended the local Methodist church on Sunday evenings, where members avoided and scorned her rather than offering her the acceptance, forgiveness, and salvation she desired. Following the service she walked through town past the post office and the men who lingered there, a subtle advertisement that she was now open for business. A trickle of men would follow her to the cemetery for sex.[1]

In Boston, a liberal Protestant watchdog group known as the Watch and Ward Society condemned "Hatrack" as obscene. The society exercised considerable power over the city's literature, and in 1915 had helped create the Boston Booksellers Committee, comprised of three members representing the bookstores of Boston and three from the Watch and Ward Society. The committee screened published materials that were believed to be obscene. Fearing prosecution under Massachusetts's obscenity law, bookstores typically shied away from anything the Committee condemned, which included "Hatrack." The Watch and Ward Society, working through the Booksellers Committee, exercised enough cultural influence in Boston to keep obscenity under wraps.

Having heard that his magazine had been effectively banned in Boston, Mencken traveled there to test the obscenity law. Secretary of the Watch and Ward Society J. Frank Chase agreed to cooperate with Mencken to bring the issue to the courts in a test case. Chase volunteered to purchase a copy of the magazine from Mencken at Brimstone Corner, on Boston Common, across the street from the renowned evangelical Park Street Church. Thousands of people turned out to witness the arrest, which they knew was imminent as Mencken's departure from Baltimore had been heralded in newspapers the day before. Once arrested, Mencken was taken immediately before a judge who announced that he would personally read "Hatrack" and rule whether the story was obscene. The courtroom was packed as the multitude who had witnessed the magazine sale tried to enter. One court official said it was as if Boston were having its own version of the Scopes trial. In response to the charges, Mencken and his attorney filed a $50,000 suit against Chase and the Watch and Ward Society for interfering with business.

The suit implied that the society had been after Mencken since the previous September when he published an article by A. L. S. Wood entitled "Keeping the Puritans Pure." Wood laid out in unflattering detail how Chase and the Watch and Ward Society controlled the Boston literary world. Two months later an article by Charles Angoff entitled "Boston Twilight" began: "Once the Athens of America, Boston now plunges downward toward the cultural level of Port au Prince and Knoxville, Tenn. . . . [L]outs and fakes and rogues have overrun the town, and an idea would feel as much at home here as the Pope at a Ku Klux Konklave." The article referred to the Watch and Ward Society as a group of "smut hounds" hell bent on keeping Boston in the gutter.[2] "Hatrack," the articles by Wood and Angoff, the arrest on the Common, and the lawsuit were all part of Mencken's effort to end what he called the Watch and Ward Society's "organized terrorism." In short, Mencken had declared culture war.[3]

In Farmington, Missouri, the chamber of commerce did not appreciate the notoriety "Hatrack" brought the town. In a meeting attended by local ministers, the chamber passed a resolution requesting that U.S. Postmaster General Harry S. New bar the story from the U.S. mails and also urged local magazine dealers to boycott that month's *American Mercury.* The U.S. Postmaster complied, ordering not only that the April issue of *American Mercury* be barred from the mails but also that every newspaper and magazine that had reprinted "Hatrack" be similarly banned. The postmaster's directive came two days after Mencken's case was tossed out of court by Judge Parmenter, who decided that "Hatrack" was not obscene. "I have read every article in the magazine given me yesterday and find them all intellectual and of a serious nature," the judge said in his ruling. Commenting on "Hatrack" specifically he added, "It is a rather frank expression, but at the same time an intellectual description of prostitution in a small town, and I found nothing in it that would arouse sexual impulses or lascivious thoughts, as prohibited by the [Massachusetts obscenity] statute."[4]

Off the hook for criminal obscenity, Mencken's attorney convinced a second judge, Judge Morton, to issue a temporary restraining order against Chase and the Watch and Ward Society. In issuing the injunction, Morton asked, "May an official organization, actuated by a sincere desire to benefit the public and to strengthen the administration of the law, carry out its purpose by threatening with criminal prosecution those who deal in magazines which it regards as illegal?"[5] Within a month a federal judge had issued a restraining order against the U.S. Postmaster General that ended the ban on sending "Hatrack" through the U.S. mails. By that time a playwright had obtained the rights to the story, and plans were in the works to turn it into a stage production.

The Watch and Ward Society was to censorship what the Anti-Saloon League was to Prohibition. Both organizations sought to outlaw something they believed was injurious to society—liquor for the Anti-Saloon League and salacious and obscene literature and films for the Watch and Ward Society. Those who opposed both organizations used an argument based on the modern, liberal view of individual freedom of expression. Before the mid-1920s, the American Civil Liberties Union (ACLU), founded in 1917, focused on defending only political speech under the free speech clause of the First Amendment. The organization's defense of Mencken and "Hatrack" marked the beginning of a new emphasis on defending the right of artistic expression against Victorian censorship.[6] This was another front in the culture wars of the Roaring Twenties.

TWO VIEWS OF RIGHTS

Prohibition engaged the question over what kind of freedom America should have. That struggle saw fundamentalist and liberal Protestants on the same side working as allies against Catholics, ethnic Protestants, and secular liberals who argued for the personal freedom to drink alcohol. On the issue of censorship, liberal Protestants led the way, with fundamentalists and Roman Catholics cheering from the sidelines. Opposing this coalition were cultural liberals (also called cultural modernists) who believed in individual freedom. Cultural liberals were distinguished from theological liberals precisely on this issue of censorship. Theological liberals retained the Protestant idea that they were the custodians of society and responsible for public morality, while cultural liberals believed that an individual's freedom of expression trumped corporate notions of morality.

The liberal Protestant journal *Christian Century* occasionally weighed in on the censorship issue and conveyed the custodial idea. In 1923 the magazine's editor made the explicit comparison between censorship and Prohibition, favoring both against the argument for personal liberty. "The personal liberty argument," the editor wrote, "so long as it is kept in general terms, is either perfectly meaningless or perfectly anarchistic." In the editor's view the personal liberty argument rested on "the concealed major premise that every person has a right to do anything that he pleases."[7] The editor acknowledged that neither Prohibition nor censorship laws would necessarily produce upright behavior, but he stressed that such laws helped create conditions where high morals were likely. The editor also noted that both Prohibition and censorship could violate personal liberty. For the *Christian Century* editor, the question was how to balance a proper understanding of personal freedom with the need for society to reinforce its values. Moreover, he repeatedly argued that "it is of no use to argue for or against specific proposals with rhetorical appeals and general principles, or by mouthing of such watchwords as liberty on one side and purity on the other."[8]

The editor believed that these issues should be considered on a case-by-case basis. Prohibition was a simpler matter than censorship. Alcoholic beverages were a readily identifiable commodity, whereas it was difficult to say exactly what constituted obscenity and therefore difficult to determine what should be censored. For this reason the cultural liberals argued for maximum personal liberty lest an individual's freedom of expression be squelched unjustly. The *Christian Century* editor, however, was not so willing to err on the side of freedom. Rather, he argued that no matter how difficult, policing obscenity was necessary. "The interests involved are too great to be ignored," the editor argued. "One who does not see that the children of today are being exposed to most demoralizing influences in some of the moving pictures and some of the periodicals which fall just short of being illegally indecent must either be very blind or must himself have very low standards of decency."[9]

Mencken's attorney in the "Hatrack" affair was Arthur Garfield Hays of the ACLU; he saw things quite differently from the *Christian Century* editor. As a cultural liberal, Hays argued that censoring Mencken's magazine was a violation of liberty. "It is getting down to the fundamentals of American society," he told the judge. He then asked whether a small group of people such as the Watch and Ward Society could set itself up as the "custodians of the morals of the majority." "Shall this minority, which gets a certain reaction from the reading of certain articles because of its state of mind, then impose its decision upon the majority?" he asked.[10] Ironically, just eight months earlier Hays had been part of the ACLU's defense team at the Scopes trial in Dayton, Tennessee. In Dayton, William Jennings Bryan and the prosecution had asked the same question Hays was now asking—whether the minority should be permitted to impose its views on the majority. Only a small minority of people in Tennessee wanted evolution taught in the schools, Bryan had argued, yet Hays and the ACLU claimed that the minority had the right to teach it.

Hays was not necessarily inconsistent. At Dayton he and the other ACLU lawyers argued that the majority could not violate Scopes's right to teach evolution, while in Boston he argued that a minority, such as the Watch and Ward Society, could not deny Mencken's right to publish "Hatrack." Hays and the ACLU believed this was the same battle, and they believed that the starting point for adjudicating such matters was the individual and his or her rights. The power of the state, they believed, could not be used to repress Scopes's academic freedom to teach evolution anymore than Mencken's freedom of press to publish the article "Hatrack."

Chase, the Watch and Ward Society, and the *Christian Century* saw the issue in a different way. They operated from an older, communitarian system of values in which the starting place for considering public morality was the family and community, not the individual and his or her rights. They believed that no individual had the right to corrupt the morals of society. The attorney for the Watch and Ward Society argued that "Hatrack" was an immoral story that would have an adverse effect on society, especially on its youth. As such, the story undermined the notion of a good society, which could be fashioned only when there was an agreed-upon baseline of public morality.

BACKGROUND

The Massachusetts obscenity law under which Mencken was prosecuted was enacted in 1881 with the help of the Watch and Ward Society. The law made it illegal to import, publish, or distribute books, pamphlets, songs, pictures, or any other printed items that contained "obscene, indecent or impure language" or that tended "to corrupt the morals of youths."[11] This was by no means the first law that Massachusetts had against obscenity. The state's history of obscenity laws extended well back into the colonial period. Like many other states, Massachusetts passed its 1881 statute in the wake of the federal Comstock Law of 1873, which forbade selling or distributing obscene literature and art and also made it illegal to send through the mail materials having to do with abortion and birth control. As was the case with Prohibition, a national law was buttressed by state and local statutes that local authorities could enforce.

Founded in 1878, the Watch and Ward Society consisted of ministers, educators, and other prominent citizens. They operated as reformers, and the most important actors in the organization were liberal Protestants, although there were Catholics and conservative Protestants represented as well. For society members, as was the case with alcohol, obscenity was a social problem that needed to be addressed and eradicated. The motivation was not so much to control people's private lives as to shore up the community's moral foundation. Censorship of the kind pushed by the Watch and Ward Society was by no means unique to Boston. Many localities had similar organizations, and some denominational agencies tackled Prohibition and censorship together. Such was the case for the Methodist Board of Temperance, Prohibition, and Moral Reform, which worked nationally to suppress obscenity and started a major censorship campaign in the mid-1920s. Organizations working against obscenity also sought to eradicate gambling, illegal drugs, and "white slavery," which was a form of forced prostitution.[12]

By the 1920s, historian P. C. Kemeny argues, there was a growing group of intellectuals who rebelled against liberal Protestant domination of Boston. Although critics of censorship had been around since the nineteenth century, they had reached critical mass by this time, were now funded by a growing list of publishing companies, and had the support of civil libertarians such as the ACLU. For the first time, in other words, the cultural liberals had the clout to take on Boston's Protestant establishment, made up in large part of liberal Protestants.[13] Liberal Protestantism was created to harmonize Protestant theology with modern modes of thought, but the cultural liberals did not see liberal Protestants as allies. Rather, in some cases they saw liberal Protestants as worse than fundamentalists. It would be hard to imagine anyone in American history who hated fundamentalists more than Mencken, but he cared not a wit for liberal Protestants either, as his attempt to destroy the Watch and Ward Society shows. In 1931 he wrote that liberal Protestants, by "depriving revelation of all force and authority, [robbed] their so-called religion of every dignity." He was not saying he preferred fundamentalism with its high regard for the authority of scripture and its belief in the supernatural. Rather, as he continued, "[Liberal religion] becomes, in their hands, a mere romantic imposture, unsatisfying to the pious and unconvincing to the judicious."[14]

In short, Mencken and the other cultural liberals disliked Protestant liberal moralists as much as they despised fundamentalists and were not about to let either group set the moral tone for society. Cultural liberals, therefore, entered into a full-scale assault against Victorian values, and they carried out their war with a deep hatred for what they believed was nothing other than a modern form of New England Puritanism. Just as the ACLU had attempted unsuccessfully in the Scopes trial of 1925 to eradicate anti-evolution laws, so the next year Mencken sought to deal a death blow to the Watch and Ward Society and the obscenity law the organization helped enforce. As Kemeny puts it, "The ban on *American Mercury* turned Mencken from a typewriting iconoclast into a secularizing activist. Mencken was the one who began to break the Watch and Ward Society's stranglehold on reading consumption in New England."[15]

But the Watch and Ward Society would not go down without a fight. Religious groups that see themselves as custodians of culture often exert their greatest energy as they feel their authority slipping away, and this is exactly what happened in Boston.

THE BOSTON BOOK WAR

The battle between the ACLU on one side and the Watch and Ward Society with its ally the Boston Booksellers Committee on the other heated up again a year after the "Hatrack" affair. The controversy with Mencken had taken a tremendous toll on Chase, who died in November 1926. Without his steady hand and reasoned voice, the society and the committee increasingly turned to the district attorney and police commissioner for help in regulating obscenity. Early in 1927 the Boston police notified the Booksellers Committee about suspect books, hoping it would handle matters. The committee then put word out to all book dealers. Arthur Garfield Hays traveled to Boston in early March to look into the case of *The Hardboiled Virgin,* which was the first book banned this time around. He then returned to New York to confer with the book's publisher about a test case similar to the one Mencken engaged in the year before over "Hatrack." Hays called the police threat of prosecution "intimidation," but the head of the Booksellers Committee characterized the action as commonsense notification that the books might be subject to scrutiny.[16]

By April the list of books banned in Boston had grown to nine, and some leaders became increasingly embarrassed over the city's reputation. Representatives from the *Atlantic Monthly* and the Boston publishing firm Little, Brown, and Company issued a statement reading, in part: "We wish publicly and seriously to protest against the high-handed, erratic and ill-advised interference of certain public officials with the sale and distribution of books, many of them of recognized standing and freely sold elsewhere through the United States." The statement suggested that the action of the Booksellers Committee did not reflect well on the citizens of Boston and "does not represent the best sentiment of this community."[17]

Most of the books were banned because of sexually suggestive content. The novel *Elmer Gantry,* however, contained sex and hostility to religion. By traditional standards the book was both obscene and blasphemous. There have been suggestions throughout the years concerning which of the preachers of the Roaring Twenties Lewis used as a model for the fraudulent Elmer Gantry. One of the characters in the book is Sister Sharon Falconer, who seems to have been patterned after Aimee Semple McPherson. Lewis began writing the book before McPherson's great disappearance scandal of 1926, and the book came out just months after her case had been dismissed by the Los Angeles district attorney. Like McPherson, the Falconer character built a giant white tabernacle complete with a lighted cross on top, just like Angelus Temple.[18]

If Sister Falconer represents McPherson, some have suggested that J. Frank Norris was Lewis's model for the Gantry character. Norris's killing of D. E. Chipps and the subsequent murder trial also took place contemporaneously with Lewis's penning of the novel. Lewis knew of Norris by reputation but had not heard the fiery fundamentalist preach before writing *Elmer Gantry.* Ten years after the book appeared the author traveled to First Baptist Fort Worth to hear Norris. Following the service Lewis remarked that he had "satisfied a desire of a great many years standing—I went to hear Dr. J. Frank Norris preach. . . . I have never seen before so many people at church at once."[19] No doubt, Gantry was a composite character, and Lewis certainly had much to work with in the preachers of the Roaring Twenties that were his models.

The spring before *Elmer Gantry* was published, Lewis spoke in a Kansas City church where he defied God to strike him dead if God really existed. When the novel appeared the famous Kansas journalist William Allen White said that artistically God must have accepted Lewis's offer. "So far as Sinclair Lewis the artist is concerned," White said after reading the book, "God took him at his word. [Lewis] got so excited making faces at God that he forgot his craftsmanship."[20] Yale University literature professor William Lyon Phelps agreed, saying Lewis wrote the book while in a rage against religion. "The author was literally foaming at the mouth, and a great work of art is never created that way."[21] Many other ministers, scholars, Catholic priests, and even Jewish rabbis echoed these criticisms. Cardinal O'Connell of Boston said the book was an affront to all religions. Moreover, he wrote, while the book has occasional flashes of Lewis's brilliance, it was in the main "ill-conceived, poorly constructed, badly written and insufferably dull." He attributed interest in the novel to "those two nauseating ingredients—sex appeal and religious skepticism."[22] The president of the liberal Federal Council of Churches, S. Parkes Cadman, said, "The book represents a huge ocean of mud, in which the author himself is immersed."[23] Good literature or not, the book was taken quite seriously, as would be any novel that was written by a recent Pulitzer Prize (and soon to be Nobel Prize) winner. Libraries around the country began to ban

Elmer Gantry in mid-March, and the censors of Boston swung into action a month later. On April 12 District Attorney William Foley notified the Booksellers Committee that any bookstore that sold *Elmer Gantry* would be prosecuted for peddling "obscene and indecent literature." Bookstores promptly removed the book from their shelves.

While the controversy over *Elmer Gantry* unfolded in 1927, Theodore Dreiser's novel *An American Tragedy* served as another test case in the courts. Dreiser was at least as hostile to religion as Lewis. As he would say a few years later to an El Paso reporter, "Religion in America is just a total loss . . . . Boot out your El Paso ministers along with all other religionists and your city and America will be much better off. At least you will have cleared this country of just so much pure dogmatic bunk. That is all this religion is—just fool dogmatic bunk."[24]

Dreiser had been a controversial literary figure since his first novel was published in 1900. *Sister Carrie* was the story of a woman who lived in sexual sin with two men, in clear defiance of Victorian morality. She nevertheless prospered as a successful actress. Dreiser's publisher, Doubleday, tried to back out of the contract when the managing editor realized how controversial the book would be, but Dreiser was as militant for cultural liberalism as any fundamentalist was for conservative theology. He threatened to sue, and the publisher eventually relented. The book was panned as immoral and offensive by reviewers and sold very poorly. Discouraged, Dreiser waited a decade before writing another novel.[25]

By the 1920s writers such as Dreiser and others in the American intelligentsia shared values that were in direct opposition to Victorian norms. Essentially they were committed to expressing what they believed was the truth about human behavior.[26] For the Victorian mind, what was true was the ideal of Christian morality lived out in community. That was what literary figures should place before the public as something toward which people should strive. In the nineteenth century many authors did just that. For many in the literary class of the 1920s, however, the truth about human nature was revealed in the way people really lived, which is often in direct violation of Victorian ideals. Hence, Dreiser wrote *Sister Carrie,* and other literary figures wrote equally "obscene" books. When the Watch and Ward Society tried to ban such works, writers believed this was censorship of the truth, a violation of their right to engage in honest self-expression. Traditionalists, by contrast, believed censorship was merely a justifiable suppression of obscenity.

Like Sinclair Lewis, the publisher of Dreiser's *An American Tragedy,* Boni and Liveright, was interested in generating controversy and therefore book sales, but Dreiser also wanted to fight censorship. Dreiser's attorney was Arthur Garfield Hays, who wanted a reenactment of the H. L. Mencken "Hatrack" affair of the previous year. With Secretary Chase gone, however, neither the Watch and Ward Society nor the police were up for another banned book purchase on Boston Common. Instead, Hays arranged for a test case that started with a lower profile. A lieutenant from the Boston vice squad purchased a copy of *An American Tragedy* from Boni and Liveright vice president Donald Friede in the quiet office of the police superintendent. The police took a complaint to a municipal court judge asking for a ruling on the book's obscenity.[27] After taking the weekend to read the book, the municipal judge fined Boni and Liveright $100. Hays appealed the case.

Two years to the day after his arrest at police headquarters, Friede's appeals trial began. On the second day the defense team brought Clarence Darrow to the stand to read portions of Dreiser's book. He had come from Chicago to participate in the trial, just as both he and Bryan had gone to Tennessee during the Scopes trial four years before; and his presence had the same dramatic effect. A throng of people showed up hoping to get into the courtroom. When Darrow read a scene where a young woman visits a physician, the jury leaned forward in anticipation. With what one reporter called "a tenderness in his voice," Darrow read of the woman's impassioned plea for help. Hays followed, telling the jury there were over 400 passages in the Bible more risqué than the one Darrow had just read.[28] Hays's efforts notwithstanding, Friede's conviction was upheld, then he had to hurry back to New York where another book his firm had published was on trial under New York law. That book was found not to be obscene, suggesting that among the leading urban centers of the Northeast, Boston was the last bastion of censorship.

The degree to which the concern over the coarsening of literature was led by liberal Protestants was illustrated three months after Friede's appeal. Speaking at a conference in Charlottesville, Virginia, the Reverend Walter Russell Bowie denounced "the sneering estimate" of human nature that came from Dreiser and Mencken. "American history would have been an American tragedy indeed" if it had no higher interpreters than those two, he said in his keynote address. Bowie was no fundamentalist. Rather, he was the priest of Grace Episcopal Church in New York City, and the conference at which he spoke was the

Third Annual Institute of Public Affairs, convened at the University of Virginia to deal with issues of war and peace, agriculture, labor, crime, law enforcement, and other progressive concerns. Bowie made an impassioned plea for religion in public life as part of his effort to refute the intelligentsia. Referencing fundamentalists, he acknowledged, "You may think of religion as meddling interference of contentious sects. You may think of it as quarreling over dogmatic prejudices which hamper the freedom that would find the truth." Then, refuting cultural liberals who believed religion should be a private matter, Bowie cataloged the host of reforms brought about by public religion. He claimed that all of public and private life has to do with humans and therefore all areas need religious input. "Religion is needed in our public affairs because, in the first place, it helps us to believe that life means something big enough for us to be in earnest about."[29]

Bowie was not speaking against a secularist establishment that was trying to keep religion out of public life; such secularists were not yet the establishment. Rather, he was speaking for a religious establishment whose heyday was passing as it was challenged by cultural liberals. He represented the Victorians who wished to hold before society the best of what human beings could be; the secular intelligentsia, he believed, was committed to exposing the worst.

In the interim between Friede's first trial and his appeal, the book war in Boston continued. By early 1928 the list of banned books had grown to over 70. New York publishers proudly added the words "banned in Boston" to book covers, knowing it would spike sales.

However, just as public opinion turned increasingly against censorship in New York, so too did the liberal Protestant custodians of public morals eventually lose favor in Boston. One letter writer to the Boston *Herald* spoke for many when he said that censorship made Boston look like "the hickest hick town in the United States."[30] Increasingly the cultural liberals and civil libertarians used culture war tactics, such as ridicule and delegitimation, to move public opinion against the moral guardians. On the eve of Friede's appeal in 1929, Boston's intelligentsia held a Ford Hall Frolic, mocking censorship. Harvard historian Arthur Schlesinger Sr. was the occasion's toastmaster, and many notables appeared on stage, including Arthur Garfield Hays. Margaret Sanger, who had once been arrested for sending "obscene" birth control information through the mail, appeared gagged with a cloth rag. Upton Sinclair sent a telegram that was read to the audience, saying "I would rather be banned in

Boston than read anywhere else," and Clarence Darrow told the audience that the religious censors advocated waiting until we get to heaven to have fun. "[B]ut personally," he said, "I have always hated to wait that long. What if there isn't any?"[31]

In a more serious vein, the Massachusetts state chapter of the ACLU launched a major civil liberties campaign to end censorship. Many joined, including two Harvard law professors, Zechariah Chafee and Felix Frankfurter, the latter a future Supreme Court Justice. The forces opposed to censorship were gaining cultural capital practically by the day. ACLU director Roger Baldwin came to town to encourage the fight. Increasingly, opposition to censorship centered on ideas of free speech, the rights of individuals, and the First Amendment,[32] but the ACLU view of these rights was not nearly as expansive as today. In a pamphlet called "Censorship in Boston" the organization called for an end to prior restraint of the kind being practiced by the Watch and Ward Society working in conjunction with government officials. Still, ACLU activists acknowledged that indecency and obscenity could be prosecuted. The ACLU strategy was to shift adjudication from government bureaucrats to juries, believing that the latter would be more tolerant.[33]

In the fall of 1929 there erupted another phase of the Boston book controversy when a representative from the Watch and Ward Society purchased a copy of British author D. H. Lawrence's novel *Lady Chatterley's Lover*. The book and subsequent film were arguably the most controversial of the twentieth century. Lawrence had trouble finding a publisher in Britain and so had the book printed in Florence, Italy, but within two years there were four bootlegged editions circulating in the United States and United Kingdom, something that maddened Lawrence, as he made no royalties. Lawrence died in 1930 after suffering various maladies for five years, most seriously tuberculosis. Shortly thereafter expurgated versions of the book were published in New York and London that omitted the most sexually explicit passages. In the 1940s the full version of the book was published but could not be sold openly in the United States or Britain. New publishers in both countries produced the book for the express purpose of challenging its legal ban. Subsequent to the new book editions, the first of several film versions appeared in 1955 and was promptly banned by the New York State censorship board. Four years later a U.S. judge ruled that the book was not obscene, and that same year the U.S. Supreme Court overturned New York's ban on the film. The following year a jury in London ruled likewise on the book.[34]

When the Watch and Ward Society representative tried to purchase a copy of *Lady Chatterley's Lover* at the Dunster House Book Shop near Harvard Square in Cambridge in 1929, he did so under an assumed name and was told the bookstore did not carry the book. The Watch and Ward censor persisted until the bookstore ordered a copy and sold it. The society then reported the sale to police. At the trial the defense made much of the fact that the Watch and Ward Society had used subterfuge to obtain the book, much as Prohibition officials sometimes used disguises to catch bootleggers. Putting the Watch and Ward Society into the same class as Prohibition officials was a tactic intended to damage the society's reputation, and it worked. Still, the Dunster House owner was fined $500 and sentenced to a month in prison, but not before Judge Frederick Fosdick (no relation to Harry Emerson Fosdick) roundly criticized the society for its tactics. The Dunster House owner's conviction was upheld on appeal, but District Attorney Bushnell then convinced Judge Fosdick to drop the prison time, and an anticensorship organization stepped in and paid the fine. Although some conservative preachers criticized Bushnell for not upholding the law, the Dunster House defense attorney called the district attorney a hero for his stand against censorship.

Public opinion increasingly turned against the Watch and Ward Society as the decade wore on. Some prominent members quit, and contributions began to fall in large part because of the onset of the Great Depression. In the face of the society's decline, a group called the Massachusetts Citizens Committee stepped up its advocacy for revision of the state obscenity law. After extended debate, the legislature changed the law so that only a book that was considered obscene in its entirety would be restricted rather than any book merely "containing obscene, indecent or impure language or manifestly tending to corrupt the morals of youths," as had been the wording of the old law. Admitting defeat in the wake of the obscenity law's revision, in 1931 the Watch and Ward Society wrote in its annual report that it "does no more advance book censoring and cannot justly be criticized in the future on this score."[35] Mencken had won.

While the battle over *Lady Chatterley's Lover* raged in Boston, the U.S. Senate debated an amendment to the infamous Smoot-Hawley Tariff of 1929. The amendment was intended to strip customs agents of their authority to seize obscene literature shipped to American ports. In response to the proposed changes, Reed Smoot (R-Utah) threatened to read obscene passages of banned books from the Senate floor. In March 1930 crowds packed the U.S.

Senate chamber for the debate over obscenity. Smoot opened by saying "This question is one that strikes at the morals of every young boy or girl in the U.S. . . . I did not believe there were such books printed in the world. They are lower than the beasts. . . . I'd rather have a child of mine use opium than read these books." Smoot characterized *Lady Chatterley's Lover* as "damnable" and its author as a man "with a diseased mind."

Senator Bronson Cutting (R–New Mexico), who had authored the amendment that would have weakened censorship, framed the issue differently, saying "This is not a question of indecent literature; it is a question of freedom of speech and freedom of thought." Coleman Blease (D–South Carolina) responded by saying, "I'd rather see the democratic and republican form of government forever destroyed if necessary to protect the womanhood of America." *Time* magazine characterized the Senate debate between Smoot and Cutting as a clash of the new West and the old West. Smoot was "Utah-born, Mormon-educated, moral, [and] righteous," while Cutting was "New York–born, Harvard-educated, sophisticated, [and] broadminded." The final compromise restored customs agents' authority to seize suspect books but stipulated that only a judge or jury in U.S. District Court could render final judgment as to whether the works were obscene.[36] The fight over obscenity laws would continue into the 1930s and beyond in various states and at the federal level.

A SECULAR REVOLUTION

By the late 1920s there was growing resistance to Prohibition's restrictions on what people could drink. Similarly, sentiment against restricting what people could read was also on the rise. P. C. Kemeny points out that the same week in 1933 that saw the repeal of the Eighteenth Amendment also saw the forces that opposed obscenity laws win a legal battle that allowed the importation of James Joyce's previously banned book, *Ulysses*. As Kemeny puts it, the demise of cultural authority of groups such as the Watch and Ward Society resulted from "a secular revolution."[37] This secular revolution that began in the Roaring Twenties eventually succeeded in making individual rights and freedom of expression the foundation of liberal democracy. The older communitarian, Victorian way of organizing society came to be viewed as puritanical and oppressive. Cultural authority shifted from religious to secular and from a corporate and communitarian view of values to the view that individual rights alone are a sufficient foundation for democracy.[38]

Culture wars over obscenity and censorship continue in our own time but with a difference. Today, religious and communitarian forces have to make their case as outsiders arguing against a legal establishment, university culture, and media that tout individual freedom as the only possible foundation for democracy in a pluralistic culture. In the 1920s the reverse was true. The religious and communitarian forces were the establishment, but their cultural influence was fading. By the 1930s liberal Protestant forces were gravitating more and more toward the secular view of individual rights. This is because Protestants had a long history as custodians of culture. In order to maintain custodianship, liberal Protestantism needed to adjust or it would be marginalized. Moreover, liberal Protestantism had always been driven by the perceived need to adjust theology to modern modes of thought. That, in fact, is the historical definition of liberal or modernist Protestantism. During the shift toward individual rights and freedom of expression, theological liberals moved in the same direction as cultural liberals in an effort to maintain their legitimacy. Fundamentalist Protestants, by contrast, had largely forgotten what it was like to be culturally dominant and thus by the 1930s relinquished hope of shaping the culture. As has already been said, they retreated from public view while reorganizing and building institutions that would serve them when they reentered the culture wars in the 1980s, hoping once again to be a cultural force, which they did, but this time as outsiders.

CHAPTER 10

THE ELECTION OF 1928

In the midst of the Boston book wars, the nation experienced a historic election with its first Catholic presidential candidate. As was the case with the obscenity wars and Prohibition, fundamentalists and liberal Protestants fought together in the election of 1928 against their age-old Catholic rivals. Ironically, cultural liberals who opposed Protestants in the obscenity wars joined them against the Catholic candidate. All three groups—fundamentalists, liberal Protestants, and cultural liberals—appropriated the secular liberal language of individual rights against the Catholic view of church authority and communitarian values. Culture wars create odd bedfellows and ever-shifting alliances.

During his campaign Al Smith was dogged by reporters about an encyclical Pope Leo XIII had issued in 1885 condemning separation of church and state, among other things. Asked repeatedly by reporters, "What do you have to say about the pope's encyclical?" Smith at one point responded in exasperation, "Will someone please tell me what the hell an encyclical is?" The election of 1928 was one of the low points in American history for Protestant anti-Catholicism. Many Protestants worried that a Catholic president would take marching orders from the pope, and many refused to believe that Catholics could be truly American.

THE HAPPY WARRIOR

Born in 1873, Alfred E. Smith Jr. was the grandson of immigrants. His mother's parents were from Ireland, his father's from Germany. He was born and reared on New York City's Lower East Side. His father died when he was 12 years old, and the family pressures created by his father's passing required Al to start working after the seventh grade. It was just as well, given that Al was not much of a student. He became a "truck chaser," which meant that he ran along the waterfront chasing his employer's horse-drawn trucks so he could tell them where to go next. During the 1880s and 1890s he progressed from truck chaser to office boy, took a job at the fish market, then moved to the Davison Steam Pump Works in Brooklyn, improving his salary with each move. With a booming voice and a gift for gab, Smith was hired as an announcer for the John Sullivan–James Corbett boxing match in 1892. The bout, billed as the Battle of New Orleans, marked the end of the bare-knuckled era. Reading the blow-by-blow description via teletype, Smith relayed the action to a throng of Irish American boxing fans who idolized their hero Sullivan. Smith used this same gift to talk himself out of many a jam, usually employing an excellent sense of humor. While not large or powerful as his father had been, Al was athletic. When bicycling became the rage in the 1870s, riding clubs appeared across the country. Smith entered coasting races and also became a member of the Century Club by riding 100 miles in a single day.[1]

As a young man Smith was mentored by Henry Campbell, a wealthy grocery store owner who often took orphans and fatherless boys under his wing. Campbell was a major Democratic Party donor and friend to President Grover Cleveland. In 1895 Campbell secured Smith a position with the new mayor's office serving as a commissioner of jurors. In that job Smith tracked down people who had not appeared for jury duty. His association with Campbell and subsequent work in the mayor's office put Smith squarely in the middle of a political effort to reform the corrupt political machine known as Tammany Hall, so named for the hall where the group's meetings originally took place. Smith worked his way up the ladder of appointive positions in city government, and in 1903 party leaders nominated him to run as the Democratic candidate for the New York State Assembly. Smith won easily and in January 1904 went off to Albany for his first stint as an elected official.

As a state assemblyman Smith became a practical-minded and hardworking legislator. In his early years the upstate Republicans dominated the assembly, leaving Democrats from New York City as a minority on committees and with little power. Shoved to the side, Smith spent most of his first year with little to do but observe and try to figure out how the state legislature worked.

With his conversational skills and generally gregarious nature, he ingratiated himself with both Democrats and Republicans. In his second year he gained recognition when the newly elected progressive Republican assembly speaker appointed him chair of the Committee on Insurance. Smith distinguished himself in that role, and Tammany leaders as well as New York City reformers began to take notice. While Smith's activities on the floor of the assembly usually put him at odds with Republicans, he nevertheless cultivated friendships with his adversaries after hours by inviting them to a weekly dinner he hosted. With his humor and charm he forged alliances across party lines that would serve him well in the future. By the end of the decade Smith was called "the Bowery statesman" for his leadership among the minority Democrats at the state capital of Albany. Despite his efforts as a reformer, he was opposed by Progressives who would never trust Tammany Hall.

In 1910 New York state politics changed dramatically. As was the case in several states across the country, the Democratic Party made significant gains in New York, winning both houses of the legislature. Smith became majority leader of the assembly. Immigration was largely responsible for the Democratic victories of 1910. The Republican Party had been historically the party of Anglo-Protestant insiders, so immigrants and their offspring gravitated to the Democrats. Republicans lost about half of the assembly seats that represented the city. The Democrats who replaced them were like Smith, Tammany Hall politicians. Progressive reformers usually opposed Smith because he was a Tammany man, but he continued to evolve as a reformer himself. In 1911 the Triangle Shirtwaist Company fire resulted in the deaths of 146 New York City residents, 125 of them women. In the wake of the tragedy, women's rights activist Frances Perkins went to Albany pushing for a bill that would limit the working hours of women in industry. Smith befriended Perkins and became vice chair of a commission that investigated working conditions. The commission helped change the way people in New York perceived government, leading many to accept the state's role in regulating the workplace. Several pieces of legislation the commission recommended became law, giving New York the most progressive labor laws in the country. Smith led the effort, and New Yorkers took notice.

Smith's increased stature resulted in his becoming Speaker of the assembly in 1913, further indication of his ability to work across the lines that divided Tammany Hall from Progressives. Republicans took back control of the state legislature in 1914, making Smith an opposition leader once again. When the

Republicans attempted to scale back labor legislation, Smith rose in defense of workers, especially the laws limiting working hours for women, whom he called the state's most valued natural resource. When a bill providing pensions for widows went before the legislature, many believed such a provision was beyond the proper role of government. Smith, however, called it a law to preserve the family that would keep the children of widows from being shuffled off to orphanages. Having grown up the son of a poor widow, this issue became personal for him. In arguing for the bill he reminded the assembly, "[B]y the adoption of this policy, we are sending to Him a prayer of thanksgiving for the innumerable blessings that He has showered upon us, particularly in light of the words of the Savior Himself, who said: 'Suffer little children to come unto me, and forbid them not, for of such is the kingdom of heaven.'"[2]

Although Smith did not talk in such religious terms frequently, his Catholic faith was a natural part of his life. He had grown up as a traditional urban Irish Catholic in the St. James Parish, which had 16,000 communicants. Religion was not something one did or an experience one had, as was the case for many Protestants. Rather, religion was part and parcel of life itself, infusing every activity. St. James had 15 different social organizations, everything from a drama society to a rifle club. Community life revolved around parish activities. Not only did Smith attend mass on Saturday or Sunday, but his neighborhood activities and recreation were usually organized by the parish, and the priests of St. James served as his role models. In the evenings, as children played in the streets, at 9:00 p.m. Father Kean would throw open the window of the rectory and shout, "Everybody home," and everyone obeyed.[3] Father Kean also banned liquor and cracked down on local establishments that served it. When Smith was a boy, highlights of the year included the St. Patrick's Day parade and Thanksgiving competitions sponsored by the parish.

Having distinguished himself in Albany as a Tammany man who could also be a reformer, by 1916 Smith was one of the leading politicians in New York City and became the Democratic nominee for sheriff. The position carried a healthy salary, plus bonuses, and the duties were relatively light. It was one of Tammany Hall's plum jobs, and Smith was nominated as a reward for his 14 years in Albany. Even the anti-Tammany New York *Times* acknowledged that Smith was "a man of quite unusual ability for that office."[4] The position of sheriff was a way station on Smith's road to higher things. In 1918 he served as president of the city's Board of Aldermen, the second most powerful position in city government, then the state Democratic Party nominated him as its candidate for governor. He ran against long odds. It had been more than 30 years since a Democrat had defeated a Republican for governor in a two-man race. Democrats had won only when a third party candidate split the Republican vote.

During the campaign the Republican incumbent, Charles Whitman, charged that Smith was a professional Tammany Hall politician who had never worked a real job. Smith responded by saying "When [the governor] was an Amherst College student, I was working in the Fulton Fish Market at the hardest labor that any man could do. I started before sunrise and worked until dark night. I know labor's needs."[5] Although a product of Tammany Hall, Smith was clearly a man of the people. In sum, according to Smith, the incumbent governor's main argument was that his challenger was unfit for office because he was born on the Lower East Side. Smith was not of proper social station to be governor, in other words. Smith said this was true. He was born on the Lower East Side and was proud of it. Moreover, he said, "When I am governor of this state and when I come home to New York they can meet me and find me in my old neighborhood and talk to me. They won't have to break through hundreds of pounds of gold lace in the St. Regis Hotel to make known their troubles."[6] Smith won by 15,000 votes. His biographer calls his arrival at the governor's mansion in Albany "nothing less than a social revolution in the politics of New York State."[7]

Smith was defeated for reelection in 1920. That year the Harding Republican landslide swept Democrats from office all over the country. President Woodrow Wilson had led the country through World War I only to botch the peace proceedings. The U.S. Senate refused to ratify the treaty Wilson negotiated in Paris because it included the League of Nations, Wilson's most cherished idea. The country was already growing disillusioned with its participation in the war and was in no mood for joining hands with Europeans in the League. Under these conditions, Republicans did well across much of the country, including New York. Smith kept the contest close, but his streak of 15 straight electoral victories came to an end, and he was as statesmanlike in defeat as in victory.

Even though Smith lost in 1920, he gained a national reputation as a result of his feud with William Randolph Hearst. Hearst's newspapers had bashed Smith so badly in 1919 that the governor challenged the newspaper magnate to a debate at Carnegie Hall. Hearst failed to show, so Smith gave a rousing speech of his own that was covered by Hearst newspapers across the country and helped raise Smith's national profile. He intended to retire from politics, but in 1922 Hearst announced he would run for the Democratic Party nomination for governor himself, so Smith jumped into the race, beating back Hearst's challenge in the primaries. He then won the general election handily and returned victorious to Albany. Some began to talk of Smith as a possible presidential candidate. At the 1924 Democratic National Convention in New York City, Smith was one of several candidates up for the presidential nomination. By then he had become a symbol of the growing urban opposition to Prohibition. In 1923 he had supported then signed into law a repeal of the Mullen-Gage Act, which was New York's version of the Volstead Act. Repeal of the law left enforcement of Prohibition largely in the hands of understaffed federal authorities.

Smith's longtime friend Franklin D. Roosevelt gave a rousing speech nominating Smith, but the 1924 convention was bitterly divided over a proposed condemnation of the Ku Klux Klan. Success of the anti-Klan resolution would have alienated Democrats in the South, and it was defeated by a single vote out of the nearly 500 cast. William Jennings Bryan opposed the anti-Klan resolution, an act nearly as unpopular with liberals as his role in the Scopes trial the next year. In a convention so divided, Smith appeared too much a part of the anti-Prohibition, anti-Klan, Northeast, urban, and Catholic wing of the party. After 103 ballots over nine days of deadlock, the party settled on John Davis, a New York attorney originally from West Virginia. Nebraska governor Charles Bryan, William Jennings Bryan's brother, became the vice presidential candidate. In October, following the Democratic convention, Smith denounced the Klan to an overflow Boston audience. "That thing can't live in this country," he shouted as he pounded on the podium and the audience leapt to its feet. "The Catholic can stand it, so can the Jew and the Negro, but the United States of America can never stand it."[8] Smith ran for reelection as governor of New York and won handily while the Democratic presidential ticket lost New York by 850,000 votes.

Having won reelection, Smith helped engineer a Tammany sweep of the most important elections in New York City the following year. His friend Jimmy Walker became mayor. Smith also pushed through by popular vote a set of constitutional amendments that were central to his aims and did so over bitter opposition from the Republicans in the state legislature. The New York

Times said the 1925 accomplishments "cap the climax of an unbroken record of success established by Mr. Smith during the generation he has spent in politics and public life." Then, to emphasize the point, the *Times* reporter added, "Alfred E. Smith today is the most powerful leader the Democratic Party has ever had in the greatest state in the Union."[9] Smith not only had a lock on New York Democrats, he had substantial support among state Republicans as well. Hardly given to hyperbole, Walter Lippmann cast similar sentiments in the New York *World* as he attempted to understand how Smith "holds these crowds as no man can hold them. He holds them without promise of a millennium, without a radical program, without appeal to their hatreds, without bribes and doles and circuses." Then how? Lippmann asked. "The answer, I think, is that they feel he has become the incarnation of their own hope and pride." As Lippmann saw it, Smith had dared to go into the world, where others feared to go, and in so doing had lifted from the masses "their secret sense of inferiority."[10] In short, Smith was now presidential timber.

NOMINATION

As an Irish Catholic, Smith knew what it meant to be a minority in public life. He once told the Friendly Sons of St. Patrick in 1923, "We are watched a little more than anybody else. We have to be just a bit better than the other fellow. . . . Let us do everything we can to keep Irish names off the calendars of the police courts and divorce courts."[11] That same year, on a warm spring day, Smith thought he was speaking off the record when he told some reporters, "Wouldn't you like to have your foot on the rail and blow the foam off some suds?," a comment that would be used against him by Prohibition forces when he ran for president in 1928.[12] By the time he ran Smith was the candidate who had pulled himself up from the poverty of the Bowery to be governor of New York for four terms. A product of Tammany Hall, he had nevertheless become a champion of reform aimed at improving life for the working-class masses of New York City and beyond. On the other hand, he was also stigmatized among many Protestants as the leader of the anti-Prohibition forces, urban Americans of non-Anglo Saxon origin, and Catholic immigrants. That was the problem.

As Lippmann put it in 1925, there brewed a looming conflict between Smith and "that older American civilization of town and country which dreads him and will resist him." Smith was the first of the "new immigrants" who could be considered suitable for president. New immigrants were those who came to America as late as the mid-nineteenth century. As long as no one from that class was likely to be nominated, Americans persisted in the fiction that all offices were open to men of talent, Lippmann argued. In reality, the new immigrants were "half enfranchised Americans" and in the person of Al Smith were making their first bid for presidential power. Smith would be opposed by the old-stock Americans, white Anglo-Saxon Protestants who supported Prohibition and believed that the cities represented the degradation of American culture. Each of Smith's political victories, Lippmann wrote, was like a premonition of a conflict on the horizon that would have Smith at its center as a tragic figure. "Here are the new people, clamoring to be admitted to America," Lippmann continued, "and there are the older people defending their household gods."[13]

Smith won the nomination on the first ballot at the 1928 Democratic National Convention in Houston, Texas. Franklin Roosevelt once again served as the official nominator, giving a vigorous speech on Smith's behalf. As was the custom in those days, likely nominees stayed away from the convention. Smith and his family listened to the delegate vote over the radio in the governor's mansion in Albany, the governor wearing a ten-gallon cowboy hat. Six weeks later Albany held an official kickoff before Smith embarked on a remarkable campaign that saw thousands in major cities exhibit unbridled enthusiasm for him. In the absence of modern polling data to show otherwise, the enthusiasm Smith witnessed on the campaign trail convinced him he would win. But there was fierce opposition as well, usually running along two fronts, Prohibition and religion, and they were related. The election of 1928 was a clash of cultures. At stake were competing conceptions of morality, religious authority, individual freedom, and even the meaning of America.

THE SERIOUS RELIGIOUS ISSUE IN 1928

In March 1927, more than a year before Smith actually won the Democratic nomination, the *Atlantic Monthly* published an essay entitled "An Open Letter to the Honorable Alfred E. Smith," written by New York attorney Charles C. Marshall. Previously unknown, Marshall became an anti-Smith celebrity. He prefaced his inquiry into the relationship between the Catholic church and the state by acknowledging Smith's "great record of public trusts successfully and honestly discharged" as well as Smith's "spirit of fair play." Moreover, Marshall said that the issue of religion was one that could be taken up with great rancor and bigotry, but to avoid the question of Smith's Catholicism would be "to neglect the profoundest interests in our national welfare."[14]

The crux of Marshall's essay was the Catholic doctrine of the "two powers" or two swords, enunciated first by Pope Gelasius in the fifth century. In the two powers theory, the state rules in civil matters and the church in the spiritual realm, but where there is conflict, the church is supreme. Marshall did not mention Pope Gelasius by name, but he referenced Popes Pius IX and Leo XIII several times because in the late nineteenth century both had reaffirmed church supremacy and even condemned separation of church and state. Pius rejected democracy and separation of church and state along with socialism, communism, and other dangerous modern ideas in his infamous Syllabus of Errors of 1864. In light of Pius's and Leo's statements, Marshall wanted to know what would happen if there was a clash between church and state during a Smith presidency. "Here arises the irrepressible conflict," Marshall wrote. "Shall the state or the Roman Catholic Church determine?" The U.S. Constitution, Marshall argued, claimed that it was the highest law of the land, but the Catholic church denied this. What was Smith's view?

Moreover, the Constitution stipulated that all religions were equal before the law, while the popes claimed the Catholic faith was the one true religion that should be favored by the state. To Marshall's way of thinking, religions other than Catholicism were, according to the Catholic church, allowed to exist by favor and not by right, while the Constitution said that all religions had a right to free exercise in America. As Marshall put the case concerning the two powers, "We are satisfied if [Catholics] will but concede that those claims, unless modified and historically redressed, precipitate an inevitable conflict between the Roman Catholic Church and the American State irreconcilable with domestic peace."[15]

Never one to run from a challenge, Smith immediately began composing a reply that was contracted to the *Atlantic Monthly*. When excerpts of his essay were leaked to newspapers, the magazine released its May issue a week earlier than planned to avoid being scooped completely. Editors at the *Atlantic* included a preface in which they praised Smith, saying he had answered Marshall "not deviously and with indirection, but straightforwardly, bravely, with the clear ring of candor."[16]

Reminding readers that he was neither a theologian nor a presidential candidate, at least not yet, Smith claimed that Marshall had mischaracterized the views of Catholics, calling into question their patriotism. In developing his response, Smith called on Father Francis P. Duffy for theological advice. Duffy had won several military awards, including the Distinguished Service Medal for serving as chaplain to the nearly all-Catholic 165th Army Regiment in World War I. Duffy's patriotism could not be impugned, Smith reminded Marshall. Smith then wrote of his own record in New York politics. He had taken an oath of office 19 times. Seeing no conflict between his faith and public service, the people of New York had elected him to the highest state office four times. He had always supported public education as one of the "foremost functions of government," Smith maintained in response to Marshall's concern that Catholic schools would be given preference under a Catholic president. In short, Smith argued, he saw nothing in his faith that could possibly conflict with his duty to country: "The essence of my faith is built on the commandments of God. The law of the land is built on the commandments of God. There can be no conflict between them."[17]

In his response Smith admitted that even though he had been a Catholic all his life, he had never heard of Pius's Syllabus of Errors until he read Marshall's letter. Smith's point was that American Catholics do not follow papal encyclicals and other church documents slavishly. "You seem to think," Smith told Marshall, "that Catholics must be all alike in mind and in heart, as though they had been poured into and taken out of the same mold." Demanding that a Catholic defend every statement or document issuing forth from a pope was like demanding that Marshall defend every statement made by one of his own Episcopal bishops. At this point Smith sounded as if he believed in an individual's freedom to accept or reject church teaching. That was certainly not the church's position, as Marshall accurately pointed out, but Smith was no more intellectually Catholic than he was intellectually anything else. He was a pragmatic politician who happened to be both devout and culturally Catholic. He had never entertained the idea that there could be any tension between being American and being Catholic.

Smith included lengthy sections dealing specifically with religious liberty and the separation of church and state, and on these he obviously had the help of Father Duffy. Responding to Marshall's reference to Pope Leo XIII's encyclical of 1885, Smith referred to Father John Ryan. Ryan was professor of moral theology at Catholic University of America, and his text *The State and the Church* was considered the best scholarly interpretation of Catholic teaching as it pertained to church-state relations. Ryan taught a view known as the thesis-hypothesis theory. The thesis was that the Roman Catholic Church was the true church and should therefore be recognized and supported by the state. Leo and Pius rearticulated this thesis in the nineteenth century, but its origin could be traced at least back to the great theologian Thomas Aquinas of the Middle Ages. The hypothesis was that Catholics were a minority in the United States, and it would be unjust, therefore, should the state prefer the church of the minority. As long as they were the minority, Catholics were happy to accept the hypothesis that the Catholic faith would not be the nation's official religion. On these matters, Smith quoted Father Ryan: "Pope Pius IX did not intend to declare that separation [of church and state] is always unadvisable, for he had more than once expressed his satisfaction with the arrangement obtaining in the United States."[18]

As for Protestant fear of the thesis, Father Ryan put the case this way: "[T]he danger of religious intolerance toward non-Catholics in the United States is so improbable and so far in the future that it should not occupy [Protestants'] time or attention."[19] Ryan suggested that only "zealots and bigots" could possibly worry about an occurrence that was "five thousand years hence." Still, for some of those zealots and bigots, and for some who were not, Ryan's view failed to satisfy. The idea that a Catholic establishment was theologically acceptable but impractical at the moment troubled some thoughtful non-Catholics. Protestants such as Marshall interpreted this view as meaning that Catholics rejected the First Amendment's dictum "Congress shall make no law respecting an establishment of religion," because deep down they longed for the day when the Catholic church would become both the majority and the official religion of America. Moreover, as Marshall wrote, the thesis-hypothesis theory sounded to him like the Catholic church did not acknowledge religious liberty for Protestants as a right but only as favor in this time when Catholics happened to be the minority.

Smith, of course, did not believe this and tried to allay the fear by quoting several prominent American Catholic leaders, such as Boston's William Cardinal O'Connell, the late Archbishop John Ireland of St. Paul, and his successor, Archbishop Dowling. All were part of the so-called Americanist Party within the country's Catholic hierarchy and had affirmed on numerous occasions their full support for the First Amendment. Dowling said that the conditions for the thesis were lacking not only in the United States but in virtually every nation on the globe, even Spain. Smith quoted Dowling as saying "[T]he thesis may well be relegated to the limbo of defunct controversies," and he quoted Ireland as saying "Religious freedom is the basic life of America, the cement running through all its walls and battlements, the safeguard of its peace and prosperity."[20] Smith also leaned on America's most influential Catholic, the late James Cardinal Gibbons, quoting him as saying "American Catholics rejoice in our separation of church and state, and I can conceive of no combination or circumstances likely to arise which would make a union desirable to either church or state. For ourselves, we thank God that we live in America."

Smith argued that any scenario Marshall could conjure "in the wildest dreams of your imagination," whereby church teaching would conflict with one's political duty, would be so extreme that such a teaching would violate "the common morality of all God-fearing men." In such a case both Catholics and Protestants would need to follow the guidance of individual conscience. Moreover, as Smith quoted Cardinal Gibbons, because the state and the church are both ordained by God, the pope does not properly issue directives in purely civil matters. If he did, Gibbons wrote, "He would be offending not only against civil society but against God, and violating an authority as truly from God as his own." In such a case, Gibbons concluded, a Catholic "would not be bound to obey the Pope."[21]

The final section of Smith's reply to Marshall consisted of Smith's own creed with regard to church-state relations. Smith recognized no power of the church to interfere in "the operations of the Constitution of the United States or the enforcement of the law of the land." Speaking most directly, he wrote, "I believe in the absolute freedom of conscience for all men and in the equality of all churches, all sects, and all beliefs before the law as a matter of right and not as a matter of favor." Then he professed his belief in the First Amendment's religion clauses, saying "I believe in the absolute separation of church and state and in the strict enforcement of the provisions of the Constitution that Congress shall make no law respecting the establishment of religion or prohibiting the free exercise thereof." He concluded his statement with a plea: "In this spirit I join with fellow-Americans of all creeds in a fervent prayer that never again in this land will any public servant be challenged because of the faith in which he has tried to walk humbly with his God."[22] Smith's prayer was not answered.

FUNDAMENTALISTS ATTACK SMITH

Smith's reply to Marshall satisfied many people but certainly not all, and many who attacked him went well beyond Marshall's carefully crafted concerns. Fundamentalists in particular trotted out some of the most virile anti-Catholic tropes the nation had seen in some time.

J. Frank Norris was among the most extreme fundamentalists in his opposition to Smith. By 1928 Norris had fully recovered from his murder trial of 1926 and was once again at the helm of a growing church and thriving revivalist ministry. With his own newspaper and regular radio broadcasts, he was a fundamentalist figure to be reckoned with across the Southwest and beyond. He began speaking out against Smith in 1926 when suggestions surfaced that the New York governor would likely be the Democratic presidential nominee. Then, during the summer of 1928, Norris suspended all other aspects of his ministry in order to barnstorm Texas and Oklahoma for Smith's Republican opponent, Herbert Hoover. Norris took it upon himself to lead the anti-Smith campaign in his region of the country.

By itself, Smith's position on Prohibition would have been enough to warrant Norris's fierce opposition. Likewise, Smith's Catholicism alone would have sufficed. The combination of those two issues served to ratchet up the stakes to monumental and even hysterical proportions for Norris. When Smith was in the running for the 1924 nomination, Norris said that while the U.S. Constitution protected people of all religions, even Muslims and Buddhists, the country should require Catholics to renounce their allegiance to the pope.[23] When Smith's name circulated again in 1926, Norris combined Prohibition and anti-Catholicism in a sermon entitled "The Conspiracy of Rum and Romanism to Rule This Government." He was refused use of a city auditorium in Lexington, Kentucky, when he advertised the sermon for a revival there. Prohibition, of course, had never been popular with the bourbon distillers of the Bluegrass State. Printing a version of these sermons in his weekly newspaper, soon called *The Fundamentalist,* Norris claimed that the Catholic church held three ideas that made members unfit for public office: (1) church supremacy in all things, (2) papal infallibility, and (3) that church teachings were unalterable. "Are we ready to permit a man to occupy the highest office, the chief magistracy over this Government, who owes his first allegiance to a foreign power which claims these three things?" Norris asked.[24] He was just getting started. A few months later Norris claimed, "Roman Catholics Plan Huge Broadcasting Scheme to Make 'The United States a Catholic Country.'"

During the spring of 1927 Norris corresponded privately with a Texas member of the Republican National Committee, volunteering to campaign across the solidly Democratic region in support of Coolidge, Hoover, or whoever became the Republican nominee. That summer Norris published a booklet on why Smith should not be president, and by the end of the year he had prepared to campaign extensively should the New York governor get the nomination the following summer, something Norris was sure would happen. During summer and fall of 1928 Norris traveled full time giving anti-Smith addresses. Norris raised the serious church-state issues that troubled Protestants, and he even reprinted Marshall's widely circulated "Open Letter" but not Smith's response. Much of Norris's anti-Smith campaign, however, was given over to scare tactics, the most outrageous of which was his reference to the St. Bartholomew's Day Massacre of 1572. Coming in the midst of the French Wars of Religion in which Catholics and Protestants butchered each other for three decades, the St. Bartholomew's Day Massacre was the worst of the bloodletting. Over a three-week period beginning in August Catholic forces slaughtered somewhere between 10,000 and 30,000 Protestant Huguenots. Norris told audiences that the same thing would happen today if Catholics amassed enough political power. Norris also circulated bogus charges peddled by anti-Smith forces across the country. One quoted Abraham Lincoln as fearing Catholic power, and another claimed that Smith was an alcoholic who had been seen drunk in public on several occasions.

Norris used the campaign to attack other Southern Baptist leaders with whom he was at war continuously throughout his career. They also opposed Smith but too timidly for Norris's tastes. George Truett of First Baptist Dallas was the leading statesman in the Southern Baptist Convention. He believed it unseemly to engage in partisan politics from the pulpit and therefore refused to denounce Smith or endorse Hoover by name. He did, however, state publicly that he could never vote for any candidate who opposed Prohibition.[25] Such indirect endorsement of Hoover was not enough for Norris. Truett's attorney brother supported Smith, so Norris used guilt by association and demanded that George Truett come out publicly against his brother by endorsing Hoover by name. Taking its lead from Truett, the state Baptist newspaper came out for Prohibition but also refused to endorse Hoover explicitly, leading Norris to issue headlines such as "Your Attitude Is Distinctly Cowardly," and "Will the Baptists of Texas Submit to the Compromise of Their Paper on Al Smith and Tammany Hall?" Then Norris went after his alma mater, Baylor, for harboring a student-run Al Smith Club. Norris ran a headline claiming "They Have Defiled the Oldest and Greatest Baptist University."

When Hoover became the Republican nominee in June, Norris printed an article titled "The Republicans Nominate a Democrat"—this despite the fact that Hoover had worked in the Harding and Coolidge administrations. Norris then extolled the virtues of Hoover's Quaker faith and gave the candidate a fundamentalist makeover. Norris pronounced Hoover orthodox on the trinity, the deity of Christ, conversion, and the work of the Holy Spirit. In remembering Hoover's World War I relief efforts, especially his organization of food delivery to war-ravaged Belgium, Norris wrote, "It is not far to see the religious influences that have entered the life of Herbert Hoover. One of the outstanding characteristics of Quakerism is justice for all men."[26] Norris then fired off another letter to state Republican officials urging them to enlist the Protestant ministers of the state, create a pro-Hoover press bureau, send pro-Hoover campaign materials to small-town newspapers, and set up a separate women's brigade of pro-Hoover campaigners. A bewildered Republican official wrote back reminding Norris that the state party had limited resources.

Throughout the summer and fall Norris was in full swing. During a single week in September he gave speeches in nine cities and estimated that he had spoken to 30,000 people. "I am speaking every day and night against [Smith]," he wrote to a friend in Brooklyn, New York, "and speaking to crowds of from five to ten thousand." He predicted privately that Smith would take only a few southern states.[27] At a stop in Dallas a woman rose to take issue with Norris's attacks, using profanity as she approached the platform. Ushers intercepted her and escorted her from the premises. Norris responded, "Now, we are prepared to have order here tonight. We are not surprised at the lowdown whiskey-soaked imps of Hell. The toe-kissing, Tammnanyites are here for the purpose of creating a disturbance, and I will serve notice on you now that this is Texas and not Mexico." He then told any other potential disturbers to "get up on your hind feet where we can see you," before urging all "red-blooded white folks here tonight, who love God, who love the flag, and who love order," to exercise their rights by suppressing any disturbances made by the "ring-kissing Tammany Hall gang."[28]

Playing the race card, Norris often went into great detail arguing that a Smith victory threatened segregation in the South and raised the likelihood of a flood of non-Anglo immigrants who would take jobs from white Americans. "The dregs of southern Europe" would become foot soldiers for corrupt political machines such as Tammany Hall. "What a conglomeration," he wrote in an article two weeks before the election. "Tammany Hall, Roman Catholicism, bootleggers, carpet bag politicians and negros [sic]. What will the white people of Texas do?"[29]

The white people of Texas went Republican for the first time since Reconstruction. During a celebration at First Baptist Church in Fort Worth following the election, state Republicans presented Norris with an engraved watch, saying that he had done more than anyone to help Hoover win the state. Proving to be a sore winner, Norris sent a telegram to Democratic Party chair and Smith friend John Jacob Raskob. It read in part: "I hope you will understand the meaning of the handwriting on the wall, the unmistakable verdict of the American people against you and all others who called Prohibition a damnable affliction, and who made the un-American and unfair threat against the ministry of America." Noting that he was scheduled to preach in New York City the following week, Norris invited Raskob to be present.[30] The next spring Hoover's campaign organizers invited Norris to the inauguration in Washington, D.C., which he attended.

While Norris campaigned for Hoover regionally, Billy Sunday did so on a national stage. The difference, however, is that Sunday was not nearly as anti-Catholic as Norris and kept his message centered on Prohibition most of the time. He told reporter John T. Brady of Boston in a 1927 interview that Coolidge was the man for 1928. On Smith he said, "I've never met Al Smith personally, but undoubtedly he is a good fellow and a most able man. But the fact that he is the mouthpiece of Tammany Hall and is known to be a wet will hurt him more, I think, than the fact that he is a Catholic, although his religion is bound to hurt him in some sections of the South. I don't think he would be able to overcome all three things unless his Republican opponent was terribly weak timber."[31]

Having identified openly as a Republican for years, Sunday saw a sinister plot afoot in the press when revelations of former President Harding's scandals surfaced just as Smith was positioning himself for the presidency. "And this damnable rot about Harding," he said in St. Louis early in 1928. "Why, I ask you, why did they wait until both Harding and his wife were dead before they uttered their gross slander?"[32] His central concern for Prohibition then came to the fore as he joked, "And, sir, if the Democrats nominate Al Smith or Jim Reed for President, or the Republicans nominate a wet, I'll run. They'll know I'm in the race, too, you can bet."[33] Later in the St. Louis revival he predicted confidently that because Hoover favored the Eighteenth Amendment and the Volstead Act, "he is as good as elected. He will go in with a bang."[34] When Hoover won the nomination at the Republican National Convention, Sunday was quick to endorse him. He then told a camp meeting audience near New York City that he was ready to fight against Al Smith. He stressed, however, that his main problem with Smith was Prohibition. "I have no personal fight against Al Smith as a man, but I would be against my own brother if he were wet. I'm fighting Al on the temperance issue alone." He then predicted that religion would not be a primary issue in the election and followed with "I certainly am not against Smith myself because he is Catholic." [35]

This did not, however, mean that Sunday would go easy on Smith. Moving from New York across the river into New Jersey, Sunday managed to stir up a religion and politics controversy in the historic Methodist camp meeting town of Ocean Grove. From the pulpit of town's famous tabernacle, Sunday criticized Smith for repudiating his own party's platform. Sunday recalled that the governor's position had always been that the party writes the platform and the candidate stands on it. But "[w]hen the Democratic Party advocated a dry platform, does he stand upon it?" Sunday asked rhetorically. "No. [He] repudiates it." Stating up front that this was a political sermon, Sunday lashed out at "crooks, cork screwers, bootleggers, [and] whisky politicians. They shall not pass—even to the White House."[36] In his farewell sermon for the brief revival, Sunday told his Ocean Grove audience that Al Smith had no more chance being elected than the pope had being named Imperial Wizard of the Ku Klux Klan.[37]

Two weeks later Democratic New York state senator William Love spoke from the same pulpit in Ocean Grove. In an address to 4,000 children and their parents gathered for a youth rally, the senator digressed from his inspirational speech to rebut Sunday. He said that while it was bad enough when politicians slandered each other, it was worse when a preacher "prostitutes the pulpit" to attack a politician of unimpeachable integrity and family values, such as Smith. Sectarianism was one of the nation's greatest dangers, Senator Love said. "It breeds bigotry and intolerance as readily as a stagnant pool breeds malaria."

The next day the Asbury Park Council of Religious Education, which had invited Love to speak, issued a letter of apology to the Ocean Grove Campmeeting Association expressing dismay at the injection of politics into what was supposed to be an inspirational talk. Love responded that he was merely defending his governor against Sunday's injection of politics into a religious gathering. "I spoke of Billy Sunday's remarks in the interest of fair play," Love told the press.[38] The controversy passed, but it stands as an example of how religion and politics get played out in heated elections.

After the election Sunday sent a congratulatory letter to the vice president elect, Hoover's running mate Senator Charles Curtis. Curtis replied to Sunday, "I know you were of great help in the campaign and I am thankful for your valued assistance. I heard of your good work in the South. . . . Mr. Hoover and I are under great obligations to you for your good work."[39] After the inauguration Sunday received a letter from President Hoover's secretary saying "You may be sure that the President will be glad to see you and Mrs. Sunday when you come to Washington."[40]

Lacking the religious bigotry of Norris and some other fundamentalists, after the election Sunday was actually accused of being pro-Catholic. In a pamphlet entitled "Billy Sunday Unmasked," an obscure anti-Catholic activist suggested that Sunday might be a Jesuit in disguise and that his attitude toward Catholicism was "void of red-blooded patriotism."[41] Rail Splitter Press, which published the pamphlet, might well have tagged Norris with the same charge come the 1940s. Once his interests turned to rabid anticommunism, Norris praised the Catholic church and had his famous audience with Pope Pius XII in 1947.[42]

Like Sunday, Aimee Semple McPherson took the high road. By 1928 she was recovering well from her scandal two years before and was beginning to test the political waters by supporting various issues and candidates. She endorsed Hoover, and like Sunday, said that the religious differences were not the reason. In an editorial in her magazine she either wrote or approved this statement: "Laying aside entirely the matter of religious differences, Mr. Hoover is the man of the hour right now." The editorial went on to praise Hoover's business acumen and said that other than religion there was nothing "quite so important in the world now as the business of the United States of America."[43] McPherson was out of the country for most of the presidential campaign. Touring Great Britain in a five-week crusade, she had little more to say about the election.

A contemporary journalist held up McPherson as the one fundamentalist leader who refused to jump into the political war against Al Smith even when doing so might have diverted attention from the memory of her recent scandal. That journalist was apparently unaware that the most erudite scholar on the fundamentalist side not only refused to join the campaign against Smith but had actually voted for the Catholic candidate. J. Gresham Machen of Princeton Seminary was the one prominent fundamentalist who opposed Prohibition. Moreover, he was a longtime Democrat who also opposed efforts to use the public schools to inculcate morality and religious practices. These were matters for churches. Machen also opposed vigorously efforts of some to eliminate the teaching of foreign languages. He valued classical languages and believed the English-only campaign was misguided. Machen wrote letters of support to Smith when the governor helped repeal New York's laws regulating language instruction.[44] As was so often the case, Machen disagreed with other fundamentalists on everything except theology.

JOHN ROACH STRATON VERSUS CANDIDATE SMITH

Along with Norris, one of the nation's leading fundamentalists was Al Smith's fellow New Yorker John Roach Straton of Calvary Baptist Church. Like Machen, Straton usually voted Democrat, but this time he opposed Al Smith, although not on religious grounds. Rather, in a highly publicized August 5 sermon Straton accused his governor of lawlessness and corruption. By lawlessness Straton meant Smith's opposition to Prohibition and his support for repeal of the Mullen-Gage Act. Straton's corruption charge referred to Smith's Tammany Hall ties. Straton said that "whether wittingly or unwittingly," Smith was "the best friend of the forces of reaction, immorality, vice and crime, in the land today." He alluded to corruption charges made by well-known Republican newspaper editor William Allen White, saying that while White had retracted the charges, Straton stood by them. When controversy erupted between Straton and Smith, however, White jumped back in, cabling from Europe that he was retracting his retraction.[45]

Referencing the disconnect between Smith and the Democratic platform's dry plank, Straton accused the party of making "a covenant with death and an agreement with hell" in its nomination of Smith. Even with such a negative assessment, Straton acknowledged Smith's genial disposition and his economic success as governor. As a Baptist pastor in a city that had as many Catholics as Protestants, Straton never mentioned Smith's Catholicism.[46] Straton lacked the luxury of being ensconced in the anti-Catholic South, as Norris was. As controversy ensued over his accusations against Smith, Straton vowed to avoid religion and focus on the issue of corruption.

Incensed by Straton's charges, Smith fired off a letter demanding an opportunity to come to Calvary Baptist for debate. The governor also accused Straton of "bearing false witness against thy neighbor," a direct violation of the Ninth Commandment. Smith identified the commandment as one of Jesus's sayings, a technical error Straton seized on in a reply two days later. Straton initially agreed to the debate, saying he would repeat the sermon in Smith's presence, and Smith could then make a full reply. Even though Calvary Baptist was one of the largest churches in New York City, Straton believed his church would not be big enough to accommodate the crowd, so he suggested they meet at Madison Square Garden instead, then take the show on a swing through the South.[47]

The controversy between Straton and Smith took a new turn when New York State Supreme Court Justice William Harmon Black publicly defended Smith. Black was a member of Straton's church and as a Baptist defended his pastor's right to say whatever he believed, so long as he was factually correct. It was on the facts, however, that Black disagreed with Straton. Acknowledging that Straton knew "more about the Bible in a minute than I will ever know," Black quickly added, "I know more about political history than he will ever know." He then called Smith "the cleanest, most loyal man in politics today." Black was not the only person associated with Calvary Baptist who disagreed with Straton. The pastor's former secretary, Walter Soderstrom, said he would probably be thrown out of the church for his views, but "Christians have grown sick and tired of pulpiteers and publicity seekers seizing upon Alfred E. Smith and the Democratic platform as a background for their un-Christian and un-chivalric messages. Christians are starving for the gospel." There was probably a reason that Soderstrom was Straton's "former" secretary. Although not a member of Straton's church, state senator Love, who took on Sunday in Ocean Grove, said that his father and grandfather were Baptist ministers like Straton, but they would never have stooped to attack the legislative record of a politician as clean as Smith.[48]

Straton and Smith continued to argue through the pages of the New York *Times*. Smith insisted that he be allowed rebuttal at Calvary Baptist. Straton continued to push for Madison Square Garden but also suggested two debates, one at Calvary and one at St. Patrick's Cathedral "because I do not like to have my Catholic friends suppose for a minute that I believe a Baptist church is more holy ground than their cathedral."[49] Catholics seized on Straton's blunder as Straton had on Smith's alleged misquotation of Jesus. Straton should know, they pointed out, that a Catholic church is never used for anything but worship and that Smith was not a parishioner at St. Patrick's and would not be allowed to speak there, even if the cathedral were given to political debate. The rector of St. Francis Xavier then defended Smith on the Ninth Commandment. He cited Matthew 19:18 where Jesus quotes the commandment, "Thou shall not bear false witness against thy neighbor" and chided Straton for not acknowledging that Jesus made the commandment part of his own teachings. Others chimed in with Mark 10:17–19 and Luke 17:18—20 (only the former of these two verses actually addresses the issue in question).[50]

Having accepted a debate at Calvary Baptist on August 10, Straton reversed himself the next day to avoid a rift with his own trustees, who opposed letting the circus continue and wanted no part of a Straton-Smith debate at their church. Straton, meanwhile, said his agreement to bring Smith to Calvary was a misunderstanding born of a poor telephone connection when he spoke to the New York *Times* reporter the day before from his Greenwood Lake summer home outside the city. Straton claimed that he was joking when he suggested a debate at St. Patrick's but that his humorous tone got lost in the static.[51] As Straton got heat from his own board of trustees at Calvary, other Protestant ministers in New York City joined against him as well. After a week of controversy a Lutheran pastor in Brooklyn criticized Straton's un-Christian spirit and remarked, "If Dr. Straton were typical of Protestantism, then a Catholic president would be a blessing."[52] Three weeks later Dan Brummitt, the well-known editor of the Methodist newspaper the *Northwestern Christian Advocate* in Chicago, defended Smith's character even though he opposed the governor on Prohibition. Brummit paired Straton with "Two-gun Norris" and wrote, "[W]e are sorry that Governor Smith has paid any attention to Straton and we hope he will ignore the Texas gunman pulpiteer. . . . They live on headlines and cannot endure the obscurity which is their rightful abode."[53] Norris liked being linked with Straton and reported the Smith-Straton controversy in his own newspaper with headlines such as "Dr. Straton versus Governor Smith."

As the debate over the debate moved into its second week, the tone degenerated. Smith continued to insist that any exchange between himself and Straton take place at Calvary Baptist. With reporters chasing Straton across Greenwood Lake in rowboats to get a reply, Straton called the candidate's intransigence "just childish." Straton said he would rent a large hall and hold the debate whether Smith attended or not, and he portrayed Smith as running away from a challenge. But the press saw it differently. At one point reporters sitting outside Straton's cottage could hear the pastor in his study whistling Smith's campaign battle tune, "The Sidewalks of New York." Straton then appeared, said he had nothing to say, and asked the reporters to join him for a swim. The New York *World* ran a cartoon showing Straton fleeing to a storm cellar with a cyclone representing Smith in hot pursuit. Straton responding by calling the cyclone governor nothing but "a May day whirlwind."[54]

As the fiasco with Smith continued, Straton completed the purchase of a hotel at Greenwood Lake that he intended to convert into a Christian community similar to Ocean Grove, New Jersey. Ten days after the purchase, while the hotel was still under lease to the previous proprietor, a reporter for the New York *World* bought a quart of liquor at the hotel bar, then reported his purchase to Straton. Straton called it a "frame up" and demanded the arrest of those engaged in bootlegging. Two months later he sued the *World* for $200,000. Two weeks after the suit was filed, and four days after Smith's defeat, the hotel burned to the ground. Noting that six years earlier his home had burned after he publicly battled against cabarets and nightclubs, Straton blamed this blaze on people who were angry at him for his opposition to Smith.[55]

The prospects for a Smith-Straton debate died in late August, and Straton was free to fire away. When the parade in Albany celebrating Smith's nomination was rained out, Straton called it "a fizzle in a drizzle" and an omen of Smith's sure defeat in November.[56] Straton spent the rest of the campaign attacking Smith and renewing offers to debate the candidate anywhere but Calvary Baptist. In September Straton barnstormed the South and Southwest on the tab of the Woman's Christian Temperance Union and the Anti-Saloon League. In Raleigh, North Carolina, the home of former Secretary of the Navy Josephus Daniels, Straton urged Daniels and Georgia Senator Walter George to abandon the Democratic Party and support Hoover.[57] After preaching against Smith in Florida and Georgia, Straton headed west to Oklahoma City, where he and Smith actually came close to having the debate they had been threatening for over a month.

Smith headed to Oklahoma City the same time as Straton. He arrived on September 20 to an estimated 70,000 supporters, who boisterously welcomed him, standing several rows deep on city sidewalks. Even the local Republican newspaper acknowledged the occasion as one of the most enthusiastic greetings any public figure had ever received in Oklahoma. Ten thousand jammed the City Coliseum to hear Smith denounce a "whispering campaign" against his religion. Calling the attack on Tammany Hall and corruption a red herring, Smith said, "I know what lies behind all this and I shall tell you." He then addressed the religion issue directly, accusing Oklahoma Democratic Party leaders of joining the Hoover forces because of religious prejudice. Diving headlong into religion, Smith risked a southern backlash, and advisors were divided on the move. Smith dove in anyway, saying "[A]ny person who votes against me simply because of my religion is not, to my way of thinking, a good citizen." Smith was riled because several prominent Oklahoma politicians had bolted the party to become Hoover Democrats. He accused Oklahoma senator Robert Owen and others of injecting "bigotry, hatred, intolerance, and sectarian division" into the campaign.

Smith also responded to the Ku Klux Klan. Of all the organizations in America, the Klan was particularly active in the bigotry department, along with publications such as *The Rail Splitter* and *Fellowship Forum*. When Smith's train had crossed into Oklahoma from Arkansas the night before, there was a large cross burning in a field near the railroad tracks. Smith and his family were asleep and did not see the sight for themselves, but it was widely reported. With the cross burning still fresh on his mind, Smith lashed out at the Klan. "Totally ignorant of the history and tradition of this country and its institutions and in the name of Americanism," he thundered, "they breathe into the hearts of their members hatred of millions of their fellow countrymen because of their religious belief. Nothing could be so out of line with the spirit of America." He then referred briefly to the teachings of Thomas Jefferson and even Jesus, adding "Nothing could be so false to the teachings of our Divine Lord Himself. . . . The world knows no greater mockery than the use of the blazing cross, the cross upon which Christ died, as a symbol to instill into the hearts of men a hatred of their brethren while Christ preached and died for the love and brotherhood of man." As Smith spoke and the audience cheered, Straton sat silently on the back row of the platform with his friend Mordecai Ham, Oklahoma City's leading Baptist preacher. Even with a ticket to the function, Straton was almost denied entrance by an organizer who recognized him.[58]

The next night Straton mounted the same platform, this time preaching from the front rather than grousing silently in the back. He joked that he was there to "do some more whispering." "I have had quite an interesting time 'whispering' to people about the present presidential campaign, not only up in New York but down through Dixie as well." Chastened by the pro-Smith adulation he had witnessed the night before, Straton acknowledged that Smith would never knowingly vote to further the cause of corruption, lawlessness, and vice. He then went into great detail explaining the long history of Tammany Hall going back to the infamous Boss Tweed in the late nineteenth century. Absolving Oklahoma's Hoover Democrats for crossing party lines, he told how reform-minded Democrats such as Grover Cleveland and Woodrow Wilson had opposed Tammany. Smith, Straton argued, was utterly a creature of the infamous political machine. Referring to his many battles over evolution, Straton said he had finally found the missing link. "It is this miserable monstrosity, this hybrid impertinence produced by the crossing of the Democratic donkey with the Tammany tiger."[59] Straton spoke the next night, as well, and accused Smith of dragging the religious issue into the campaign. To Straton's way of thinking, since Smith had brought religion into the debate, now he could as well. Rather than saying himself that Smith might take orders from Rome, however, Straton told the story of New York mayor Jimmy Walker. Allegedly, when asked whether his friend Al Smith would take orders from Rome should he become president, Walker replied, "I hope so."[60] That was as close as Straton came to saying people should vote against Smith because he was Catholic.

From Oklahoma City Straton headed south to J. Frank Norris country, preaching to a packed house at First Baptist Fort Worth. Frequently prompted by Norris as he spoke, Straton told his Texas audience that back in New York he had "double dog dared" Smith to debate him at Madison Square Garden, not mentioning of course that Smith had agreed to debate at Calvary Baptist. In addition to his standard critique of Tammany Hall corruption, Straton injected race into the campaign, saying that in the "negro heaven" of Harlem, "All the corrupt Negroes are behind Smith."[61] "Good bye Al," Norris shouted in response.

Straton returned to New York in mid-October and continued to rap Smith in his weekly sermons. The night before the election Calvary Baptist held a special prayer and fasting service, ostensibly for the continuation of Prohibition, but better understood as a prayer meeting for Hoover and the Republicans. Woman's Christian Temperance Union chapters did likewise. Four days after Hoover won the election, Chicago radio preacher Paul Rader filled Straton's pulpit at Calvary and called the election "a great big moral sweep." Rader believed the election indicated that there were more people than ever longing for "a real old-fashioned revival that will sweep the country." Norris preached at Calvary Baptist the following March.[62]

After all of Straton's efforts to "swing around the South," Smith still won Alabama, Arkansas, Georgia, Louisiana, Mississippi, and South Carolina. The South was still solidly Democratic, owing to bitterness stemming from the Civil War and Reconstruction. Not even the threat of a Catholic in the White House could scare up enough southern Republicans to give Hoover an edge. Oklahoma, the site of the great Straton-Smith duel, joined Norris's Texas in the Republican column. Smith could not even win his own (and Straton's) state, but as governor he had always faced Republican odds stacked against him outside New York City.

CHAPTER 11

HOW THE ROARING TWENTIES SET THE STAGE FOR THE CULTURE WARS OF OUR OWN TIME

The significance of the election of 1928 goes well beyond the question of who won and why. That year the country stumbled into a controversy that ran far deeper than Al Smith, Charles Marshall, Billy Sunday, Aimee Semple McPherson, J. Frank Norris, or John Roach Straton. The election of 1928 is a microcosm of the central elements of the culture wars of our own time. In the 1920s, Protestants charged that Catholics could not hold full loyalty to the country because they had a prior political allegiance to the pope. For Catholics, however, the real question was not where they stood with regard to the state and the pope but where they stood with regard to American freedom. As one Catholic historian argued recently, the issue for Catholics in America has always been the tension between their faith and the modern notion of freedom that is based on individual autonomy.[1] Emanating from the eighteenth-century Enlightenment, autonomy affirms each individual's freedom to make up his or her own mind about important matters, unencumbered by external authority. Today, we call this "freedom of choice."

Popes Pius and Leo in the late nineteenth century believed that separation of church and state in America was based on individual autonomy, which meant it freed individuals from the authority of the Catholic church—hence the encyclicals and Pius's Syllabus of Errors. It took Catholic theologian John Courtney Murray to show in the 1960s that individual autonomy was not the only way to conceive of religious liberty and separation of church and state. Murray interpreted the First Amendment to the U.S. Constitution as disallowing state supremacy over the consciences of individuals so they could properly obey the church without interference from the state. In other words, Catholics could embrace the American idea of religious freedom without embracing individual autonomy. Murray's ideas became the basis for the Catholic church's 1965 Declaration on Religious Freedom. He wrote the declaration, and it became the church's official position at the Vatican II Council. The declaration states forthrightly that "the human person has a right to religious freedom." Al Smith could have used an authoritative statement such as that in 1928, but Protestants would not have believed it anyway. Many Protestants in the 1960s and since have hailed the declaration of 1965 as a shift away from the ideas of Pius and Leo, but at least one thing has not changed. The Catholic church is still supreme, not in the sense of demanding that the state acknowledge it officially but in the sense that the state has a responsibility under God to protect religious liberty so that individuals can stay properly under the ultimate authority of the church. This is not individual autonomy.

In 1928 John Courtney Murray and the Declaration on Religious Freedom were well in the future. In the meantime, the week after the presidential election, the editor of the liberal Protestant journal *Christian Century* offered a remarkable analysis. Throughout the election the *Century* had consistently denounced "bigoted anti-Catholicism" and rejected wholeheartedly the notion that a Catholic was necessarily unfit for the presidency. At the same time, the journal framed the election as a contest between those who advocated a conscience "formed under ecclesiastical authority" and those who touted a "conscience individually formed." There was little doubt that the *Christian Century* editor preferred a conscience individually formed. Most Protestants at the time, whether fundamentalist or liberal, thought the difference between themselves and Catholics was that Protestants believed in consciences free from the sort of ecclesiastical authority that bound Catholics. To prefer candidates who believed in the conscience individually formed was not bigotry, the *Christian Century* editor wrote, "but the reasonable application of the voter's religious convictions to his judgment of men."[2]

The conundrum that went unacknowledged by the *Christian Century* editor was apparent when he discussed Prohibition, the issue with which the election of 1928 was tightly bound. The *Century* editor said that only a few wets fought for freedom in order to build a better society. "[M]ore of them were fighting for a personal privilege regardless of public welfare," he charged. This is the same journal that the next year denounced the individual freedom argument when the obscenity wars raged in Boston. Against cultural liberals who espoused the right of authors to write about sex, the *Christian Century* was consistent in its position that an argument was insufficient if based on individual freedom of expression without proper concern for the corporate well-being of society. In other words, individual freedom was not an end in and of itself, as cultural liberals believed. Rather, the proper end of politics was a good society, and a good society depended on a set of deeply held community values. The drys had them; the wets did not, the editor wrote. "The drys were fighting for a policy and a program which they conceived to have deep moral significance and to which they attached the sanctions of religion," he continued. "Religious conviction attaching itself to a practical program for social betterment is both legitimate and indispensable."[3] This is the Victorian, communitarian position that had reigned supreme in the nineteenth century but had come under assault by the 1920s.

The irony here is that having pitted a conscience "formed under ecclesiastical authority" against a conscience "individually formed," the *Christian Century* editor preferred the latter. Yet he still believed that free individuals could deliberate together to form a good society. He had not yet thought about the tension present in such an argument. Essentially, it is this: If consciences are to be individually formed, how can free individuals deliberate together to restrict the freedom of other individuals in order to produce a good society? Prohibition restricted the freedom of individuals. Under what authority could consciences "individually formed" possess the right to curb the freedom of other consciences "individually formed"? It would seem that such consciences would need to recognize an authority to which all individuals were responsible, an authority that says what constitutes a good society, in which case those consciences would be formed by that authority and would therefore not be "individually formed."

This brings us to one of the great ironies of the 1920s. Neither liberal nor fundamentalist Protestants could appreciate the tension between American freedom and religious authority that thoughtful Catholics experienced. Liberal Protestantism like that of the *Christian Century* adjusted theology according to modern modes of thought. A chief component of modern thought was the notion of freedom based on individual autonomy, in other words a conscience individually formed. Yet liberal Protestants still believed that reasonable individuals could deliberate together around common values to produce a good society. They did not foresee a time later in the century when freedom would be reduced to the maxim that one can do whatever he or she wants so long as it does not inhibit another's freedom. By the late twentieth century, American freedom meant that individual autonomy trumps efforts to build a good society or even to decide what a good society would look like. The idea of the good must be left to individuals to decide for themselves. If there happens to be a clash between an individual's rights and the group's effort to build a good society, individual rights prevail. Accustomed as they were to a broad moral consensus that had existed throughout American history, liberal Protestants in the 1920s could not have envisioned deep moral disagreement; nor could they have envisioned that freedom alone, especially when it is based on individual autonomy, was an insufficient basis for a good society. In the 1920s liberal Protestants never quite understood that Catholic immigrants who were serious about their faith loved America because it gave them greater freedom to submit themselves to the church—that is, to be good Catholics.

Cultural liberals should not be let off the hook either. Just as Protestant liberals assumed that consciences individually formed would somehow, as if by magic, always produce a good society, in the obscenity wars cultural liberals defended the individual right of self-expression because they assumed such freedom would always be uplifting for humanity. They defended the literary exploration of human sexuality because they valued human beings in all their complexity. When exploration of human sexuality gave way to exploitation of sex in the form of hard-core pornography that degraded and victimized women and children, it was tough to make an argument based on freedom that there should be even minimal limits on pornography.[4]

Fundamentalists may have seen the dilemma a bit more clearly than liberal Protestants, when fundamentalists were not acting according to anti-Catholic and anti-liberal prejudice, which was not very often. They and their more moderate evangelical heirs cannot accept individual autonomy any more than Catholics can. Fundamentalists and evangelicals believe that some things have been settled by the Bible, and the Bible trumps both individual freedom and individual experience. Living under the last vestiges of a quasi-Protestant establishment, however, fundamentalists failed to see that Catholics argued essentially the same thing. Moreover, it was inconceivable to fundamentalists in the 1920s that the Bible and a political decision based on American freedom could ever be at odds. They happily championed American freedom as if it was the same thing as religious liberty to bind oneself to the Bible.

By the end of the twentieth century this had all changed. Once the issue was no longer Prohibition but abortion, evangelical Protestants and traditional Catholics recognized their common ground. Evangelicals now see as clearly as Catholics that religion can be at odds with individual autonomy. Abortion became the clearest example where the individual's autonomous right to choose clashed with religious authority that said the fetus is human and endowed by its creator with the right to life. Moreover, evangelicals argued publicly in the 1980s that the state is under the authority of God, roughly the same thing Catholics had been saying throughout the century. In 1994 the two groups even formed a project called Evangelicals and Catholics Together, which became a venue for discussing theology and politics. The clarity over their shared worldview developed as the cultural liberalism we saw in the obscenity wars of the 1920s became the dominant political force in America. In recent decades liberal political theorists have emphasized more forcefully than ever that American freedom is based on individual autonomy. This cultural liberalism is today known as political liberalism, and its leading theoretician was the late John Rawls of Harvard University. The constitutional right to choose an abortion made clear to evangelicals that there were limits to their allegiance to this sort of freedom, something traditional Catholics had always known at least instinctively. Evangelicals and Catholics now understand more than ever before that they are under a religious authority that has settled deeply moral issues, such as abortion or, for that matter, gay rights. The decision to have an abortion or to live a gay lifestyle, therefore, cannot be left to the individual acting autonomously.

Liberal Protestants, however, both in the 1920s and today, are more apt to make peace with political liberalism and individual autonomy because, for them, personal religious experience stands as their central authority. The essential difference between the liberal and fundamentalist Protestants of the 1920s was that liberals sought to harmonize Protestant theology with modern ways of thinking while fundamentalists were at war with modernity. In the 1920s, the old Protestant-Catholic culture war was still strong enough to blur the new culture war over the meaning of freedom itself. As a result, liberal and fundamentalist Protestants were on the same side of the election of 1928, the obscenity wars, and Prohibition. Beneath the surface, however, lay the question of how to affirm a transcendent moral order while giving individuals the right to choose virtually anything. Liberal Protestants were not yet forced to face that question, so the *Christian Century* editor could extol the virtues of both a conscience "individually formed" and society's corporate values to which all individual consciences were responsible. He never noticed the tension between these two positions.

Today's culture war makes slightly more sense as it pits the evangelical heirs of 1920s fundamentalists on one side of virtually every important public issue and liberal Protestants on the other. In the 1920s the situation was more complex as fundamentalists and liberals opposed each other in the fundamentalist-modernist controversy and the Scopes trial, only to be aligned with each other in the election of 1928, the obscenity wars, and Prohibition. After their pitched denominational battles and the Scopes trial of 1925, they were uneasy allies for the rest of the decade against the cultural liberals who led the secular revolution. Although the stated issues that divided fundamentalist and liberal Protestants in the first half of the decade were particular points of doctrine, views of the Bible, and whether the acceptability of evolution, the underlying issue was always authority. Fundamentalists recognized the Bible; liberal Protestants looked to individual religious experience. On the issue of authority, by the late 1920s fundamentalists were closer to Catholics than they were to liberal Protestants. And liberal Protestants, touting "consciences individually formed," were closer to the cultural liberals they fought against in the obscenity wars. Protestant anti-Catholicism, however, thwarted a new alignment that would have pitted Catholics and fundamentalists on one side against liberal Protestants and cultural liberals on the other.

The culture war over authority and individual autonomy of the Roaring Twenties calmed down considerably during the 1930s, only to be revived in slightly altered form in the last quarter of the twentieth century. During the middle third of the century Americans rallied together to defend liberal freedom, first against the onslaught of Nazi aggression during World War II and then against Soviet communism in the Cold War. Nazism and communism sought nothing less than the destruction of the liberal ideal of freedom based on individual autonomy. While they fought fascists and communists, all groups simply assumed they meant the same thing when they used the word "freedom." The fact that communism sought to eliminate the Christian faith as well as the liberal view of freedom also helped hold fundamentalists in the Cold War alliance with liberal Protestants. Catholics, Protestants of both liberal and fundamentalist stripes, and secular liberals could all agree that communism threatened everything held dear by Americans. Historian Richard Hofstadter once remarked that a single generation of post–World War II consensus caused Americans to forget decades of turmoil.

To the extent that there were culture wars fueled by religion between 1930 and the 1970s, they tended to run along Protestant-Catholic lines with religious liberty the issue. In 1949 Paul Blanshard authored a popular book entitled *American Freedom and Catholic Power,* which trotted out at length the kinds of issues Charles Marshall had covered in his open letter to Al Smith in 1927. Just prior to Blanshard's book, clergy and scholars had founded an organization dedicated to religious liberty and church-state separation called Protestants and Other Americans United for Separation of Church and State. Coming almost 20 years before the Catholic church's Declaration on Religious Freedom, the very name of this organization suggested that Catholics might not be fully American. The organization found its members among secular liberals, Jews, liberal Protestants, and some Southern Baptist leaders who had never seen a form of separation of church and state they did not like. As anti-Catholicism became a bigoted taboo during the 1960s, the name of the organization changed from Protestants and Other Americans to, simply, Americans United. In the meantime, Catholics distinguished themselves as fully American by solidly opposing communism during the Cold War and getting one of their own, John F. Kennedy, elected president.

In order to be elected in 1960, Kennedy had to go to Houston, Texas, the so-called buckle of the Bible Belt and the site of Al Smith's nomination in 1928. There, Kennedy told Protestants, "I believe in a President whose views on religion are his own private affair."[5] Kennedy's statement was more sweeping than Al Smith's claim in 1928: "I should be a poor American and a poor Catholic alike if I injected religious discussion into a political campaign."[6] In his response to Charles Marshall, Smith argued that there was no conflict between his faith and his political duties. Moreover, he said that different religions should tolerate each other, that all religions were equal before the law, that individuals had the right of conscience, and that there should be complete separation of church and state. But he never claimed that religion was merely a private affair. Rather, he extolled the virtues of religion in public life and said America needed more of it, especially among the youth.

By Kennedy's day, the belief that religion was a private matter was commonly paired with the idea that freedom was premised on the autonomy of the individual. The private nature of religion and the autonomy of the individual are the twin pillars of what I have called in this book "cultural liberalism," which was just beginning to take hold in the 1920s but was emerging as dominant by the time Kennedy ran for president. In contrast to the idea that religion was private, Smith went so far as to say "The law of the land is built upon the Commandments of God," something Christian Right activists argued with vigor after their reemergence on the political scene in 1980. Smith may have believed it unseemly or unmannerly to inject religion into a political campaign, and he knew that what drove Protestants to do so was often intolerance of Catholics. But he was not saying that America had a secular state or that religion was a private matter.

This is not to say that no one in the 1920s viewed religion as private. Clearly, Warren Harding did. Religion was both private and relatively unimportant for him, but he was never pressured to make such a claim as he campaigned for the presidency. It would have sounded odd and even ominous had he done so. There were also those such as Dudley Field Malone who said explicitly in the Scopes trial that people should keep their Bibles "in the world of your own conscience, in the world of your individual judgment." Malone was part of the culturally liberal minority, however, arguing a position he hoped might someday dominate the public landscape. Privatized religion had not yet become the dominant view. This would change over the course of the next four decades, the same decades that saw the autonomy of the individual become the dominant definition of American freedom.

The Cold War was the last historical era that allowed Americans of different religious persuasions to harbor the fiction that they all meant the same thing when they used the word "freedom." Without a communist bogeyman to hold the liberal-Protestant-secular coalition together, the old fault lines of the 1920s resurfaced, but with a twist.[7] Liberal Protestants switched sides, joining the ranks of the secular cultural liberals in affirming the autonomy of the indi-

vidual, or what the 1928 *Christian Century* editor called "the conscience individually formed." Liberal Catholics joined them, affirming with John F.
Kennedy that religion is a private matter. As then New York governor Mario
Cuomo told a 1984 Notre Dame University audience, "The values derived from
religious belief will not—and should not—be accepted as part of the public
morality unless they are shared by the pluralistic community at large, by consensus."[8] For Cuomo and other liberal Catholic politicians this means that while
they follow the teachings of the Catholic church by opposing abortion privately,
publicly they are pro-choice because each autonomous individual must decide
for herself whether to have an abortion or not. In other words, while privately
Catholic, publicly they follow the line of cultural or political liberalism. Like
the *Christian Century* editor of 1928, Cuomo held out the hope that we could
arrive at a consensus about what constitutes a good society, but thus far no one
on either side of today's culture wars has figured out how autonomous individuals can do that.

Evangelicals also switched sides in the recent culture wars, joining conservative Catholics in acknowledging that religious authority (the Bible, the
church, or both) stands above the individual conscience. The combatants in
America's culture wars have realigned, and the Protestant-Catholic divide that
seemed so central in the 1920s has dropped out of sight. New cultural issues
have emerged—abortion and gay rights to name two—while others from the
1920s are still with us. Among the latter are the relationship between science
and religion, what constitutes obscenity, and the intramural squabbling between
liberal and evangelical/fundamentalist Protestants. The underlying issue in
America's culture wars has not changed, however. Differing definitions of
human freedom were central in the Roaring Twenties, and they still are today.
As to the question of whether religion is a private matter, the quarter century
after 1980 has seen a return to the dominant view of the 1920s. Religion is, once
again, very public.

In 1980 three presidential candidates—Democrat Jimmy Carter, Republican Ronald Reagan, and independent John Anderson—all claimed publicly that
they were born-again Christians. Cultural liberals howled that religion was a
private matter. They might well have said that these candidates were taking us
back to the 1920s. From 1980 until 2000 the status of religion in presidential
campaigns was contested, with some candidates baring their religious souls
while others declined to go public with their faith. In 2000 there were again

three very publicly religious candidates in the presidential campaign: Republican George W. Bush, Democrat Al Gore, and Democratic vice presidential candidate Joseph Lieberman. Bush is a self-professed born-again evangelical, Gore an active Southern Baptist, and Lieberman an Orthodox Jew. It seemed as if the three competed to see who could most clearly articulate how his religious views shaped public policy. In 2004 Catholic Democratic presidential candidate John Kerry realized too late in his campaign that Kennedy's and Cuomo's cultural-liberal line about private religion would not do. A devout Roman Catholic privately, Kerry was nevertheless unaccustomed to talking about religion in public, quite possibly because he hailed from a section of the country where cultural liberalism was still dominant. Roundly denounced by bishops in his own church for his pro-choice stance on abortion, he tried late and feebly to articulate how religion played a role in his public life. This illustrates how much things had changed from 1960 when Kennedy ran. Kennedy needed to tell Americans how religion would not influence his politics; Kerry had to say how it would.

As Kerry's experience shows, after 2000 religious full disclosure was no longer optional. In 2008 candidates John McCain and Barack Obama talked openly about religion. Before they ever met face-to-face in debate, they both traveled to Saddleback Church, an evangelical megachurch in California, where they participated in nationally televised interviews with evangelical pastor Rick Warren. Both professed faith in Jesus Christ as their personal savior. Meanwhile both candidates had preacher problems. Obama had to answer for the odd, controversial, and borderline racist views of his pastor, Jeremiah Wright, while McCain had to distance himself from the fundamentalist endorsement of the Reverend John Hagee. A self-proclaimed Christian Zionist and end-times prophecy expert, Hagee on one occasion seemed to imply that God engineered the Holocaust to facilitate the creation of modern Israel, a nation that plays a central role in evangelical end-times prophecy. Newscasts ran video clips of Wright claiming the U.S. government spread AIDS in black communities, that the 911 terrorist attacks were God's judgment on America for racism, and that African Americans might well sing "God Damn America" rather than God Bless America.

While still a contender in the Republican primaries, Mitt Romney traveled to Texas and reprised Kennedy's speech from 1960. This was because evangelicals on the Christian Right were as worried about Romney's Mormonism as they had been about Kennedy's Catholicism. Rather than arguing that religion was merely a private affair as Kennedy had done, however, Romney said that the morality of his religion that would influence his potential presidency was the same morality touted by evangelicals and traditional Catholics. He was, in other words, publicly religious but only privately Mormon.[9] In this respect he sounded more like Al Smith than John F. Kennedy.

While evangelicals join traditional Catholics in applauding the forthrightness of candidates' public expressions of religion, cultural and political liberals continue to argue that religion is a private matter that should be left in the realm of autonomous individuals. Most of the liberal arguments are made in the halls of academia through scholarly articles that appear in journals that the wider public never reads. The idea that religion is private and should be kept out of politics has lost the popular favor it held in the 1960s and 1970s. As was the case in the 1920s, the liberal insistence that religion remain private is once again in the minority. At the popular level liberal pundits may argue why a particular candidate's religious views are detrimental to public welfare, but such pundits know they will get nowhere with the blanket claim that religion is a private matter. Kennedy's position from 1960 satisfies few today, and polls show that a majority of the American people want their president to be a person of deep religious faith.[10]

The status of religion has gone from public in the 1920s, to private at mid-century, then back to public after 1980. The related issue of freedom has seen a similar but not identical flip-flop. Freedom as individual autonomy was the minority view in the 1920s, advocated by cultural liberals against a waning Victorian, communitarian establishment. Today, the reverse is true: Autonomy is the publicly dominant view of freedom with communitarians of evangelical and traditional Catholic stripes holding forth a hearty critique. No one has yet solved the conundrum characterized by the *Christian Century* editor of 1928 as a contest between a "conscience individually formed" versus a "conscience formed under ecclesiastical [or biblical] authority." For better or worse, the culture war battles over the place of religion in public or private and the nature of American freedom are with us no less today than in the Roaring Twenties.

NOTES

CHAPTER 1

1. Harding's most extensive biography is Francis Russell, *The Shadow of Blooming Grove: Warren G. Harding in His Times* (New York: McGraw-Hill, 1968). Except where otherwise noted, the following story of Harding's affairs comes from Russell.
2. Russell tells this story in the final chapter of his biography; see ibid., 650–666. See also Robenalt, James, *The Harding Affair: Love and Espionage During the Great War* (New York: Palgrave Macmillan, 2009), 4–5 and 345–346.
3. Russell, Shadow of Blooming Grove, 93.
4. Ibid., 84–85.
5. Quoted in ibid., 401.
6. Unless otherwise noted, the story of Harding's relationship with Nan Britton comes from Britton's book, *The President's Daughter* (New York: Elizabeth Ann Guild, 1927).
7. Britton includes her entire letter and quotes from Harding's reply. See ibid., 23–24.
8. Russell, *Shadow of Blooming Grove*, 345.
9. Although there are some who doubt that Nan Britton's daughter was Harding's, recent historian, after analyzing the evidence, concludes it highly likely that Harding and Nan did have an affair. See Phillip Payne, *Dead Last: The Public Memory of Warren G. Harding's Scandalous Legacy* (Athens: Ohio University Press, 2009), 154.
10. Quoted in Britton, *President's Daughter,* 46–47
11. Ibid., 79.
12. Ibid., 124
13. Paraphrased in ibid., 132.
14. Ibid., 137.
15. Quoted in Russell, *Shadow of Blooming Grove,* 632.
16. Unless otherwise noted, my rendition of this story comes from M. R. Werner and John Starr, *Teapot Dome* (New York: Viking Press, 1959), and Laton McCartney, *The Teapot Dome Scandal: How Big Oil Bought the Harding White House and Tried to Steal the Country* (New York: Random House, 2008).
17. Quoted in McCartney, *Teapot Dome Scandal,* 109.
18. Ibid., 115.
19. Quoted in ibid., 140.
20. Werner and Starr, *Teapot Dome,* 94–95.
21. Quoted in ibid., 113.
22. Quoted in ibid., 154.
23. Quoted in ibid., 229–230.
24. Ibid., 281.
25. Quoted in ibid., 105.

26. Quoted in ibid., 105. (They cite Longworth's book *Crowded Hours* [New York: Scribner, 1934] but do not list the page number.)

27. Russell, *Shadow of Blooming Grove*, 168.

CHAPTER 2

1. Michael Lerner, *Dry Manhattan: Prohibition in New York City* (Cambridge, MA: Harvard University Press, 2007), 1–3; William Jennings Bryan, "Prohibition," *Outlook*, February 7, 1923, 262–265. This article can be found in Ray Ginger, *William Jennings Bryan: Selections* (Indianapolis: Bobbs-Merrill, 1967), 214–215.

2. Quoted in Norman H. Clark, *Deliver Us from Evil: An Interpretation of American Prohibition* (New York: W. W. Norton, 1976), 10.

3. James Timberlake, *Prohibition and the Progressive Movement, 1900–1920* (Cambridge, MA: Harvard University Press, 1963), 2.

4. Clark, *Deliver Us from Evil*, 13.

5. W. J. Rorabaugh, *The Alcoholic Republic: An American Tradition* (New York: Oxford University Press, 1979), 10.

6. Ibid.

7. Except where otherwise noted, I am following Clark in this overview of the Prohibition history.

8. Quoted in Lucile Sheppard Keyes, "Morris Sheppard" (Washington, DC: typed, manuscript, 1950), 111. This manuscript was compiled by Sheppard's daughter, who received a Ph.D. from Radcliffe College in 1948.

9. Quoted in Timberlake, *Prohibition and the Progressive Movement*, 179.

10. Billy Sunday, "Booze," in Barry Hankins, ed., *Evangelicalism and Fundamentalism: A Documentary Reader* (New York: New York University Press, 2008), 119–120.

11. Ibid., 120–121.

12. Quoted in Clark, *Deliver Us from Evil*, 60.

13. Ibid., 7.

14. Quoted in ibid., 41–42.

15. Quoted in ibid., 95.

16. D. G. Hart, *Defending the Faith: J. Gresham Machen and the Crisis of Conservative Protestantism in Modern America* (Baltimore MD: Johns Hopkins University Press, 1994), 135–139.

17. Quoted in Timberlake, *Prohibition and the Progressive Movement*, 22.

18. Robert Moats Miller, *Harry Emerson Fosdick: Preacher, Pastor, Prophet* (New York: Oxford University Press, 1985), 434.

19. Harry Emerson Fosdick, *Christianity and Progress* (New York: Fleming H. Revell, 1922), 135.

20. Charles Stelzle, *A Son of the Bowery: The Life Story of an East Side American* (Freeport, NY: Books for Libraries Press, 1926; reprinted 1971), 192–193.

21. Quoted in Stelzle, *A Son of the Bowery*, 203–204. Stelzle here quotes from his 1925 Detroit speech.

22. Quoted in ibid., 207.

23. Barry Hankins, *God's Rascal: J. Frank Norris and the Beginnings of Southern Fundamentalism* (Lexington: University Press of Kentucky, 1996), 46–49.

24. Quoted in ibid., 49–50.

25. Quoted in Clark, *Prohibition and the Progressive Movement*, 199.

26. Quoted in Dale E. Soden, *The Reverend Mark Matthews: An Activist in the Progressive Era* (Seattle: University of Washington Press, 2001), 189.

27. Quoted in Soden, *Reverend Mark Matthews*, 190.

28. Ibid., 190; and Norman Clark, *The Dry Years: Prohibition and Social Change in Washington* (Seattle: University of Washington Press, 1965), 209.

29. Quoted in "Prohibition Sectarianism," *Christian Century,* January 26, 1928, 104.

30. Ibid., 104.

31. Walter Lippmann, *A Preface to Morals* (New York: Time Inc., 1929; reprinted in 1964), 29.

32. Ibid., 258–259.

33. Stanwood Lee Henderson, "Failure of Dry Law," New York *Times,* February 1925, 18.

34. Ibid.

35. Quoted in Clark, *Dry Years,* 144.

36. Gifford Gordon, "A Dry Law Investigation," New York *Times,* February 9, 1925, 16.

37. Clark, *Dry Years,* 146.

38. For a discussion of the effectiveness of Prohibition, see ibid., 145–157.

39. Ibid., 158.

40. Morison and Taylor quoted in ibid., 144–145.

41. Ibid., 145.

42. I am partly indebted to Norman Clark for this interpretation. See ibid., 170–179.

CHAPTER 3

1. New York *Times,* March 12, 1920, 3.

2. "Sunday for Wood," New York *Times,* May 17, 1920, 13.

3. "Congratulated by Billy Sunday," New York *Times,* June 23, 1920, 2.

4. Unless otherwise noted, this overview of Sunday's life is based on William McLoughlin Jr., *Billy Sunday Was His Real Name* (Chicago: University of Chicago Press, 1955); Lyle W. Dorsett, *Billy Sunday and the Redemption of Urban America* (Grand Rapids, MI: Eerdmans, 1990; reprinted Macon, GA: Mercer University Press, 2004); and Robert F. Martin, *Hero of the Heartland: Billy Sunday and the Transformation of American Society, 1862–1935* (Bloomington: Indiana University Press, 2002).

5. Quoted in McLoughlin, *Billy Sunday Was His Real Name,* 6.

6. Newspaper clipping. Papers of William and Helen Sunday, Box 12, Folder 2, CN 61, Reel No. 19. Billy Graham Center, Wheaton College, Wheaton, Illinois.

7. *The Evangel,* October 16, 1895, 1. Papers of William and Helen Sunday, Box 12, Folder 4, CN 61, Reel No. 61.

8. Newspaper clipping, Papers of William and Helen Sunday, Box 12, Folder 4, CN 61, Reel No. 19.

9. Quoted in "Sunday Finishes His Work Here," New York *Times,* June 18, 1917, 9.

10. John D. Rockefeller Jr. to William A. Sunday, June 23, 1917, William and Helen Sunday Papers.

11. Frank P. Spellman to Mr. Billy Sunday, February 28, 1917; and Sunday to Spellman, n.d., William and Helen Sunday Papers, Reel 1.

12. Quoted in McLoughlin, *Billy Sunday Was His Real Name,* 45.

13. "Sidelights on Sunday as Orator-Gymnast," St. Louis *Globe Democrat,* January 9, 1928, 1.

14. Billy Sunday, "The All-America Professional Baseball Team," *Collier's,* October 14, 1911, 19–20; and Billy Sunday, "My All-Star Nine," *Collier's,* October 18, 1913, 19 and 30, quote on 30.

15. Quoted in Clifford Putney, *Muscular Christianity: Manhood and Sports in Protestant America, 1880–1920* (Cambridge, MA: Harvard University Press, 2003), 172.

16. Quoted in ibid., 200.

17. Ibid., 5–6 and 114.

18. Quoted in McLoughlin, *Billy Sunday Was His Real Name,* 64.

19. Quoted in "Here Is Billy Sunday's Story of Battle Waged on Platform," Atlanta *Journal,* December 22, 1917. Sunday was wired by the New York *Evening World* for his side of the story. Papers of William and Helen Sunday, Scrapbooks, 17–19, CN 61, Reel 26.

20. "Assailant Indicted on Three Counts," Atlanta *Journal,* December 21, 1917. Papers of William and Helen Sunday, Scrapbooks, 17–19, CN 61, Reel 26.

21. Quoted in "Wildly Excited Throng Threatens Life of Man Who Assails Evangelist, Atlanta *Journal,* December 21, 1927. Papers of William and Helen Sunday, Scrapbooks, 17–19 CN 61, Reel 26.

22. Quoted in McLoughlin, *Billy Sunday Was His Real Name,* 139.

23. Quoted in ibid., 131.

24. Quoted in ibid., 133.

25. Quoted in ibid., 133.

26. Quoted in ibid., 147.

27. Quoted in ibid., 149.

28. Billy Sunday to Helen, n.d. Papers of William and Helen Sunday.

29. Quoted in "Billy Urges Husbands to Give Their Wives a Few Bouquets While They Are Still Alive," St. Louis *Globe-Democrat,* January 12, 1928, 1.

30. Ma Sunday, "Should a Wife Work for a Living?" Bell Syndicate, September 24, 1917.

31. "9000 at 'Woman Only' Meeting See Sunday Do the Black Bottom," St. Louis *Globe-Democrat,* February 19, 1928, 1 and 4.

32. "Sunday Son Tries to Die," New York *Times,* November 19, 1923, 3; and Roger Bruns, *Preacher: Billy Sunday and Big-Time American Evangelism* (Urbana: University of Illinois Press, 1992), 276–277.

33. "Sues Billy Sunday, Jr.," New York *Times,* September 6, 1929, 2; "Mrs. Billy Sunday, Jr. to Wed," New York *Times,* July 19, 1930, N4.

34. Quoted in Bruns, *Preacher,* 285; and "G.M. Sunday Is Arrested," New York *Times,* November 25, 1929, 18; "Son of Billy Sunday Held," New York *Times,* March 27, 1930, 12.

35. "Billy Sunday's Son Near Death in Fall," New York *Times,* September 8, 1933, 40; "Billy Sunday's Son Dies," September 12, 1933, 3; and Bruns, 276–277 and 284–285.

36. Quoted in Dorsett, *Billy Sunday and the Redemption of Urban America,* 127.

37. "Evangelist Warns Nation Faces Ruin by Reckless Youth," Philadelphia *Inquirer,* September 13, 1926; article reprinted in Rader's magazine, *World Wide Christian Courier* (October 1926): 11–12

38. "Evangelist Warns Nation," 11–12.

39. "Evangelist Warns Nation," 12. For more on Rader, see: Larry Eskridge, "Only Believe: Paul Rader and the Chicago Gospel Tabernacle, 1922–1933," M.A. thesis, University of Maryland, 1985.

40. Eskridge, "Only Believe," 18–43.

41. Quoted in ibid., 76.

42. "Says Fight Would Shock Founders," *World Wide Christian Courier* (November 1926): 16.

43. Paul Rader, "A Perfecting Program," *Good News* (November 1918): 2.

44. Quoted in Tona Hangen, *Redeeming the Dial: Radio, Religion and Popular Culture in America* (Chapel Hill: University of North Carolina Press, 2002), 41.

45. "Athletics and Christians?" *World Wide Christian Courier* (June 1928): 15; and "Flaming Youth, No Indeed, Not at the Tabernacle, But We Have Youth Aflame," *World Wide Christian Courier* (June 1928): 5.

46. Ibid.

47. Quoted in Eskridge, "Only Believe," 173.

48. Paul Rader, "Events and Comments," *World Wide Christian Courier* (August 1927): 18.
49. Quoted in Hangen, *Redeeming the Dial,* 48.
50. Ibid., 43–45.
51. Eskridge, "Only Believe," 123.
52. Ibid., 120–123.
53. "Bible Foretold Radio, Says Pastor," *World Wide Christian Courier* (September 1928): 7. This article was put out on the wire by the Newspaper Enterprises Association and could be picked up by newspapers around the country.
54. See Terry Lindvall, *Sanctuary Cinema: Origins of the Christian Film Industry* (New York: New York University Press), 2007, 105–106 and 117–177.
55. Homer Rodeheaver, "Billy Sunday and Paul Rader at Winona Lake, Ind.," *World Wide Christian Courier,* September 1928, 8–9 and 28; and "Billy Sunday to Be in Movietone," New York *Times,* August 12, 1928, 26.

CHAPTER 4

1. Quoted in George Marsden, *Fundamentalism and American Culture: The Shaping of Twentieth-Century Evangelicalism, 1870–1925* (New York: Oxford University Press, 1980), 25.
2. Quoted in Robert Moats Miller, *Harry Emerson Fosdick: Preacher, Pastor, Prophet* (New York: Oxford University Press, 1985), 58. Unless otherwise noted, the biographical information on Fosdick comes from Miller.
3. Quoted in ibid., 40.
4. Quoted in ibid., 41.
5. Harry Emerson Fosdick, "Shall the Fundamentalists Win?" in Barry Hankins, ed., *Evangelicalism and Fundamentalism: A Documentary Reader* (New York: New York University Press, 2008), 52–58.
6. Quoted in Miller, *Harry Emerson Fosdick,* 116.
7. Quoted in Bradley J. Longfield, *The Presbyterian Controversy: Fundamentalists, Modernists, and Moderates* (New York: Oxford University Press, 1991), 11.
8. J. Gresham Machen, *Christianity and Liberalism* (Grand Rapids, MI: Eerdmans, 1923), 2 and 6–7.
9. Walter Lippmann, *A Preface to Morals* (New York: Macmillan, 1929; reprinted, Time Inc., 1964), 30.
10. Quoted in D. G. Hart, *Defending the Faith: J. Gresham Machen and the Crisis of Conservative Protestantism in Modern America* (Baltimore: Johns Hopkins University Press, 1994), 79.
11. Quoted in Longfield, *Presbyterian Controversy,* 74.
12. Quoted in ibid., 76.
13. Quoted in ibid.
14. Quoted in ibid., 79.
15. Quoted in ibid., 101–102.
16. "Dr. Fosdick's Case Sent to Committee," New York *Times,* May 24, 1924, 20.
17. "Presbyterian Head is Fundamentalist," New York *Times,* May 23, 1924, 7.
18. Quoted in Longfield, *Presbyterian Controversy,* 104.
19. Quoted in ibid., 125.
20. "Presbyterian Head is Fundamentalist," 7.
21. Quoted in Longfield, *Presbyterian Controversy,* 126.
22. Coffin letter quoted in "First Church Asks Dr. Fosdick to Join," New York *Times,* June 2, 1924, 10; also quoted in Longfield, *Presbyterian Controversy,* 126.

23. "Presbyterians Ask Dr. Fosdick to Join," New York *Times,* May 29, 1924, 1.

24. "Fosdick Decision Pleases Both Sides," New York *Times,* May 30, 1924, 6.

25. "New Fight Looms in Fosdick Case," New York *Times,* August 11, 1924, 8.

26. Fosdick letter reproduced in "Dr. Fosdick Resigns, Refuses to Accept Presbyterian Faith," New York *Times,* October 7, 1924, 1 and 3; quote on 3.

27. Longfield, *Presbyterian Controversy,* 149–151.

28. Quoted in "Billy Sunday Again Hits the Trail Here," New York *Times,* April 16, 1925, 14.

29. Longfield, *Presbyterian Controversy,* 152.

30. "Dr. Wishart Condemns Extreme Surgery," New York *Times,* May 26, 1924, 19.

31. Walter Lippmann, *American Inquisitors: A Commentary on Dayton and Chicago* (New York: Macmillan, 1928), 65–66; also quoted in Miller, *Harry Emerson Fosdick,* 177.

32. Lippmann, *A Preface to Morals,* 31.

33. Miller, *Harry Emerson Fosdick,* 112.

34. Quoted in ibid., 162.

35. Quoted in ibid., 390.

36. H. Richard Niebuhr, *The Kingdom of God in America* (Chicago: Willett, Clark, and Co., 1937), 193.

37. Ibid., 195.

38. See Joel Carpenter, *Revive Us Again: The Reawakening of Fundamentalism* (New York: Oxford University Press, 1997).

CHAPTER 5

1. "Presbyterians Open 136th Session Today," New York *Times,* May 22, 1924, 19.

2. Quoted in David Livingstone, *Darwin's Forgotten Defenders: The Encounter Between Evangelical Theology and Evolutionary Thought* (Grand Rapids, MI: Eerdmans, 1987), 118. See Barry Hankins, *American Evangelicals: A Contemporary History of a Mainstream Religious Movement* (Lanham, MD: Rowman and Littlefield, 2008), 49–82.

3. Quoted in Livingstone, *Darwin's Forgotten Defenders,* 105.

4. See James Orr, "Science and Christian Faith," and Henry Beach, "The Decadence of Darwinism." Both articles can be found in Barry Hankins, ed., *Evangelicalism and Fundamentalism: A Documentary Reader* (New York: New York University Press, 2008), 71–84.

5. David Lindberg and Ronald Numbers, "Beyond War and Peace: A Reappraisal of the Encounter between Christianity and Science," *Church History* 55, no. 3 (September 1986): 347.

6. Quoted in "Billy Sunday Hits Modernism and Wets," New York *Times,* December 21, 1925, 15.

7. This argument was first developed by George Marsden, *Fundamentalism and American Culture* (New York: Oxford University Press, 1980). It is still part of the standard argument for the development of fundamentalism. A twenty-fifth anniversary edition of the book was published in 2005.

8. Quoted in Edward Larson, *Summer for the Gods: The Scopes Trial and America's Continuing Debate Over Science and Religion* (New York: Basic Books, 1997), 32.

9. William Jennings Bryan, *In His Image* (New York: Fleming and Revell, 1922), 88.

10. Ibid., 118.

11. Ibid., 94.

12. Charles McD. Puckette, "The Evolution Arena at Dayton," New York *Times,* July 5, 1925, SM1 and 22; quotes on 22.

13. "Bryan in Dayton, Calls Scopes Trial 'Duel to the Death,'" New York *Times,* July 8, 1925, 1 and 6; quotes on 6.

14. Walter Lippmann, *American Inquisitors: A Commentary on Dayton and Chicago* (New York: Macmillan, 1928), 14. See also Michael Kazin, *A Godly Hero: The Life of William Jennings Bryan* (New York: Knopf, 2006), 275. Kazin covers Bryan's arguments nicely.

15. Lippmann, *American Inquisitors,* 10.

16. Quoted in "Bryan Threatens National Campaign to Bar Evolution," New York *Times,* July 9, 1925, 1 and 4; quotes on 4.

17. Quoted in ibid.

18. "Mencken Epithets Rouse Dayton's Ire," New York *Times,* July 17, 1925, 3.

19. "Bryan Threatens National Campaign to Bar Evolution."

20. "Full Text of Mr. Bryan's Argument Against Evidence of Scientists," New York *Times,* July 17, 1925, 1–2; quote on 2.

21. "Malone Demands Freedom of Mind," New York *Times,* July 17, 1925, 3.

22. Quoted in Larson, *Summer for the Gods,* 179.

23. "State's View of Evolution," New York *Times,* July 17, 1925, 1.

24. "Dramatic Scenes in Trial," New York *Times,* July 21, 1925, 1.

25. The complete trial transcript is available as an e-book as *The Complete Scopes Trial Transcript* (n.p.: n.d.); An edited version of the transcript is available at www.law.umkc .edu/faculty/projects/ftrials/scopes/day7.htm.

26. Quoted in Larson, *Summer for the Gods,* 189.

27. Quoted in ibid., 207.

28. Robert Moats Miller, *Harry Emerson Fosdick: Preacher, Pastor, Prophet* (New York: Oxford University Press, 1985), 308.

29. "Dramatic Scenes in Trial," New York *Times,* July 21, 1925, 1. I am quoting from the trial transcript. The *Times* reporter had the words slightly different.

30. "Final Scenes Dramatic," New York *Times,* July 22, 1925, 1.

31. Quoted in Larson, *Summer for the Gods,* 200.

32. Ibid., 220–221.

33. Quoted in ibid., 206.

34. Ibid., 226.

35. "Dayton Keyed Up for Opening Day of Scopes Trial," New York *Times,* July 10, 1925, 1 and 6; quote on 6.

36. "Cranks and Freaks Flock to Dayton," New York *Times,* July 11, 1925, 1–2; quote on 2.

37. Joseph Wood Krutch, "The Monkey Trial," *Commentary* 43, no. 5 (May 1967): 83.

38. "Inherit the Wind," *Time,* October 17, 1960, 95; and Stanley Kauffmann, "O Come All Ye Faithful," *The New Republic,* October 31, 1960, 30.

39. Quoted in Larson, *Summer for the* Gods, 242.

40. Roderick Nash quoted in ibid., 227. See Roderick Nash, *The Nervous Generation: American Thought, 1917–1930* (Chicago: Rand McNally, 1970), 5–8.

41. Quoted in Larson, *Summer for the Gods,* 242.

42. Stephen Jay Gould, *Hen's Teeth and Horse's Toes* (New York: Norton, 1983), 270.

43. "Malone Demands Freedom of Mind," New York *Times,* July 17, 1925, 3.

CHAPTER 6

1. Carey McWilliams, "Aimee Semple McPherson: 'Sunlight in My Soul,'" in *The Aspirin Age, 1919–1941,* ed. Isabel Leighton (New York: Simon and Schuster, 1949), 60.

2. Unless otherwise noted, information on Aimee's early life comes from Edith L. Blumhofer, *Aimee Semple McPherson: Everybody's Sister* (Grand Rapids, MI: Eerd-

mans, 1993). Another recent biography focuses more on her later career. See Matthew Sutton, *Aimee Semple McPherson and the Resurrection of Christian America* (Cambridge, MA: Harvard University Press, 2007).

3. Blumhofer, *Everybody's Sister,* 59.
4. Quoted in ibid., 238–239.
5. Quoted in ibid., 262.
6. See Harry Stout, The *Divine Dramatist: George Whitefield and the Rise of Modern Evangelicalism* (Grand Rapids, MI: Eerdmans, 1991).
7. Blumhofer, *Everybody's Sister,* tells this dramatic story superbly on 268–269.
8. "Divers Seek Body of Woman Preacher," New York *Times,* May 21, 1926, 14; and "Search Sea Bed for Body of Aimee McPherson; Thousands Join Hunt for Noted Evangelist," New York *Times,* May 24, 1926, 3.
9. "New Hunt Started for Mrs. M'Pherson," New York *Times,* June 4, 1926, 6.
10. "Beach Patrol Quits Hunt for Evangelist," New York *Times,* June 5, 1926, 14.
11. "Woman Evangelist Escapes Abductors," New York *Times,* June 24, 1926, 1 and 5.
12. "Mother Hurries to Her Side," New York *Times,* June 24, 1926, 5.
13. "Her Prison Sought by Mrs. M'Pherson," New York *Times,* June 25, 1926, 3; "Mrs. M'Pherson Fails to Find Prison Cabin," New York *Times,* June 26, 1926, 15; and "Aboard Train with Aimee Semple McPherson, Near Gila," New York *Times,* June 27, 1926, 12.
14. "Los Angeles Hails Aimee M'Pherson," New York *Times,* June 27, 1926, 12.
15. "Two Juries Start M'Pherson Inquiry," New York *Times,* July 3, 1926, 13; "Woman Evangelist Summoned by Jury," New York *Times,* July 7, 1926, 14; and "Aimee Case Laid Before Jury," New York *Times,* July 8, 1926, 8.
16. Sutton tells the story of McPherson's kidnapping: *Aimee Semple McPherson,* 90–151.
17. "Mother Collapses in M'Pherson Trial," 1. Minnie's collapse took place in the second grand jury inquiry while this exchange between Keyes and Aimee from the first grand jury was being read into the record.
18. "Mrs. M'Pherson Tells Story to Grand Jury," New York *Times,* July 9, 1926, 40; and "Mother Is Questioned in M'Pherson Case," New York *Times,* July 14, 1926, 3.
19. "Says Mrs. M'Pherson Was with Ormiston," New York *Times,* July 16, 1926, 4; and "Kidnapped Evangelist in Perjury Inquiry," New York *Times,* July 29, 1926, 18.
20. "Says She 'Doubled' for Mrs. M'Pherson," New York *Times,* September 14, 1926, 3.
21. "Aimee M'Pherson Ordered Arrested," New York *Times,* September 16, 1926, 1 and 18.
22. "Aimee M'Pherson Cheered and Jeered as She Is Arraigned," New York *Times,* September 18, 1926, 1 and 5; quote on 5.
23. "Fail to Recognize Mrs. M'Pherson," New York *Times,* September 28, 1926, 1 and 12.
24. "Mother Collapses in M'Pherson Trial," 1; and "Ormiston Linked to Mrs. M'Pherson," New York *Times,* October 1, 1926, 25. Quote from letter in October 1 article.
25. "Will Arrest Seven in M'Pherson Case," New York *Times,* September 18, 1926, 2.
26. Richard Creedon, "Evangelist's Daughter in Tragic Scene," Seattle *Post Intellingencer,* September 27, 1926, 1.
27. "Martyr Show Given By Mrs. M'Pherson," New York *Times,* October 4, 1926, 25.
28. "Warrant Is Ready for Mrs. M'Pherson," New York *Times,* September 19, 1926, 28.
29. "Says Mrs. M'Pherson Can Find Ormiston," New York *Times,* October 28, 1926, 18. Emphasis in original.
30. Quoted in Sutton, *Aimee Semple McPherson,* 134.
31. "Says Hair Is Clue in M'Pherson Case," New York *Times,* October 30, 1926, 19; and "Seized Trunk Here Left by Ormiston," New York *Times,* October 29, 1926, 25.
32. "Rich Feminine Garb in Ormiston Trunk," New York *Times,* November 2, 1926, 29.
33. "Finds New Letters in M'Pherson Case," New York *Times,* October 31, 1926, 12.
34. "Find Second Trunk in M'Pherson Case," New York *Times,* November 3, 1926, 14.

35. "Aimee M'Pherson Is Held for Trial," New York *Times*, November 4, 1926, 29.

36. "Ormiston Quoted in M'Pherson Case," New York *Times*, October 9, 1926, 5; "Ormiston Is Caught After Long Search," New York *Times*, December 10, 1926, 1 and 15; and "Parents to Stand by Him," New York *Times*, December 19, 1926, 15.

37. "Ormiston Gives Up in Los Angeles," New York *Times*, December 18, 1926, 3; and "Ormiston Surrenders and Is Held on Bail," New York *Times*, December 19, 1926, 24. Quote in "Ormiston Surrenders."

38. "M'Pherson Lawyer Accuses Witness," New York *Times*, October 12, 1926, 20.

39. "Opens New Inquiry in M'Pherson Case," New York *Times*, December 30, 1926, 10.

40. "Prosecutor Frees Aimee M'Pherson," New York *Times*, January 11, 1927, 26. See also "Opens New Inquiry in M'Pherson Case"; "New Charges Wait in M'Pherson Case," New York *Times*, December 31, 1926, 3; "Will Try Mrs. Aimee," New York *Times*, January 1, 1927, 3; "Ormiston Tells of 'Miss X' Trip," New York *Times*, January 2, 1927, 28.

41. Sutton, *Aimee Semple McPherson*, 137.

42. Ibid., 138–139; Louis Pizzitola, *Hearst over Hollywood: Power Passion, and Propaganda in the Movies* (New York: Columbia University Press, 2002), 223–224; "Keyes Guilty of Bribery and Conspiracy: Aides of Los Angeles Prosecutor Convicted," New York *Times*, February 9, 1929, 1; and "$800,000 Hush Fund Laid to Evangelist: Los Angeles Grand Jury Delves into Story of Prosecution of Aimee McPherson," New York *Times*, November 13, 1928, 20.

43. Blumhofer, *Everybody's Sister*, 300.

44. Sutton, *Aimee Semple McPherson*, 141.

45. Ibid., 273–274.

46. "Aimee McPherson Invades Broadway," New York *Times*, September 19, 1933, 23.

47. "Aimee McPherson Marries on Yuma Flight," New York *Times*, September 14, 1931, 1. Kennedy quoted in Sutton, *Aimee Semple McPherson*, 170.

48. "Aimee Hutton Sued by Singer Husband," New York *Times*, July 18, 1933, 19; and "Aimee M'Pherson Files Divorce Suit," New York *Times*, December 21, 1933, 22.

49. Quoted in Blumhofer, *Everybody's Sister*, 346.

50. Sutton, *Aimee Semple McPherson*, 192.

51. Quoted in ibid., 223. Aimee's efforts to restore a Christian America are central to Sutton's interpretation of her.

52. Joel Carpenter, *Revive Us Again: The Reawakening of Fundamentalism* (New York: Oxford University Press, 1997).

53. Blumhofer, *Everybody's Sister*, 376–379; and "Aimee M'Pherson Rites," New York *Times*, October 10, 1944, 23. Photo layout and article covering McPherson's funeral appeared in major newsmagazines. See Aimee Semple McPherson Ephemera file in Billy Graham Center/Archives, CN 103, Box 1, Billy Graham Center, Wheaton College, Wheaton, Illinois.

CHAPTER 7

1. For a biography of Norris, see Barry Hankins, *God's Rascal: J. Frank Norris and the Beginnings of Southern Fundamentalism* (Lexington: University Press of Kentucky, 1996).

2. "Burning of Norris's Home Is Shrouded in Mystery, Officers Without a Clue," Fort Worth *Record*, March 3, 1912, 1.

3. Quoted in Hankins, *God's Rascal*, 28.

4. "Six Members of First Baptist Church Fired by L.B. Haughey, Roman Catholic Manager of Meacham Dry Goods Co.," *Searchlight*, July 16, 1926, 1, 2, and 5.

5. "J. Frank Norris Under $10,000 Bond; Fort Worth Man Slain," Dallas *Morning News*, July 18, 1926, 1–2.

6. "Slayer Preaches to Packed Church," New York *Times,* July 19, 1926, 1 and 3; "Hear Frank Norris in Pulpit after Tragedy," Dallas *Morning News,* July 19, 1926, 1.

7. Charlotte *Observer,* July 19, 1926, 1.

8. "Plot to Kill Norris Charged by Church," New York *Times,* July 20, 1926, 9; "Norris Demands Murder Indictment," New York *Times,* July 21, 1926, 8; "Dr. Norris Charges New Evidence of a Plot," New York *Times,* July 22, 1926, 6; Norris Asks to Be Indicted, Dallas *Morning News,* July 21, 1926, 1 and last page sec. 1; "Mayor Defends Slain Friend," Dallas *Morning News,* July 22, 1926, 1.

9. "Norris Demands Change of Venue," Dallas *Morning News,* November 2, 1926, 1–2, quote on 2.

10. "State Rests Case in Norris Trial," Dallas *Morning News,* January 15, 1926, 1 and 3.

11. "Chipps Threat to Kill Norris Told on Stand," Dallas *Morning News,* January 16, 1927, 1 and 4; "Two Swear Chipps Threatened Norris," New York *Times,* January 16, 1927, 1 and 19.

12. "Chipps Called Quarrelsome by Witnesses," Dallas *Morning News,* January 18, 1927, 1 and last page of section.

13. "Woman Describes Threats on Norris," New York *Times,* January 20, 1927, 2. I am using the New York *Times* here because the available Dallas *Morning News* edition is illegible.

14. "'I Feared for My Life and I Killed Him,'" Dallas *Morning News,* January 22, 1927, 1 and 3; and "Norris, Amid Sobs, Tells of Killing," New York *Times,* January 22, 1927, 1 and 7.

15. "Asks Death Penalty for Pastor," New York *Times,* January 25, 1927, 25; "Not Guilty Jury Finds Dr. Norris in Quick Verdict," Dallas *Morning News,* January 26, 1927, 1; and "Norris Acquitted in Swift Verdict," New York *Times,* January 26, 1927, 1.

16. "First Baptist Church Burns at Fort Worth," Dallas *Morning News,* January 13, 1929, 1 and 3.

17. Quoted in Hankins, *God's Rascal,* 152.

18. Quoted in "Baptists See Pope, Back Truman View," New York *Times,* September 6, 1947, 7.

19. Quoted in Hankins, *God's Rascal,* 135.

20. "Norris Blast Stirs Baptists," Dallas *Morning News,* May 7, 1947, 1.

21. Ralph McGill, "Editorial," Atlanta *Journal Constitution,* May 8, 1947; and "Baptist Meeting Thrown into Disorder as Rev. J. Frank Norris Makes Query," Atlanta *Journal Constitution,* May 7, 1947.

22. "Jury Finds Norris Guilty of Malicious Libel," *Amazing Grace,* September 27, 1940, 1; and Record of Norris Libel Payment, Norris File, Roberts Library, Southwestern Baptist Theological Seminary, Fort Worth, Texas. This document is a handwritten note on Texas Baptist Historical Library stationery saying "J. Frank Norris paid D.F. Park $2000 to satisfy the libel judgment secured by R.E. White from the 73rd District Court in San Antonio, Texas. See County Clerk, Tarrant County, Texas, instrument recorded March 5, 1945 at 2:35 p.m."

23. Jerry Falwell, "New Foreword," in Louis Entzminger, *The J. Frank Norris I Have Known for 34 Years* (Fort Worth, TX: New Testament Ministries, n.d.), 4. This book has no publication date listed on the title page or elsewhere. It appears to have been published in the early 1970s. Falwell wrote and signed the "New Foreword."

CHAPTER 8

1. Quoted in Marie W. Dallam, *Daddy Grace: A Celebrity Preacher and His House of Prayer* (New York: New York University Press, 2007), 46. Unless otherwise noted, the biographical material on Grace comes from Dallam.

2. Ibid., 39.

3. Quoted in ibid., 48.

4. "'Healer' Stirs Negro Frenzy," Charlotte *Observer*, July 1, 1926, 3 and 6; and "Negroes Still Bow at Shrine of 'Faith Man,'" Charlotte *Observer*, July 8, 1926, 3.

5. Quoted in "Spiritual Life Not for Wife, So Daddy's Marriage Ended," Charlotte, *Observer*, January 13, 1960. Black was being interviewed for an article done when Grace died that month. This article is in the Grace File, Charlotte *Observer* Library.

6. Quoted in Dallam, *Daddy Grace*, 51–52.

7. Quoted in ibid., 54–55.

8. Quoted in Don Oberdorfer, "Grace Meant 'Faith' to Followers," Charlotte *Observer*, February 5, 1960. Oberdorfer was the religion editor for the *Observer* and followed Grace's career for many years, writing several articles. In this one he was quoting Grace from a black newspaper.

9. Don Oberdorfer, "Daddy Grace Profited by Being a Prophet," Charlotte *Observer*, February 1960, in Grace File, Charlotte *Observer* Library.

10. Dallam, *Daddy Grace*, 133.

11. Don Oberdorfer, "U.S. Claims Daddy Owes $5,990,600," Charlotte *Observer*, February 2, 1960; "$1.9 Million Is Offered from Grace Estate," Charlotte *Observer*, February 1, 1961; and "Daddy Grace Estate Pays $1.94 Million," Charlotte *Observer*, June 3, 1961. In Grace File, Charlotte *Observer* Library.

12. "Negro Bishop Convicted," New York *Times*, March 17, 1934, 9; and "Negro Bishop Gets Year," New York *Times*, March 22, 1924, 7.

13. Dallam, *Daddy Grace*, 96–105.

14. Quoted in ibid., 102.

15. Ibid., 103.

16. Quotes from ibid., 86–90.

17. Quoted in Robert Weisbrot, *Father Divine and the Struggle for Racial Equality* (Urbana: University of Illinois Press, 1983), 19. Unless otherwise noted, the biographical information on Father Divine comes from Weisbrot.

18. Quoted in ibid, 19.

19. Quoted in ibid.

20. Study cited in ibid., 43. The study was Seth Scheiner, "The Negro Church and the Northern City, 1890–1930," in *Seven on Black: Reflections on the Negro Experience in America*, ed. William Shade and Roy Herrenkohl (Philadelphia: J. B. Lippincot, 1969), 100–101.

21. Quoted in Weisbrot, *Father Divine*, 47.

22. "Defense of 'Heaven' Jeered by Villagers," New York *Times*, November 22, 1931, 69.

23. "Offers His Aid to 'Heaven,'" New York *Times*, November 29, 1931, 31.

24. Quoted in "Disorder in 'Heaven' Convicts Evangelist," New York *Times*, May 26, 1932, 27.

25. "Leader of 'Heaven' Gets Year in Jail," New York *Times*, June 5, 1932, 5; and "Justice L.J. Smith Dies Unexpectedly," New York *Times*, June 9, 1932, 21.

26. "Convert Repays Relief," New York *Times*, August 14, 1938, 3.

27. Quoted in Weisbrot, *Father Divine*, 92–93.

28. Quoted in "Must Drop Divine Names," New York *Times*, June 1, 1938, 5.

29. "Divine's Adherent Loses," New York *Times*, August 26, 1938, 19; and "Divine Disciples Barred," New York *Times*, September 21, 1938, 20.

30. "Rioting in Heaven, Police Hunt Divine," New York *Times*, April 21, 1937, 1; "Father Divine Routed Out by Police from Hiding Place Behind Furnace," New York *Times*, April 23, 1937, 1.

31. "Divine Is Deserted by Head 'Angel,'" New York *Times*, April 22, 1937, 1; "Divine's Heaven Upstate Burned," New York *Times*, April 25, 1937, 1; "Divine Aide Surrenders," New York *Times*, April 29, 1937, 3.

32. "Rival Casts Eye on Divine's Flock," New York *Times*, February 22, 1938, 23.

33. Quoted in Dallam, *Daddy Grace*, 126.

34. Weisbrot, *Father Divine*, 122–123.

35. "Divine's Heaven Bought By Rival," New York *Times*, February 21, 1938, 21.

36. "Rival Takes Title to Divine 'Heaven,'" New York *Times*, March 4, 1938, 25.

37. "Father Divine Group Buys 'Krum Elbow' Estate Facing Roosevelt's on the Hudson," July 29, 1938, 1; "50 Room City Home Bought for Divine," New York *Times*, August 4, 1938, 3; and Robert Bird, "The Divine Movement Waxes," New York *Times*, August 7, 1938, 62.

38. Quoted in Weisbrot, *Father Divine*, 212.

39. Quoted in ibid., 213.

40. Quoted in ibid., 214.

CHAPTER 9

1. Herbert Asbury, "Hatrack," *American Mercury* (April 1926): 479–483. For an excellent discussion of this and other similar incidents, see P. C. Kemeny, "Power, Ridicule, and the Destruction of Religious Moral Reform Politics in the 1920s," in *The Secular Revolution: Power, Interests, and Conflict in the Secularization of American Public Life*, ed. Christian Smith (Berkeley: University of California Press, 2003), 216–268.

2. Charles Angoff, "Boston Twilight," *American Mercury* (December 1925): 439 and 441.

3. Quoted in Kemeny, "Power, Ridicule, and the Destruction of Religious Moral Reform Politics," 232, from an unpublished manuscript by Mencken. See also A. L. S. Wood, "Keeping the Puritans Pure," *American Mercury* (September 1925): 74–78.

4. Quoted in "Mencken Acquitted in Boston Court," New York *Times*, April 8, 1926, 27.

5. Quoted in "Injunction Granted on Mencken Plea," New York *Times*, April 15, 1926, 14.

6. Samuel Walker, *In Defense of Liberties: A History of the ACLU* (New York: Oxford University Press, 1990), 82.

7. "Censorship and Prohibition," *Christian Century*, July 19, 1923, 901.

8. Ibid., 902.

9. Ibid., *Christian Century*, July 19, 1923, 902.

10. Quoted in "Judge Read Piece in Mencken Case," New York *Times*, April 7, 1926, 25.

11. Quoted in Kemeny, "Power, Ridicule, and the Destruction of Religious Moral Reform Politics," 217.

12. Ibid., 226.

13. Ibid., 229.

14. Quoted in ibid., 231.

15. Ibid., 235.

16. "Confer in Boston on Banned Books," New York *Times*, March 13, 1927, 2. The story of the Boston Book War can also be found in Paul Boyer, *Purity in Print: Book Censorship in America from the Gilded Age to the Computer Age*, 2nd ed. (Madison: University of Wisconsin Press, 2002), 167–206. The book chapter is titled "Bannned in Boston."

17. "Publishers Protest Book Ban," New York *Times*, April 15, 1927, 2.

18. Matthew Sutton, *Aimee Semple McPherson and the Resurrection of Christian America* (Cambridge, MA: Harvard University Press, 2007), 146–147.

19. Fort Worth *Star Telegram*, November 1, 1937 (morning edition only), 12. Also quoted in Barry Hankins, *God's Rascal: J. Frank Norris and the Beginnings of Southern Fundamentalism* (Lexington: University Press of Kentucky, 1996), 92.

20. Quoted in "White Hits Lewis' 'Gantry,'" New York *Times*, March 11, 1927, 4.

21. Quoted in "Elmer Gantry Not Real," New York *Times*, March 20, 1927, 19.

22. "Prosecutor Assails Booksellers," New York *Times*, April 16, 1927, 16. This article had a few paragraphs about the prosecutor; the rest covered O'Connell's review of *Elmer Gantry.*

23. Quoted in "Dr. Cadman Denounces Lewis in London Talk," New York *Times*, July 12, 1927, 7.

24. Quoted in Kemeny, "Power, Ridicule, and the Destruction of Religious Moral Reform Politics," 241.

25. Stanley Coben, *Rebellion against Victorianism: The Impetus for Cultural Change in 1920s America* (New York: Oxford University Press, 1991), 41–42.

26. Ibid., 43.

27. "Publishers Test Boston Book Ban," New York *Times*, April 17, 1927, 23; and Kemeny, "Power, Ridicule, and the Destruction of Religious Moral Reform Politics," 242–243.

28. "Darrow Reads to Jury Part of Dreiser's Book," New York *Times*, April 18, 1929, 2.

29. Quoted in "Dr. Bowie Deplores 'Sneering' Writers," New York *Times*, August 5, 1929, 14.

30. Quoted in Kemeny, "Power, Ridicule, and the Destruction of Religious Moral Reform Politics," 245.

31. Quoted in "Darrow Pokes Fun at Book Censorship," New York *Times*, April 17, 1929, 12.

32. Kemeny, "Power, Ridicule, and the Destruction of Religious Moral Reform Politics," 247.

33. Walker, *In Defense of American Liberties,* 83–84.

34. D. H. Lawrence, *Lady Chatterley's Lover,* ed. Michael Squires (Cambridge: Cambridge University Press, 1993), xxxii–xl; See also Boyer, *Purity in Print,* 340.

35. Quoted in Kemeny, "Power, Ridicule, and the Destruction of Religious Moral Reform Politics," 258–259.

36. All quotes from "Decency Squabble," *Time,* March 31, 1930.

37. Kemeny, "Power, Ridicule, and the Destruction of Religious Moral Reform Politics," 260.

38. Historian Rochelle Gurstein has discussed America's obscenity wars under the title *The Repeal of Reticence* (New York: Hill and Wang, 1996). She argues that the battle from the Gilded Age (1877–1900) through the 1930s was between the party of reticence that sought to uphold public decorum and the party of exposure that sought maximum freedom for individual expression regardless of the coarsening and vulgarizing of society that might ensue.

CHAPTER 10

1. Unless otherwise noted, background information on Smith comes from Christopher M. Finan, *Alfred E. Smith: The Happy Warrior* (New York: Hill and Wang, 2002).

2. Quoted in ibid., 100.

3. Quoted in ibid., 18.

4. Quoted in ibid., 107.

5. Quoted in ibid., 117.

6. Quoted in ibid.

7. Ibid., 119.

8. Quoted in ibid., 186.

9. "Talk of Smith for Senate," New York *Times*, November 5, 1925, 1.

10. Walter Lippmann, *Men of Destiny* (New York: Macmillan, 1927), 7.

11. Quoted in Finan, *Alfred E. Smith*, 164.

12. Quoted in ibid., 165.

13. Lippmann, *Men of Destiny*, 1–4, and 9.

14. Charles C. Marshall, "An Open Letter to the Honorable Alfred E. Smith," *Atlantic Monthly* (April 1927): 540.

15. Ibid., 548.

16. "Gov. Smith's Reply to Be out Tomorrow," New York *Times*, April 17, 1927, 1; preface to Alfred E. Smith, "Catholic and Patriot: Governor Smith Replies," *Atlantic Monthly* (May 1927): 721.

17. Smith, "Catholic and Patriot," 722–723.

18. Quoted in ibid., 735.

19. John A. Ryan and Moorhouse F. X. Millar, *The State and the Church* (New York: Macmillan, 1922), 39.

20. Quoted in Smith, "Catholic and Patriot," 725.

21. Quoted in ibid., 726.

22. Ibid., "Catholic and Patriot," 728.

23. J. Frank Norris, "Roman Catholic Control of New York," *Searchlight*, January 11, 1924, 2.

24. J. Frank Norris, "The Conspiracy of Rum and Romanism to Rule This Government," *Searchlight*, February 5, 1926, 6. Quoted in Barry Hankins, *God's Rascal: J. Frank Norris and the Beginnings of Southern Fundamentalism* (Lexington: University Press of Kentucky, 1996), 54.

25. George W. Truett, "Christian Citizenship and Baptists," Texas *Baptist Standard*, October 4, 1928, 3.

26. J. Frank Norris, "Herbert Hoover and Prohibition v. Al Smith and the Brass Rail," *Fundamentalist*, June 22, 1928, 8. Quoted in Hankins, *God's Rascal*, 62.

27. Norris to Lon F. Anderson, Brooklyn, New York, August 27, 1928, Norris Papers, Texas Collection, Baylor University, Waco, Texas. Quoted in Hankins, *God's Rascal*, 62.

28. "Six Thousand Dallasites Enthusiastically Cheer Name of Hoover Monday Night," *Fundamentalist*, August 24, 1928, 4. Quoted in Hankins, *God's Rascal*, 61.

29. "Al Smith and the Negro," *Fundamentalist*, October 19, 1928, 4.

30. Quoted in Hankins, *God's Rascal*, 64.

31. Quoted in Boston *Sunday Post*, May 29, 1927, n.p. available. Clipping found in William and Helen Sunday Papers, Billy Graham Center/Archives, Wheaton College, Wheaton, Illinois.

32. Quoted in "15,000 People Hear Billy Sunday Bombard the Devil, Lambast Divorce and Hurl Bombs at Whisky Drinkers," St. Louis *Globe Democrat*, January 9, 1928, 1 and 4; quote on 4.

33. Quoted in ibid.

34. Quoted in "Billy Sunday for Hoover," New York *Times*, June 17, 1928, 29. The *Times* article recalled this quote from Sunday's St. Louis Campaign in January-February.

35. Quoted in "Billy Sunday Says He Will Fight Al Smith," New York *Times*, August 7, 1928, 4.

36. Quoted in "Billy Sunday Scores Smith in Jersey Talk," New York *Times*, September 2, 1928, 5.

37. "Sunday Quits Ocean Grove," New York *Times*, September 4, 1928, 5.

38. Quoted in "Answers Sunday on Smith," New York *Times*, September 17, 1928, 35; "Regrets Political Talk," New York *Times*, September 19, 1928, 2; and "Denies Political Talk," New York *Times*, September 20, 1928, 3.

39. Charles Curtis to Reverend W. A. Sunday, November 10, 1928, William and Helen Sunday Papers.

40. Lawrence Richey, secretary to the president, to Reverend W. A. Sunday, March 23, 1929, William and Helen Sunday Papers.

41. Quoted in William G. McLoughlin, Jr., *Billy Sunday Was His Real Name* (Chicago: University of Chicago Press, 1955), 285.

42. Quoted in Hankins, *God's Rascal,* 151.

43. Quoted in Mark Sutton, *Aimee Semple McPherson and the Resurrection of Christian America* (Cambridge, MA: Harvard University Press, 2007), 213.

44. D. G. Hart, *Defending the Faith: J. Gresham Machen and the Crisis of Conservative Protestantism in Modern America* (Baltimore, MD: Johns Hopkins Press, 1994), 136–137.

45. "White Now Stands by Smith Charges," New York *Times,* August 15, 1928, 3.

46. "Smith Aids Vice, Straton Charges," New York *Times,* August 6, 1928, 16.

47. "Smith Demands Straton Let Him Answer Attack In Church; Pastor Willing," New York *Times,* August 8, 1928, 1.

48. "Governor Smith Insists Answer to Straton Be Made in Church," New York *Times,* August 9, 1928, 1 and 4.

49. "Straton Accepts Smith's Challenge to Debate Charges," New York *Times,* August 10, 1928, 1.

50. "Dr. Straton Agrees to Church Debate," New York *Times,* August 11, 1928, 2.

51. "Straton Now Bans Debate in Church," New York *Times,* August 12, 1928, 9; and "Straton Formally Bars Pulpit Debate," New York *Times,* August 13, 1928, 4.

52. "Offerman Scores Straton," New York *Times,* August 13, 1928, 4.

53. Quoted in "Methodist Denounces Smith Pulpit Critics," New York *Times,* September 7, 1928, 3.

54. Quoted in "'Answer Yes or No' Smith Asks Straton," New York *Times,* August 15, 1928, 1; and "Liquor in His Hotel, Dr. Straton Hears," New York *Times,* August 14, 1928, 3.

55. "Liquor in His Hotel, Dr. Straton Hears," 3; "Dr. Straton Sues on Liquor Story," New York *Times,* October 26, 1928, 28; "Straton Sees a Plot as His Hotel Burns," New York *Times,* November 11, 1928, 1; and "Straton Repeats Charge," New York *Times,* November 12, 1928, 30.

56. Quoted in "Straton Reiterates Charges Against Smith," New York *Times,* August 27, 1928, 4.

57. "Straton Flays Smith at Raleigh, Seeking Daniels as Convert," Charlotte *Observer,* September 4, 1928, 1.

58. All quotes from "Smith Assails Intolerance, Answers Foes on Record, Oklahoma Crowd Cheers," New York *Times,* September 21, 1928, 1–2.

59. Quoted in "Straton Raps Smith in Oklahoma City," New York *Times,* September 22, 1928, 4.

60. Quoted in "Straton Says Smith Dragged in Religion," New York *Times,* September 23, 1928, 12.

61. Quoted in "Star-Telegram Account of Straton's Address," *Fundamentalist,* September 28, 1928, 2. Norris here reprinted the Fort Worth *Telegram's* coverage of Straton's address at First Baptist Fort Worth.

62. Quoted in "Vote Pleases Evangelist," New York *Times,* November 10, 1928, 3; and "Ask Dry Law Victory in Prayer and Fasting," New York *Times,* November 6, 1928, 29.

CHAPTER 11

1. John McGreevy, *Catholicism and American Freedom* (New York: Norton, 2003).

2. "What Elected Hoover?" *Christian Century,* November 15, 1928, 1388.

3. Ibid.

4. For a discussion of how pornography complicates the censorship issue, especially for feminists, see Paul Boyer, *Purity in Print: Book Censorship in America from the Gilded Age to the Computer Age,* 2nd ed. (Madison: University of Wisconsin Press, 2002), 329–361.

5. John F. Kennedy, "Address to the Greater Houston Ministerial Association," September 12, 1960. Kennedy's speech can be accessed at: www.americanrhetoric.com/speeches/jfkhoustonministers.html.

6. Alfred E. Smith, "Catholic and Patriot: Governor Smith Replies," *Atlantic Monthly* (May 1927): 721. See also "Full Text of Governor Smith's Reply on Religious Issue," New York *Times,* April 18, 1927, 2.

7. George Marsden, *Religion and American Culture,* 2nd ed. (New York: Harcourt College Publishers, 2001, 1990), 188.

8. Mario Cuomo, "Religious Belief and Public Morality," University of Notre Dame, September 13, 1984. The speech can be accessed at: http://archives.nd.edu/research/texts/cuomo.htm or www.americanrhetoric.com.

9. For a discussion of this point, see Barry Hankins, "The Rule of Decorum: How Sex and Religion Became Public Issues in America," *Criswell Theological Review* 6, no. 1 (Fall 2008): 3–22.

10. A poll in early 2004 showed that nearly 60 percent of likely voters wanted the U.S. president to be a "deeply religious person." See Adelle M. Banks, "Poll: Americans Want a 'Deeply Religious' Person as President," The Pew Forum on Religion and Public Life, January 9, 2004. This article can be accessed at: http://pewforum.org/news/display.php?NewsID=3012. That percentage actually went up to 68 percent later in 2004. See John C. Green, "The American Religious Landscape and Political Attitudes: A Baseline for 2004," The Pew Forum on Religion and Public Life, n.d. The article can be accessed at: http://pewforum.org/publications/surveys/green-full.pdf .

INDEX